ADMIRAL
ARLEIGH (31-Knot) BURKE

ADMIRAL
ARLEIGH (31-Knot) BURKE

The Story of a Fighting Sailor

KEN JONES

and

HUBERT KELLEY, Jr.

BLUEJACKET BOOKS

Naval Institute Press
Annapolis, Maryland

Naval Institute Press
291 Wood Road
Annapolis, MD 21402

First Bluejacket Books printing, 2001

ISBN 13: 978-1-5575-018-2
ISBN: 978-1-61251-371-3 (eBook)

Library of Congress Cataloging-in-Publication Data
Jones, Ken, 1903 Feb. 11–
    Admiral Arleigh (31-knot) Burke : the story of a fighting sailor / Ken Jones and Hubert Kelley, Jr.
          p.   cm.
    Originally published: Philadelphia : Chilton Books, 1962.
    Includes bibliographical references and index.
    ISBN 1-55750-018-5 (alk. paper)
    1. Burke, Arleigh A., 1901– 2. Admirals—United States—Biography. 3. United States. Navy—Biography. 4. United States—History, Naval—20th century. 5. World War, 1939–1945—Naval operations, American. I. Kelley, Hubert. II. Title.
E746.B87J66   2001
359'.0092—dc21
[B]   00-051953

Printed in the United States of America on acid-free paper ∞
                        6 5 4 3 2

Dedication

The record of Arleigh Burke's life is, in its most important dimensions, a study in courage, integrity, and the purposeful conservation and development of those fundamental disciplines which, in all ages, have been characteristic of individual greatness and which inevitably fortify the thrust of human progress without which we perish.

The authors dedicate this record—this study—to the memory of

EMILY BRETTMAN SORG

As Arleigh Burke, in his career, enriched the traditions of the United States Navy and kept the faith, so also did *Emily Brettman Sorg* keep the faith and enrich a different but perhaps no less important tapestry. Despite a desperate personal sorrow, she faced life with courageous serenity and passed on to her children and her children's children a heritage of spiritual honesty, human dignity, individual responsibility, and love.

Scripta manent

Foreword

This book reflects clearly the integrity of Arleigh Burke and, at the same time, his understanding and willingness to work in harness with the combination military-and-civilian structure of the Department of Defense and the Joint Chiefs of Staff in our country's military effort.

An excellent example of the strength of Admiral Burke as an associate was revealed in the way in which he supported the reorganization of the Department of Defense in 1958 when his conscience let him do so, but opposed those parts of reorganization which he felt were contrary to the defense interests of the country. When differences existed between the Secretary of Defense and Arleigh Burke, one had to respect the way in which he put forward his views. He did not carry out his opposition covertly, but always in a forthright and open manner.

The head of an organization such as the Department of Defense needs to have articulate dissent from his immediate subordinates in order to avoid arriving at conclusions based on lack of full understanding of the pros and cons. What is important to the Secretary of Defense is that any opposition to Administration proposals be expressed openly so that the differences may be resolved after full consideration of all points of view.

Arleigh Burke was at his best in presenting his own viewpoint on defense-wide problems, pressing them until the decision was made but then accepting and operating loyally under the decision as made.

Tom Gates, who was Secretary of the Navy when I took office and who later became Deputy Secretary of Defense and then Secretary of Defense, was a civilian counterpart of Arleigh. Both of these men were straight as a die in the conduct of their individual responsibilities. They were vigorous and lucid in setting forth their views, but these views were always out in the open for full discussion and consideration. Both men were all Navy, but they had sufficient breadth to understand that at times they must accept a decision by the Secretary of Defense which might not be in full accord with the views of the Navy. These were valued associates and good friends.

I have found my reading of this book to be of interest to me not so much because of any new insight into the character of Arleigh Burke as that the relating of many incidents of Arleigh's life with which I was unfamiliar has provided additional testimony to the character of the man as I have known him.

NEIL MCELROY
Secretary of Defense, 1957–1959

Contents

ADMIRAL
ARLEIGH (31-Knot) BURKE

CHAPTER 1

Crisis in the Middle East

"Good morning, sir!"

Chief Machinist's Mate David L. ('Ham') Hamilton, USN, stood loosely erect holding open a rear door of the vintage Chrysler sedan assigned for the personal use of four-star Admiral Arleigh Burke, USN, Chief of Naval Operations. The vehicle's principal claim to modernity was a two-way radio telephone which afforded the Admiral instant communication the world around through Flag Plot, the Navy's nerve center in the Pentagon. Burke had several times been offered a current model limousine but had steadfastly refused to give up the old Chrysler which, he felt, served him adequately.

"Good morning, Ham."

The professional boss of the U.S. Navy, wearing a conservatively cut grey suit accented by a somewhat boisterous cravat which he sometimes favored, slipped agilely into the back seat. He rested across his knees the polished red-brown leather attaché case containing the papers he had worked on overnight and which he would continue to peruse and ponder on during the brief drive to his Pentagon office. Thirty-nine years of naval service and training had made Burke meticulous in all things, and the documents in the case were carefully compartmented in separate folders.

Instinctively neat and precise, although not preciously so, Arleigh Burke was a well set up, broad-shouldered six-footer of some fifty-seven years. He walked with a long-rolling and reaching stride, and his carriage was notably erect. The rectangular appearance of his face was accentuated by a short, thick neck which seemed to carry the perpendicular planes of his cheeks and the thwartwise lines of a heavy chin and jaw right down into the V of his collar. He had a wide, full mouth which smiled easily, revealing strong, white teeth. During most of his waking hours, these were clamped tight upon the bit of a straight briar pipe, of which he kept a number constantly at hand. His nose was broad and his ears, set well out from his head, might have given an old salt the fanciful impression of a Chesapeake Bay schooner sailing wing-and-wing before a spanking breeze.

1

The Admiral's hair was curly, somewhat sparse, and grey-white. His unusually high forehead rose almost majestically above attention-arresting blue eyes which looked straight and level from beneath lids permanently squinted a little in the characteristic stigmata of the officer accustomed to long sailing of sunny seas. Considering his age, Burke's face showed very few of the deep-etched lines which the years invariably bring to those charged with decision. His only jewelry was a gold watch, worn on his left wrist, and his Naval Academy class ring, worn on the third finger of his left hand.

The time was 0715 on the still fresh summer morning of Monday, July 14, 1958. The immediate locus was Admiral's House, a charming mansion set amid the landscaped lawns and terraces of the Naval Observatory at the head of Massachusetts Avenue's famed Embassy Row, and traditionally assigned as quarters for the incumbent Chief of Naval Operations. And the problem—never was there a moment without its own special problem—the problem this morning was the Middle East.

As 'Ham' eased the big car out of the portecochere and headed for the railroad-grade-crossing-type barrier which would be swung aside to permit a smooth right turn into the downhill traffic of 'Mass Avenue,' Arleigh Burke reviewed the tangled and portentous Middle Eastern situation in his mind. He started with a simple premise: *The Mid-East is on the Navy's back. If anything goes wrong in the Mid-East it's up to the Navy to fix it.*

The essentials of the immediate picture were these:

In February, 1958, Egypt's Gamal Abdel Nasser, undoubtedly cued in by Moscow, had formed the United Arab Republic (UAR) consisting of Egypt and Syria, with Nasser in the driver's seat. Iraq and Jordan had countered by forming the anti-Nasser Arab Union under King Faisal II, of Iraq. Since that time, Nasser's agents had been engaged in an all-out effort to foment revolution in Iraq and Jordan and prevent others from joining the Baghdad Pact.

Arleigh Burke knew well enough that, if the loyal governments of Iraq and Jordan were overthrown, the much larger state of Saudi Arabia might follow, and this would expose a chain of defenseless sheikdoms along the Persian Gulf to Soviet pressures. Despite the actuality of a world surplus of oil, this treasure of the Middle East was an important stake. Politically, it was agreed that the collapse of United States policy in the area could not be tolerated.

The political problem had been an expanding one for some time. Indeed, as far back as November, 1957, the Joint Chiefs of Staff had warned Admiral James L. Holloway, Jr., Commander-in-Chief, U.S. Naval Forces, Eastern Atlantic and Mediterranean (CINCNELM) that the Mid-East situation was critical; and in May, 1958, pro-Nasser rebels had become active against the government of Lebanon. Habitually farsighted, Burke saw

2

the necessity for U.S. military intervention as an inevitable eventuality. So far as he was concerned, the inevitable had become reality that morning. At ten minutes to seven, while breakfasting, he had been summoned to his study to take a call over his 'hot' line—a bright-red telephone connecting him with his headquarters. The message the duty captain gave the CNO was brief and portentous: The U.S. Naval Attaché at Beirut, capital of Lebanon, reported that Lebanese President Camille Chamoun had requested President Eisenhower to land U.S. military forces in Lebanon to protect the government against overthrow by Soviet-inspired rebels.

To Arleigh Burke, this meant the Sixth Fleet in the 'Med'—fifty ships, 25,000 men, and two hundred planes—a primed and ready force accustomed to replenishing under way, and capable of keeping the sea indefinitely. Commanding was Vice Admiral C. R. ('Cat') Brown, and as this point emerged in his review, Burke permitted himself an appreciative chuckle. 'Cat' Brown was famous in the Navy. Legend had it that, on one occasion, he and his executive officer had appeared at a formal ceremony —Brown's relief of another senior officer—spic and span in spruce uniforms, but wearing neither shoes nor socks. Pressed for an explanation, the 'Cat' reported that, upon approaching port, he had received most meticulous instructions about the uniform of the day, as prescribed by the officer he was about to relieve. These instructions, however, had not mentioned shoes or socks, so he assumed they were to be omitted! Thus was a pompous martinet deflated, and the whole Navy snickered for a considerable time. On balance, Burke concluded that the Sixth Fleet and 'Cat' Brown could hold the franchise in the Middle East, at least until they were reinforced, should that become necessary.

At 0737, two minutes behind his customary schedule, the Chief of Naval Operations entered room 4-E-644, which adjoined his Pentagon office. Without pausing, he proceeded through an inner door into his own office and took his place, standing, behind his desk. Before he had time to open his attaché case his administrative aides grouped themselves silently around the desk, pads and pencils at the ready. This matutinal and unvarying ceremony had come to be known as "the lineup," and by tradition it began when a Filipino mess boy placed a steaming cup of black coffee on the Admiral's desk at his right elbow.

Facing Burke at the lineup were a Navy captain, a commander, a lieutenant commander, and a full colonel of Marines. These four constituted his immediate administrative staff, and, in the order of their rank, they now rattled off their morning reports. Burke interrupted with a question from time to time, and handed out documents from his attaché case, sometimes accompanied by written instructions for action. There were many small slips of paper bearing cryptic notes demanding further information on matters upon which he had reflected overnight. The Admiral's relaxed

3

approach saved the situation from what otherwise might have been a strained tautness.

Now and then—not nervously but with the assurance of a man who is pacing himself—Burke glanced over the heads of his staff at a large clock high on the wall opposite his desk. The dial was calibrated Navy-style into twenty-four equal segments, and the clock had four hands. The black hand indicated Washington time. The yellow hand indicated the time in the Seventh Fleet, steaming between China and Formosa. The green hand indicated the time in the Sixth Fleet in the Mediterranean, and the red hand indicated the time at Pearl Harbor.

From long habit, Burke was an expert at correlating multiple time, and, in addition to the four variations on his special clock there automatically registered in his mind the correlation for Zulu or Greenwich mean time, used as standard throughout the world. The Admiral habitually allowed ten minutes for the lineup, which gave him a little leeway for personal phone calls before he left his office for Flag Plot and the morning briefing at 0800. It was axiomatic, around the Pentagon, that you could set your watch by Burke's punctual arrival in Flag Plot.

When his aides had left, the Chief of Naval Operations crossed his office to a couple of huge, open leather bags, searched in one for a moment, and finally abstracted a thick document. These bags he kept permanently loaded with detailed and carefully indexed summaries and reports of all problems he was currently working on, or of any matter especially hot on the Hill. Summoned suddenly to appear before a committee or a subcommittee of the Congress, Burke could steam off immediately, followed by a junior officer carrying the bags containing all the data the CNO was apt to need to give expert and accurate testimony. Long ago, in the Pacific, his doctrine for Destroyer Squadron 23 had included, with emphasis, *"Keep your ship ready for battle."* It was an old Burke characteristic. He was *always* ready for battle!

Returning to his desk, the Admiral dropped into his blue leather chair and swiveled around to a shelf behind him, where he picked up one of six telephones in five different colors. Through these telephones plus an inter-office communications system, Burke transacted an appreciable amount of the high-level Navy, political, and diplomatic business which was his responsibility.

While the colored phones were most useful to the Admiral they sometimes proved irritatingly fascinating to casual or official callers; and when one of these had departed, Burke was apt to blow off steam to an aide with the disgusted observation "Everybody wants to play with the blankety-blank telephones!"

The white phone on Burke's shelf was a direct line to the White House, and was sacrosanct to all but the CNO himself. The powder-blue phone

4

hooked him up directly with the Joint Chiefs of Staff, of which he was a member, and with Air Defense Headquarters. A grey phone and a black one permitted conventional calls. A red phone provided a direct line to all fleet commanders around the world, and a second black phone offered a direct line to the Secretary of the Navy.

Having completed a short conversation, the Chief of Naval Operations glanced at the clock, placed some secret papers in the personal safe which stood in the corner behind his left shoulder, selected a fresh pipe from the well-filled rack on his desk, and departed for Flag Plot and his regular morning briefing. Although he had little intimation of it at the moment, he was destined to spend the better part of the next thirty-six hours in this top Navy command post, issuing what amounted to battle orders at intervals through the long day and the longer night, and hoping between whiles he was not starting World War III.

The regular 0800 Flag Plot briefing begins in a fifty-seat theater located on the 'D' ring on the fourth floor of the Pentagon, in the vicinity of the sixth corridor. The whole installation is guarded around the clock by armed Marine sentries. The briefing is conducted in four parts:

1. *Intelligence*—world wide.
2. *Operations*—where ships and fleets are, and what they are doing.
3. *Weather around the world*—delivered by closed circuit television from the Navy Fleet Weather Central, at Suitland, Maryland.
4. *Press briefing*—The very latest, up-to-the-moment world and local news. (This is given factually, and no attempt is made at interpretation.)

Admiral Burke and his fifty top people from Op-Nav settled into the blue leather seats of the briefing theater. The lights dimmed, the intelligence briefing officer took his position behind a portable lectern at stage left, and the screen behind him burgeoned into life with a picture of the city of Baghdad, Iraq. The picture was projected from behind the screen.

"You see here," said the briefing officer in a pleasant voice which was carried to all corners of the small auditorium by amplifiers, "the city of Baghdad, capital of what was, until this morning, the kingdom of Iraq."

At that moment the national flag of Iraq, in full color, appeared on the screen as a small insert in the upper right-hand corner.

"At approximately zero two hundred Washington time this morning," continued the briefing officer, "an armed mob stormed the royal palace of Iraq . . ." The picture changed to show a close-up of the royal palace.

"At the time," resumed the briefing officer, "King Faisal II of Iraq was dressing, in preparation for a flight to Istanbul to attend a meeting of the Baghdad Pact nations . . ." A picture of King Faisal II appeared as an insert on the screen. "The King rushed to the courtyard just in time to

5

face armed soldiers confronting the Palace Guard. In the shooting which followed, twenty men, including the King and Crown Prince Abdul Illah, the ex-Regent, whose picture you now see beside that of the King, were killed."

The briefing officer took a sip of water as the picture changed to a closeup of the British Embassy in Baghdad. "After killing the King and Crown Prince, rebel soldiers occupied the royal palace. The mob rolled on to burn the British Embassy. They then assaulted the Baghdad Hotel, from which they took three U.S. citizens—Eugene Burns, George Calley, and Robert Alcock. Our Naval Attaché reports that these men were beaten to death."

Once more the picture changed, this time to a map of the Middle East, with a portrait of an Iraqui general in the upper right-hand corner. "As you all know," droned the briefing officer, "King Faisal II was pro-West in his sympathies. However, at this time, the nation of Iraq is in the hands of Brigadier General Aldul el Kassan, who led the coup. General Kassan has been a Mid-East 'strong man' for some time. He is pro-Nasser, anti-West, and has proclaimed Iraq a republic. Our information is that he has ample forces at his disposal to sustain his conquest. Now, are there any questions up to this point?"

There was none, and the picture on the screen changed to a map of the republic of Lebanon, with the Lebanese flag in color appearing at the lower left-hand corner. "Very well," said the briefing officer. "I shall continue, then, with the situation in the Lebanon. At 0648, Washington time this morning, the President of the United States received a request from President Camille Chamoun, of Lebanon, for the landing of U.S. military forces in his country to protect the government from Nasser-inspired rebels who are attempting to overthrow Chamoun's legitimate regime."

As the pictures of Eisenhower, Chamoun and Nasser appeared on the screen, the Chief of Naval Operations broke in with a question: "Would such intervention come under the Eisenhower Doctrine?"

"I believe so, sir. The Congressional resolution of March, 1957, authorizes the President—and I quote—to undertake, in the general area of the Middle East, military assistance problems with any nation or group of nations of that area desiring such assistance. If the President determines the necessity thereof, the United States is prepared to use armed forces to assist any such nation or group of nations requesting assistance against armed aggression, end quote."

"Or," reflected Burke thoughtfully aloud, "we could move for the protection of U.S. nationals. How many of our people are over there?"

"We have the figure as 2,500, sir."

6

"What is the status of the Lebanese military force?" another officer inquired.

"They have about ten thousand men under arms," replied the briefing officer. "It is estimated that there are a minimum of twelve thousand rebels, and that they are armed with submachine guns, mortars, and antiaircraft artillery."

"Where did these rebels come from, and how did they get the weapons?" Burke wanted to know.

"A great many of the dissidents infiltrated from Syria, sir," replied the briefing officer. "As to the weapons, Lebanon has no manufactory, so they must have come from some outside source."

"Well, that ought to cover it," said Burke. "Proceed."

The intelligence briefing, which included a perceptive rundown of the Middle East situation since 1950, when the United States, Britain, and France pledged joint action in an attempt to preserve tranquillity in the area, was concluded in another ten minutes. It was followed by the operational briefing, with emphasis upon the Sixth and Seventh Fleets, and the availability of oil and tankers. After the weather and press briefings—new Mid-East developments were beginning to emerge in some wire service reports, but had missed the morning newspapers—Admiral Burke and a phalanx of his closest advisers adjourned across the corridor to the plotting room where, should President Eisenhower call upon the Navy, the real staff work would be done. As yet, there was no word from the White House, but the President was scheduled to meet with the National Security Council at nine forty-five, and almost certainly some decision would be taken at that meeting.

It is a Burke apothegm that effective decisions rarely are difficult, if one has all the facts. Flag Plot was put together primarily with the idea of providing the Admiral with all of the facts. By the simple fact of its being, however, Flag Plot also served as a completely implemented naval command post; and the plotting room, which Burke now entered, is its amazingly complex and efficient heart.

Staffed around the clock by five captains, corresponding numbers of lesser ranks, and a precision battery of quartermaster types expert at solving intricate operational and logistic problems in a hurry, the plotting room is about thirty feet wide by some two hundred feet long. At its upper end is the status board, a dozen feet wide by about half that deep. On this board, white letters on a laminated black background give the locations and status of the First, Second, Sixth, and Seventh Fleets, together with the names of their commanders and senior assistants. Under this dominating installation, and distributed elsewhere around the room, are rank upon rank of shallow metal drawers containing large- and

7

small-scale maps and charts of the world's waters and land masses. When an 'incident' happens anywhere on the globe, such as the 'buzzing' by Soviet aircraft of the air patrol of the Seventh Fleet cruising off Formosa, the appropriate chart is broken out. Skilled plotters mark the courses ships steered or airplanes flew in the appropriate places, with speeds and times carefully indicated. The chart is then photographed, and prints are rushed to Admiral Burke and other senior officers of cognizance. Reports constantly pour in from all over the world, and Flag Plot is consistently ahead of the news. Long before bulletins of international 'incidents' reach the pages of the press, the Chief of Naval Operations has all available details, together with accurate and graphic representations of the happenings themselves.

Against one wall of the plotting room stands a battery of teleprinters. Through radio, they can be linked with any principal Navy ship anywhere in the world, affording constant two-way communications. The command desks, where the watch captains sit, are located in the center of the room toward its upper end. On these desks are multicolored telephones permitting direct communication with all fleet commanders, the Joint Chiefs of Staff, and top echelons of the Army and the Air Force.

About seventeen hundred messages are received during each twenty-four hour period. They are processed as received into subject files, and these files offer a minute-to-minute report on significant as well as seemingly obscure events the world around.

Huge metal-backed maps line the long walls on both sides of the plotting room. On these maps the location of every ship in the U.S. Navy is indicated by a small colored magnet. There are some 850 ships, and their positions are pinpointed, hour by hour.

In one corner of the lower end of the room is the locator board. On it the current location of every high government official, from the President down through the Cabinet to top military commanders of all services, and key congressional leaders is noted for ready reference. When foreign dignitaries visit the United States, their whereabouts, day by day and sometimes hour by hour, are posted on the locator board in the plotting room of Flag Plot. Near this installation, a world weather map is kept constantly current with data pouring in from the Navy's weather central.

When an 'incident' turns out to be of a continuing nature and of sufficient importance, it often is transferred to the summary boards at the lower end of the room. These are designed to give large-scale visual interpretation of significant developments world wide. There are from fifteen to twenty of these huge maps. They are ball-bearing-mounted, one behind the other, on overhead trolleys in such a manner that any desired summary board may be moved into the front position instantly, or two may be displayed side by side. When the President is flying overseas, for example, his route and hour-by-hour progress appear on a summary board, together with the locations of ships along his route and the availability of aircraft, should an emergency make assistance necessary. On another summary board, the location of every U.S. national in a critical overseas area—Iraq and Lebanon, on July 14, 1958—is pinpointed. Of course, each individual is not separately represented, but colored and numbered tabs indicate the distribution and location of groups of U.S. citizens throughout troubled areas, and the foreign firms or governments with which they are affiliated. The primary purpose of this visualization is to enable the Navy to take instant and effective action for the evacuation of U.S. nationals from any trouble spot, should such a move be required.

In a special file in the plotting room, the location of every merchant cargo ship, tanker, or liner flying the U.S. flag anywhere in the world is plotted and entered daily. Thus the Navy knows precisely where to look for U.S. ships when crisis looms. Very soon after reports were received of events in Iraq and Lebanon, this information was put to brilliant use. Private U.S. cargo ships and tankers were chartered at sea by radio and radio telephone, turned toward new destinations and missions within minutes, and the huge and complex job of sea lifting emergency military forces and their logistic support was smoothly and effectively accomplished.

On the morning of Monday, July 14, 1958, after a brief conference in a specially appointed room adjoining the CNO's office, Arleigh Burke and his Deputies entered the plotting room at precisely 0835 and settled themselves for a detailed operational briefing on the Middle East by Commander Harry Allendorfer. They were not, however, the only ones preoccupied with the developing situation in that area. Even at this early hour, waves of apprehensive tension were beginning to sweep over official Washington after the fashion of a lap dissolve on a motion picture screen. The routine concerns of a humid summer morning were swiftly and smoothly covered up and obliterated by the urgent image of crisis in the Middle East *now*. Very few in Washington knew of President Chamoun's appeal for aid, but by this time all major embassies had been advised of the coup in Iraq, and to seasoned diplomats its key implications were plain.

At 1600 Pennsylvania Avenue the President was instructing his secretariat to scrap the prepared agenda for the 9:45 meeting of the National Security Council and giving them a list of additional people to be summoned hastily to the meeting. Basically, the council consists of the President, Vice President, the Secretaries of State and Defense, and the Director of Civil and Defense Mobilization. The President had added a dozen key names to this list and decreed that the agenda would be limited to discussion of the Middle-Eastern situation.

Around the town, ambassadorial telephones sprang to life, and varia-

9

tions of the following supplied colloquies must certainly have taken place:

"What do you expect your government will do?"—an undiplomatically blunt question from the French Ambassador to his British opposite number, an expectation of candor being predicated on their long-standing personal friendship.

"Hard to tell, old fellow. It's a little early . . ." Noncommittal Albion!

"But you'll do *something* . . . ?" Impetuous Gascon.

"Oh, of course. But London hasn't told me anything yet. You know about the Lebanon business?"

"But of course!"

"Well, if the Americans go to Lebanon, we may follow them in. Or, again, we may go to Iraq. What do you hear from your people?"

"Nothing so far, beyond the bare bones of the Iraq coup and Chamoun's appeal to Eisenhower."

"Well, keep in touch . . . this should be amusing . . ." It was a fruitless probing, with no satisfaction for either side, but the effort was demanded.

In a telephone call much too early for routine diplomatic business, the Iranian Ambassador must have expressed his astonishment and sympathy to the Ambassador of Iraq. And, quite possibly, their telephone conversation crossed one between the Ambassador of India, calling from his Macomb Street residence, and the Ambassador of Israel, speaking from his residence on Massachusetts Avenue. These two did not yet know of the Chamoun appeal, but they knew full well that Western military intervention in the Middle East was only a matter of time, now that Iraq had fallen.

"We'll remain neutral, of course." The man from New Delhi was diplomatically partial either to the obvious, or to obfuscation, whichever approach would serve his purposes best. Today, it was the obvious. "What will be the position of your government?"

"Strong neutrality also, I suspect." The man from Tel Aviv knew very well the attitude his government would adopt. He had walked this tight-rope before.

"Good! Good! But what if the British go in . . . ?"

"What could we do . . . ?" This with a sigh.

"They might want to use your air space . . ."—a leading observation from the Indian Ambassador.

"I suppose so . . ." A reflective reply from the Israeli.

". . . and, as a neutral, you could prohibit overflights of Israel's territory . . . ?"

"Of course, of course! I'll even suggest it in my next dispatch."

"Good! Good! We must all work to minimize this . . . er . . . *unfortunate* business."

10

The tide of the news swirled up around Capitol Hill with ever increasing urgency. Alas, United States intelligence sources abroad had given no warning of the Iraq disorder, and news of the *fait accompli* broke upon congressional leaders, raw and dismaying. Calls from the White House, summoning selected solons to sit in the morning meeting of the NSC, whipped up a special froth to top the seething speculation; and the afternoon newsmen, with an impending crisis and, thus, banner headlines in prospect, went energetically about the job of running down the bellwethers of the Congress for interpretations, statements, and pronouncements of various sorts. It was the kind of thing made to order for the politicos of the back-home wards and warrens, and the gentlemen of the press were not disappointed. The mounting heat of the humid morning spread swiftly over an official Washington immersed in, and appreciatively savoring, its own special brand of excitement, spiced by vicariously experienced danger. The crisis was sufficiently urgent to spawn the wildest of rumors and 'I told you so's'; yet it was sufficiently remote, at least in space, to seem glamorous and colorful rather than menacing.

The pretty detachment which curled and eddied around Capitol Hill was not shared by Arleigh Burke. As he took his seat before a huge world map, something very closely akin to an electric shock pulsed through the plotting room. In the Navy portion of the Pentagon, it was a familiar phenomenon. There has been no adequate explanation of the Burke personality or the impact it had upon others. Undoubtedly it involved a mystique which cannot be fully or rationally explained. As a man, Arleigh Burke was not especially taut as were Admiral Ernie King and a hundred others of exalted rank. But he was impetuous and explosive, and one of his principal characteristics was a furious drive which swept everything before it, communicated itself to others, and often evoked a tingling sensation of anticipation (or apprehension) in those with whom he came into contact. How Burke got that way will be the burden of a latter portion of this study. Meanwhile, having arrived at the top, Admiral Arleigh Burke, Chief of Naval Operations, sat at the epicenter of the professional Navy for six long, harrowing, and eventful years. Shock waves emanated from his vicinity in a 360-degree pattern. His smile inspired men to incredible striving, and his wrath damned them to miserable lamentation.

Commander Allendorfer, pointer in hand, stepped up to the map prepared to answer questions. Allendorfer had been the project officer for Flag Plot. It was his baby. He was a trim man of medium stature, blue eyed, prematurely grey, with a probing, restless mind and an almost fanatical devotion to accuracy.

"Suppose you give us a rundown on the Sixth Fleet first," suggested the CNO.

"The Sixth Fleet," began Commander Allendorfer, as if reciting a well

11

learned lesson, "ranges the Mediterranean from the Straits of Gibraltar to Suez . . ." His pointer flashed out to tap Gibraltar and Suez on the map. ". . . and from Trieste to Tripoli. It has a nuclear capability. At this moment Task Force 60 is in Greek ports, with carrier *Essex* at Piraeus, the port of Athens. Liberty parties are ashore in Athens."

As he spoke, the Commander's pointer continued to flick from point to point illustrating his talk. "Task Force 66 is at Naples. TRANS-PHIBRON 6 * of Task Force 61 is at sea, off Lebanon, with the reinforced Second Battalion, Second Marines, combat loaded.

"TRANSPHIBRON 2, with the Third Battalion, Sixth Marines embarked, is at sea en route toward Athens from the vicinity of Suda Bay, Crete."

"That would be eighteen hundred ready Marines?" interrupted Burke.

"Approximately, sir. TRANSPHIBRON 4, with the First of the Eighth Marines is en route West through the Med toward Gibraltar. This force has been relieved and is returning Stateside."

"Knock it off for a few minutes," ordered Burke. "I want to make a phone call."

Striding to a large desk, Arleigh Burke picked up his red command telephone and requested connection with Rear Admiral Clifford Duerfeldt, Deputy Commander-in-Chief, Northeast Atlantic and Mediterranean (Deputy CINCNELM) whose headquarters were in London. While waiting for the connection, Burke calmly handed the phone to a yeoman to hold while he refilled his pipe. Connection completed, the Admiral took over:

"That you, Cliff? This is Arleigh. I suppose you've heard the news? Yes . . . well, it's more than Iraq now, Cliff. All hell's about to break loose in Lebanon. . . . you have, huh? That's good! Well, I just wanted to tell you to tighten things up, and prepare for a quick major movement of the Sixth Fleet. . . . Keep PHIBRON 4; you may need it . . . No, there's no decision here yet, but it'll come sure as fate. Keep me informed, now."

Within a half hour, six thousand miles eastward from Washington, liberty in the Sixth Fleet was canceled and shore patrols swarmed out to round up officers and men. Engine room watches aboard ships in port were put on two hours' steaming notice, and TRANSPHIBRON 6 was turned sharply from its course toward Athens and ordered to proceed at flank speed toward the waters off Lebanon. TRANSPHIBRON 4, in the western Mediterranean, heading for the United States, was turned to the East and headed to join PHIBRON 6. The majestic might of the U.S. Navy was being mustered and formed into fighting posture. Below decks in PHIBRON 4 an

* Amphibious Transport Squadron 6.

off-duty Marine Sergeant with a guitar led his mates in singing the nostalgic Marine lament:

I only want to go
Right back to Quantico;
I only want to go ho-o-o-m-m-e!

Instead of going home, they were headed for action not very far from the "shores of Tripoli" celebrated in Marine song and story.

"What about the Seventh Fleet?" demanded the CNO, returning to his seat.

"The Seventh Fleet is generally in the Japanese area, sir," reported Allendorfer, "except for one carrier and four DD's at Hong Kong. Task Force 24—forty-two ships with the annual midshipman cruise embarked, is in Scandinavian ports."

"How about the oil situation?"

"Rather mixed up, sir. The pipelines are still pumping oil, but it would appear that Nasser can interdict this flow pretty much at will. Now that he has Iraq, he can shut down at the source. Saudi Arabia is the second largest producer in the Middle East, being surpassed only by Kuwait. But the 1,070-mile pipeline from Saudi Arabia to the Mediterranean coast at Sidon crosses Lebanon. If Nasser gets Lebanon, he can tie things in knots."

"Well," said Burke turning to Vice Admiral J. M. Will, commanding the Navy's Military Sea Transport Service, "our best reliance for oil is U.S. tankers sailing through U.S.-controlled seas. How about it?"

"We're already working on it," he was told.

"What's the logistics picture?" asked Burke turning back to Allendorfer.

"Our situation in the Middle East is good, sir. The ammunition ships *Shasta* and *Wrangell* are in the Lebanon area. The *Antares,* a store ship loaded with food, is at the port of Athens. The *Rigel,* refrigerator ship loaded with fresh provisions, is there too. The *Mercury,* loaded with ship's service stores and clothing is also at the port of Athens.

"The AK *Shenandoah*—repair ship—is at Naples. We have eight tankers, carrying black oil for ship propulsion, jet fuel, aviation gas, and other POL products like lube oil and Diesel fuel, distributed around between Barcelona, Cannes, Naples, and nearby ports. These are attached to Task Force 63, which is the mobile support force for the Sixth Fleet. Backing them up are oil and supplies at Norfolk, Bayonne, New Jersey, and Newport. In the event of a protracted operation, the repair ship *Amphion* (AR-13) and the fleet tug *Atakapa* (ATF-149) are available to sail from the East Coast on short notice. Four additional mine sweepers can sail from the East Coast within a few hours. Newport has across-the-board supplies for

13

DD's. There are ample stocks of ammunition at Norfolk, Bayonne, Hingham, Massachusetts, and Earle, New Jersey. As a matter of fact, a fleet ammunition ship already has been alerted to load and stand by at Earle, should the need develop.

"So far as the Sixth Fleet is concerned, the Marines will be self-sufficient for about thirty days. And the tempo of operations envisioned will require only one extra fleet oiler from the East Coast. At full tempo, the Sixth Fleet can fight for several weeks without replenishment."

"Very well," said the Chief of Naval Operations, satisfied with his dispositions. "Now let's take a look at Beirut. Do you have any details, Allendorfer?"

"Yes, sir, I have a memorandum on Beirut. It'll just take a moment . . ." The Commander disappeared into his small office behind the status board and reappeared shortly, summary in hand. "Beirut is the only deep water port along the Lebanon Coast from Haifa on the South to Istanbul on the North," he read aloud.

"The port facilities consist of fixed moorings for six ships inside the harbor, and ten wharves with 6,514 linear feet of wharfage. There are sea berths for three tankers off shore from the Socony-Vacuum storage installation on St. George Bay, and four off the Shell plant. All are exposed areas with poor holding ground. At the wharves there are only one thousand feet of deep-water berths—four to six fathoms—inside the basin and alongside Mole de la Traverse.

"Cargo handling equipment ashore consists of two six-ton traveling portable jib cranes, two three-ton locomotive cranes, and four small fixed jib cranes. There is little suitable shore stowage."

"Hell!" exploded Arleigh Burke. "We could get mouse-trapped in a place like that! If we *do* go in it'll be over the beaches!"

The hands of the clock were creeping around, and the Chief of Naval Operations and his staff were becoming restless. There were, of course, many routine preparatory chores to claim their attention, but the question uppermost in all minds was what decisions would emerge from the meeting of the National Security Council presently in progress. Obviously, the matter had passed out of the diplomatic stage in which consultation with the Congress would have been both prudent and demanded. It had now reached the proportions of a crisis calling for quick executive decision.

The President was patient and prudent. He carefully explained all of the reasons why it was imperative that the United States take immediate and vigorous action, and summoned twenty-two congressional leaders to meet with him in his office that afternoon at two-thirty.

Rumors flew on The Hill and along Embassy Row as thick as arrows at an archer's tournament. A few even penetrated the State Department, where they were proliferated and once more set a'wing. But nothing substantial happened.

At 1045, with no word from higher authority, the CNO alerted Admiral Jerauld Wright, commanding the Atlantic Fleet, and Admiral Felix Stump, commanding the Pacific Fleet, to the acute situation in the Mid-East and the possibility of U.S. action. He then left Flag Plot to attend an emergency meeting of the Joint Chiefs of Staff.

The sense of the JCS meeting under the chairmanship of Air Force General Nathan F. Twining was unanimous. The Sixth Fleet was on the spot and, as Admiral Alfred Thayer Mahan had indicated many years before in his celebrated study of the influence of sea power upon history, the Sixth Fleet wasn't there just by accident. It was there in anticipation of precisely what was happening now, and Arleigh Burke was proud to report the Fleet combat ready. Burke's reading of the situation was precise and reflected the lessons of history. U.S. military intervention in Lebanon might, of course, precipitate armed conflict, but the Admiral was pretty confident that the Russians would endeavor to localize the action. He remembered Mussolini's invasion of Abyssinia, and Russia's invasions of Finland in 1940, South Korea in 1950, and Hungary in 1956. In each instance, the aggressors had localized the conflict, lest its spread threaten their broader schemes, and he saw the Lebanon challenge following the same pattern. The other Chiefs also doubted that Russia would go to war over the Mid-East at that time, but it was the consensus of the meeting that, if the Soviet chose to start World War III, the United States was ready. Accordingly, the JCS recommended to the President that the Marines be landed at Beirut, and that all necessary steps be taken to support the operation by Army and Air Force as well as naval backup. At the conclusion of the brief meeting, General Twining hurried to the White House to deliver his report, and Admiral Burke returned to Flag Plot.

For the CNO, the next few hours were busy ones, filled with a steady stream of incoming and outgoing messages, many of them requiring or implementing quick decisions. All fleets were alerted to the emergency, and its code designation BLUE BAT came into use. MSTS was ordered to charter privately owned tankers, cargo ships, and transports on an anticipatory basis for eventual logistical support of a combined military force. Burke ordered fleet commanders to take specific action with regard to certain ships. This included the stationing of two destroyers out of sight over the horizon off Beirut to establish direct radio communication with U.S. Ambassador Robert McClintock. The Ambassador already had started sending the dependents of embassy staff members to safety outside the Lebanon.

Gradually, despite the hum of constant action, a curious sense of detach-

15

ment seemed to take hold of those working in Flag Plot—a feeling that they were working in a vacuum. Reports and orders were flowing in and out, but the all-important message of decision did not come. The clock showed the time to be well after two thirty; the President was meeting with twenty-two congressmen. But still nothing happened. And when the word finally did come, sometime after three o'clock, it was negative: no decision had been taken; the President had called a second meeting of the National Security Council for four thirty that afternoon. Burke sighed. He did not favor imprudent action, but he saw the situation in somber tones. It was his conviction that, unless something positive was done in Iraq, detachments of Russians or at least Egyptian "volunteers" would move in. This would not only seal Lebanon's fate, but would threaten the prime oil-producing center of Kuwait, which he regarded as the key to the situation. In the thinking of the Chief of Naval Operations, prompt action was imperative, and he was distressed by the successive delays.

During the course of the afternoon Burke talked at length with Admiral James L. Holloway, Jr., Commander-in-Chief, Northeast Atlantic and Mediterranean (CINCNELM) who, in the case of U.S. military action would put on another hat—Commander-in-Chief, Specified Command (CINCSPECOMME)—and take command of the landing operation. Burke advised Holloway that the Communist Chinese, fully aware of the tense situation in the Mid-East, were making hostile threats against the Seventh Fleet cruising off the China coast. "Beakley's already got his people standing double watches, Jimmy," Burke informed Holloway. "I doubt that I can pull out any Seventh Fleet reinforcements for you. We've got five submarines in the Norwegian Sea on NATO exercises, but they're a hell of a long way from you."

"I don't need any help," replied Holloway. "I can take over all of the Lebanon if you say the word."

"I can't say the word—yet!" snapped Burke. "We will stay near Beirut, be ready to land quickly, be prepared for attacks from the north and keep our forces fully ready to protect Lebanon."

"But I've already had another proposition," said Holloway archly.

"From whom?" demanded Burke, the fuse suddenly lit on his explosive temper.

"From some Britisher. He thinks, if there's action, I should go up and take the port of Tripoli to protect their oil installations there."

The CNO let off a string of incandescent expletives. "You'll do no such thing!" he stormed. Holloway, well knowing his Chief, chuckled quietly, and the conversation drifted toward termination. There were those in the service who could pull Arleigh Burke's leg, as Holloway had done, and get away with it, but they were few and far between.

The afternoon was drawing on, and although the CNO had been gulping coffee steadily all day, he had not taken time for luncheon. He took time now to dispatch two urgent messages to Holloway, Wright, Stump, and 'Cat' Brown. The first was:

"Developments Mid-East extremely grave. Global impact cannot be foreseen but may be expected to be critical. Intervention by U.S. armed services not unlikely. I will advise you of events as situation develops."

The second was:

"Ultimate determination still in doubt, but subsequent conferences expected to result in orders for Lebanon landings within next two days. I have informed JCS and the President that two battalions of Marines are available to land on half day's notice, and that additional Marines will be intercepted en route other destinations and made available for support. PHIBRON 4 will steam toward Eastern Med at once. Units in Western Mediterranean should be prepared to steam East at maximum speed, but Dulles wants least possible indication gravity of situation until conclusive action decided upon here. Therefore units docked Western Med should not attract attention by leaving port ahead of schedule save on direct orders from me. I contemplate loading Second Marine Division plus air support for reinforcement. All here agree that a general war or at least a big one can result if this matter is not carefully handled."

Leaving these messages to be coded and sent, the Admiral returned to his own office where, over a light luncheon, he perused intelligence reports concerning various political personalities in the Lebanon. His sharp intuition and bold imagination immediately pinpointed the man to watch: General Fuad Chehab, who was both political and military.

The broad tapestry which Burke considered embraced these values: The 'American Idea' had been somewhat oversold in Lebanon a good time before by a traveling U.S. congressional hot shot. It was true, as Chamoun had reported, that arms and men had passed into Lebanon over the Syrian border. And certainly it was true that the Communists were doing everything they could to foment a rebellion which eventually might permit Nasser, as their stooge, to take over the whole Arab bloc. But, underneath it all, there was a good bit of dissatisfaction—legitimate or otherwise—among the loyal Lebanese themselves. There were great numbers who honestly felt that Lebanon's orientation should be toward the Arab countries rather than the West. The crucial point was that they did not seem to realize, or chose to disregard, the fact that this might mean Nasser and Communism, and the end of their liberties.

General Chehab, heading the Lebanese armed forces and a member of one of the oldest and proudest Christian families in the Middle East, was the idol of the troops he commanded. Obviously, he was so strong that Chamoun could not remove him. And Chehab, although honoring the outward symbols of loyalty to the Chamoun government, had, in actuality, taken a pretty much middle-of-the-road position. His troops had sought to protect the lives of citizens during the rioting and fighting which led up to the crisis of July 14, 1958. But they had not energetically attacked rebel forces, and when those forces were active, Chehab now and then had found it convenient to look the other way. Chehab, the strong man, seemed to be playing a waiting game.

Arleigh Burke returned to Flag Plot at 4:45 in the afternoon to receive the following message from Admiral Stump, commanding the Pacific Fleet:

"Civilian radio quotes American Ambassador Baghdad as saying that Iraq King and Prime Minister are missing and that they have not arrived Ankara where they were expected this morning. Am watching situation."

Burke could have told Stump that both the King and the Prime Minister were dead, but more important matters immediately pre-empted the CNO's attention. At 4:48 he was handed a query from the White House: "Can you land Marines over the beaches of Beirut at precisely nine o'clock tomorrow morning, Washington time?"

The Admiral's one word reply was instantaneous: "Affirmative!"

Still, matters hung in stays, and the tension in the plotting room was all but unbearable. Finally, at 6:15 that evening, the President took the decision to act. The Washington hour of nine o'clock on the morning of Tuesday, October 15 (3:00 P.M., Lebanon time), for the landings had been chosen to enable the President to issue a statement to the American people and the world; at the same time, Ambassador Henry Cabot Lodge made a similar announcement to the United Nations delegates in New York. Thus, the landings would be presented as a *fait accompli*.

The CNO received his enabling orders from the Joint Chiefs of Staff at 6:20. Three minutes later he messaged Holloway and 'Cat' Brown:

"Marines are to hit the beaches at exactly 151500Z. The Lebanese government is not to be informed of your intentions earlier than noon Lebanon time."

With the basic enabling order on its way, the Chief of Naval Operations and his staff settled down to a night of playing intricate chess. The pieces were ships, planes, men, and supplies. The board was the globe.

Only once before new dawn did Arleigh Burke leave Flag Plot. Entertaining at Admiral's House was a necessary concomitant of the CNO routine. Admiral and Mrs. Burke had given receptions for as many as five hundred people when the weather was fair and the spacious grounds could be pressed into service. Long ago invitations had gone out for a small dinner party at the Burke's on the evening of July 14, and the Admiral was not one to take his social obligations lightly. Actually, much high-level horse trading was accomplished at these affairs, and only on very rare occasions could the Burkes invite their close friends for an informal evening. Thus it was that, about eight o'clock, the Admiral turned Flag

18

Plot over to his Deputies and was driven swiftly to Admiral's House, where he greeted his guests amiably and gave no indication of the pressure under which he had been laboring. He chatted lightly about trivialities and he did not discuss Lebanon. After an hour, he excused himself and returned to Flag Plot, where he remained the rest of the night and most of the following day.

Surveying the situation, the CNO once more gathered the reins into his strong hands and started dictating orders and messages:

"To all commanders: Situation reports are to be sent every hour."

"To CINCNELM and COMSIXTHFLEET: American Ambassador Beirut is to be advised if landings cannot be made on schedule. Landing schedule to be confirmed to JCS by FLASH message one hour before actual landings. If any revision in time necessary let us know by FLASH message."

"From BURKE to HOLLOWAY: Advise immediately of any sign that Allied forces intend to join you in Lebanon. Should they seek to do so advise them that you lack U.S. government authorization to assume command of foreign forces but you hope they will synchronize their plans with yours. The French Ambassador may ask for your help. You should make no commitment until matter is considered and decision is reached at a meeting of the Joint Chiefs of Staff."

Where once they had seemed to crawl, the hands of the big clock in Flag Plot now raced around the dial, as Arleigh Burke maintained close liaison with the Joint Chiefs of Staff and swiftly moved the pieces of this gigantic chess game over thousands of miles of ocean to the places where they were needed or could be most effective. He ordered 'Cat' Brown to stage *Essex* planes out of Cyprus for air cover. He pulled all available Marine R5D aircraft from the West Coast to Cherry Point in order to undertake a troop lift, should it become necessary. He warned all commanders to follow the BLUE BAT concept, so far as possible, and informed them that he still had no information about what the British planned to do.

Shortly after midnight, the CNO took time out for a private message to Admiral Holloway. The message was a precautionary one, and its subject was General Chehab. No one knew at that time what attitude the General should take toward the landings, nor whether or not the Lebanese Army would oppose the Marines. Burke's feeling was that Chehab might be a disruptive factor, and he advised Holloway to establish contact with Chehab as soon as possible. Burke suggested that Admiral Holloway might want to invite Chehab aboard the Sixth Fleet flagship "where you could show him suitable honors" (and where, incidentally, he would be out of the way of the Marines).

As the early hours of the morning wore on, and despite the air conditioning, neckties and collars were loosened in Flag Plot, and the Filipino mess boys were kept busy supplying the constant demands for coffee. The situation generated its own heat and electric excitement. At his Washington headquarters, Vice Admiral Will, commanding the Navy's MSTS, was contacting U.S. flagships at sea and hiring them by radio telephone. The American Merchant Marine cooperated, and although no outside logistic support was needed for the Sixth Fleet, a total of twenty one civilian cargo ships and passenger liners, and seven tankers were eventually brought to the support of the military effort.

About two o'clock on the morning of the fifteenth the State Department advised the government of Turkey that sixty-five U.S. aircraft, carrying troops, desired to overfly Turkish territory, and that the use of Adana for staging and as a base for air operations was essential. The Turks raised no objection, but the government of Israel, receiving a similar request for permission for overflights, refused.

Orders continued to pour out of Flag Plot, and reports streamed in. The Marines making the landings were specifically ordered not to fire, unless they were directly fired upon, and, if questioned by the Lebanese, they were to state that they were there at the request of the friendly Lebanese government and to aid in its defense.

At three-thirty o'clock on the morning of Tuesday, July 15, Arleigh Burke received the dispatch he was waiting for. It informed him that the Second Battalion, Second Marines would hit Khalde Beach, near Beirut's International Airport, at nine o'clock, Washington time, that morning. The Chief of Naval Operations immediately picked up the White House telephone and left a message: "When he awakens, please inform the President that the Marines will land in Lebanon at nine o'clock this morning, on schedule."

No one left Flag Plot, and the ebb and flow of orders, messages, and situation reports did not diminish. In the event, the Marines landed precisely on time. They were unopposed, and, forty minutes after hitting the beach, they had secured the airport. But during the morning a contretemps developed which brought Admiral Holloway and General Chehab into head-on collision, as Arleigh Burke had feared would happen.

Along about mid morning of the fifteenth, President Chamoun summoned Ambassador McClintock to the Presidential Palace and asked that the Marines move into the city of Beirut proper, and not remain in their beach and airport positions. "If they don't," said the President, "the rebels have threatened to break out of their Basta stronghold and, with the help of the Army, they plan to kidnap me."

With equal vigor, General Chehab informed the Ambassador that Lebanese troops and tanks were deployed in positions along the road from the airport to the city, and that they would certainly fire on the Marines if the latter attempted to move into Beirut.

In this sticky situation, McClintock adopted an imaginative ruse. He suggested to Chehab that it was their joint duty, under such explosive circumstances, to prevent bloodshed by interposing themselves physically between the two opposing forces—the Marines and the Lebanese Army. Chehab, proud and courageous, acceded to this suggestion, and the two drove off in the ambassador's Cadillac.

They found Admiral Holloway at the head of a column of Marines drawn up and ready to march. "General," said Holloway, "I am ordering this column to advance at once. And," he added quietly, "I do not expect that there will be any resistance."

The general looked unhappy. "Would you," he asked finally, "allow fifteen minutes for me to get in touch with my headquarters and have them pull the troops back?"

"Mon Général," said the Admiral gallantly, "we will not only allow you fifteen minutes. We will escort you to the telephone!"

Holloway and McClintock did precisely that. When they returned to the column, Holloway waved his little swagger stick for emphasis and, drawing upon his Naval Academy French announced "And now, mon général, we advance *toot-dee-suitee!*"

"Permit me the honor . . ." purred McClintock in his polished French, seizing Chehab's elbow and literally propelling him into the Cadillac as Holloway climbed in from the other side. Seated up front were the chauffeur and a garishly dressed character, named Tewfik, who was the Ambassador's *kavass* or guard. Beside Tewfik sat "Golly," the Ambassador's poodle. Majestically, the Cadillac surged forward, the U.S. flag and the ambassador's flag streaming from the front fenders. The Marines followed; no shot was fired; Beirut was invested, and President Chamoun remained a free man although he was not long to remain President.

With the Lebanon operation secured and Army and Air Force reinforcements flooding in to help stabilize the situation, Arleigh Burke left Flag Plot, but he did not go home. With a full schedule of important appointments for that Tuesday, July 15, he could permit himself no rest. Instead, he returned to his own office, and he did not see Admiral's House again until after seven-thirty that night. By that time, he had been continuously on duty for thirty-six hours, and under merciless pressure the entire time. In the delicate and far-flung manipulations required by the Mid-East crisis, a wrong move by the CNO—a failure to anticipate and accommodate in advance the enemy's reply to the landings, or such primary dislocation as an interruption of the flow of oil from the Middle East —might have resulted in world crisis. Despite Burke's personal conviction

21

that Russia would seek to contain the situation, the spark of World War III indubitably was latent in the Lebanon that mid-July, and the stakes of the game were incalculable. It was, indeed, "brinkmanship" with a vengeance. While the President assumed responsibility for ultimate decision—a responsibility demanded of him, and which he could not share—it was Arleigh Burke's keen mind, sure perception, and deft control of his own forces which implemented that decision and still avoided the catastrophe of spreading hostilities.

What manner of man was this naval officer who, at age fifty-seven, moved his pieces over the global chessboard with such deft assurance and skill? His name was Burke. Did that, then, provide insight into his personality? Was he, perchance, a fighting Irishman with a rare combination of brilliant and mercurial Gaelic talents and temperaments? No, the name Burke was no clue to this man's personality, or to his talents either. His patronymic was Bjorkegren and his grandfather, Anders Petter Gustafsson Bjorkegren, was born in the parish of Herrljunga, near Göteborg, Sweden, on December 16, 1834. He landed at Boston in the spring of 1857 and eventually changed his name to Burke, simply because native Americans had difficulty pronouncing Bjorkegren, and made it sound like Burke anyway. Thus, the CNO with the Irish name was, in reality, a Swede; and under old Swedish law, even though an American citizen with his name changed, he still was the titular head of the family Bjorkegren.

It was given to Arleigh Burke to preside, as Chief of Naval Operations, over the conversion of the U.S. Navy from conventional to nuclear concepts, ships, power, weaponry, training, and strategic and tactical concepts. This was a changeover without precedent in naval history. The only comparable change—in kind perhaps, but by no means in degree—was the conversion from sail to steam. It was also Burke's lot, serving an unprecedented three successive terms as CNO, to play a leading role in the development of a far-flung free world naval capability. The free world lives only through undisputed control of the seas. This is an elementary fact of geography and political economy. In times past nations have built, trained, and deployed their naval forces in response to their own limited national needs and interests. But in the nuclear age, characterized by the powerful Soviet bloc fanatically and actively opposed to the greater, but not decisively more powerful, Western bloc, the parochial naval concepts of other days will not serve. Under the leadership of the United States, emerging from World War II as the foremost naval power on earth, the navies of friendly nations had to be fortified and coordinated into a single defensive and striking force, each nation's combatant ships playing a role complementary to all the others. Only in this way could requisite naval strength be developed for the defense of the Western coalition and its friends.

22

The job presented, to free-world naval leaders, an almost insuperably complex challenge, which included not alone the design and construction of ships and the development of weapons, but the vital matters of morale and training as well. By 1960, however, a free world naval force with a global capability was an in-being reality, and Arleigh Burke had much to do with this realization of a naval dream.

Arleigh Burke was a fighting admiral. He fought resolutely and without fear through the vicious Southwest Pacific campaign of World War II, turned in the "perfect battle" at Cape St. George, and had ships sunk under him. He was an able, aggressive negotiator, as the Red Chinese discovered when they faced him across the table during the Korean armistice talks in 1951. He has been fiercely devoted to the naval and the national interest all his life and on one occasion, although a senior officer, he showed so much zeal that the Navy itself placed him under arrest in his own Pentagon office!

As a young officer, Burke got the only black mark to mar his record, when a brazen New York woman stowed away aboard battleship *Arizona,* in which he was serving, and rode the ship to Panama for one of the most hilarious cruises in the annals of the U.S. Navy.

As a senior officer, Burke's talents were so obvious and so unique that he was selected for the high post of Chief of Naval Operations, over the heads of nearly a hundred other officers whose claims to the honor were senior to his. In that post he showed himself to be an astute diplomat in a job which demanded diplomacy as well as high technical and administrative ability. There is ample evidence to support the conclusion that Arleigh Burke will go down in history as the greatest Chief of Naval Operations in the annals of the United States naval service, and eventually will be canonized as a multidimensional naval hero, new-minted in the furnace of combat at sea, and finished in the fining pot of Washington's unremitting and crushing pressures and turbulence.

Are there keys and clues to the colorful, knowledgeable, impetuous and inspiring personality which lurks behind the four stars and briar pipe, these dominant outward and material symbols of Arleigh Albert Burke? Are there explanations of his leadership genius which constantly impelled men to do better than their best?

There are. But the roots go uncommonly deep, and the causative principles which motivated this complex man in the mid-twentieth century must be sought, at least in part, long ago, and far away . . .

CHAPTER 2

Early Days of a Viking

It was five o'clock of a warm October morning and the big man was running, shouting as he ran "Ollie! Ollie Stromberg! My wife is dying; I need help!"

The brittle edge of urgency, almost of panic, imparted a raw, rising rasp to the normally deep and even register of Oscar Burke's voice. As he ran his long blond hair tumbled down over his eyes. His hastily donned denim shirt, improperly buttoned, flopped open in front, half way down his belly. He heeded it not. Arriving at his neighbor's fence big Oscar stopped and shouted once more, "Ollie! Where in hell are you?"

Ollie was out behind his house, feeding the stock. At first he heard Oscar's tumult and shouting but dimly. Ollie was a powerful man of nearly six feet, with dark hair, grey-blue eyes, and the deep chest of a blacksmith. He was a Swede, of course, and upon first coming to the United States he'd tried railroading in the West. He'd tired of this though, and rented a farm two miles east of Boulder, Colorado and a couple of hundred yards down the road from Oscar Burke's farm, and settled to agricultural pursuits. Despite the fact that Ollie Stromberg was a bachelor and seven years his junior Oscar Burke, but one generation removed from his own native Swedish ancestry, had formed a quiet, undemonstrative attachment for his neighbor. That he would turn to Ollie in time of trouble was evidence enough of Oscar's trust in his friend, for Oscar did not give his confidence easily.

Finally, becoming conscious of the alarm in Oscar's shouting, Ollie halted his chores and came striding to the fence puzzled and anxious.

"Ollie," said Oscar, "my wife Clara's about to have a baby. There seems to be something wrong; I think she's bad off. Your horse is faster than mine; will you go for Dr. McClory?"

"Help me hook up!"

Oscar vaulted the fence and followed Ollie to the stable. Although they were friends and neighbors, it was not strange that this was the first intimation Ollie Stromberg had that Clara Mokler Burke was pregnant. They

24

were phlegmatic people, and the two men exchanged few words as they hitched Ollie's chestnut sorrel "Doll" to the buggy. "Doll" was a six-year-old and had been trained to the track for one year. She was much faster than any horse in Oscar Burke's string.

At age ninety Ollie Stromberg was to remember vividly all the color and detail of his wild ride for Dr. McClory on that Saturday morning of October 19, 1901, and to describe it in these words:

"It was a warm, sunny day, and the air was ladened with the fragrance of flowers. I had two miles to go over dirt roads. Despite the ruts, I put "Doll" flat out. We made the round trip in twenty-five minutes, which was very good time in the circumstances.

"Dr. McClory was a single man and lived in a rooming house at the corner of Twelfth and Pearl streets in Boulder. He was sitting up in bed, reading, when I arrived. I beat on the door, and when he stuck his head out the window, I explained the trouble and asked him to hurry, which he did. He was of medium height and rather portly, with dark hair and a marked professional air which was emphasized by the little black bag he seemed to carry all the time. There was not much conversation on the way back. The important thing was to get to Oscar's house as soon as possible, and I gave all my attention to "Doll." Like the intelligent horse she was, she seemed to sense that her best effort was needed, and she went a'flyin'! The doctor joined Mrs. Burke as soon as we arrived, and the baby was born fifteen minutes later. That would have been between six and seven o'clock in the morning; we'd barely made it. When the doctor was finished, I drove him back to Boulder."

Thus was born Arleigh Albert Burke, a contemporary Viking and one of the greatest fighting men and leaders the U.S. Navy ever has known. Blood spoke to blood. Although he was born close to the geographical center of the nation, surrounded by mountains and prairie, the call of his sea rover ancestors reached across half a continent to claim him for the sea. For the red infant of that morning was to become—not alone a supremely aggressive, fighting sailor, but an administrator and diplomat of rare talent as well. Wrote a colleague:

"Arleigh Burke has been the best thing to happen to the U.S. Navy since John Paul Jones." In truth the adult Burke shared many qualities with the intrepid Jones. Courage, daring, and dash were their common heritage. Jones implored "Give me a fast ship, for I mean to go in harm's way!" Arleigh Burke was to write:

"Combat is the profoundest experience of the male, corresponding to childbirth in women. Every man wants the tremendous inner satisfaction of having measured up adequately to the demands of combat. At the very least, he feels a need to face the test of combat and conduct himself like a man."

Then, he added his requirements for one who would lead men:

"The great captain must be able to project his personality so that his entire command feel they know him and follow him as an individual. The larger the command, the more flamboyant and theatrical the personality must be, to project the greater distance. We find examples of the truth of this in comparing Jeb Stuart and Jackson with Longstreet and Hill; Halsey with Spruance; Patton with Bradley."

In the years ahead, Arleigh Burke was to vindicate, and more, his appreciation of the healthy and dominant male need for participation in combat; and he was to show himself a colorful captain, whose personality projected to such distances and was felt by such numbers of people that, while still comfortably short of middle age, he became a legend in the U.S. Navy. Soon thereafter, he was to become legendary in the navies of all the Free World.

It was Clifton Fadiman, the celebrated critic, who wrote:

"A legend may be true, but it's different from a fact. You learn a fact, but the legend is something you seem to have known all your life." So it was to be with Arleigh Burke and the Navy. He presided over the creation of the modern U.S. Navy; and his spirit and leadership genius were indivisible parts of it, which seemed to have been at the core of it always.

The antecedents of this new, squalling infant were both interesting and significant. He was to grow into a complex man, and he was to face momentous decisions—decisions upon which many lives hung and, now and again, the stability of nations. As Arleigh Burke's life pattern worked out, he was to evidence a curious quality. It was almost as if his early forebears, his father and mother, and his youthful conditioning combined to wind him up and 'set' him like a peripatetic alarm clock. He was always to be 'set' in advance and in anticipation of significant happenings in which he was to participate. When the right combination of circumstances presented itself—when the hands of the 'clock' were brought into proper juxtaposition—he 'went off.' Sometimes he went off quietly; more often he went off explosively. This was true in battle, and it was manifest many times over when he faced the grievous responsibilities incident to the post of Chief of Naval Operations. Whether Burke himself recognized this singular personal attribute is moot, but, throughout life, he was to have a preoccupation with time—almost a time compulsion. He illuminated this characteristic with an epigram, when he observed that "the difference between a good officer and a poor one is about ten seconds."

Any understanding of Arleigh Burke and the heroic events in which he participated, and which he often helped to shape demands exploration of two bedrock factors in his background. First, his lineage, from whence came his courage and his joy in battle. Second, his parents and his early life in Colorado, from whence came his immediate drives, his high moral

26

rectitude and sense of responsibility, and his talent for hard, sustained work and thoroughness.

The Burke family emerges in recorded history as far back as 1750, under the name of Olofsson. These early forebears dwelt in the lower portion of Sweden, between the Skagerrak and the flinty-blue waters of the Baltic.

The Burke line comes down through Anders Gustaf Olausson Bjorkegren, born in the province of Hudene on March 15, 1810. In 1832, having become a miller by trade, Anders married Anna Stina Andersdotter and moved to the province of Herrljunga.

Anders Gustaf sired two daughters and a son—Anders Petter Gustafsson Bjorkegren—born December 16, 1834. Anders Petter, Arleigh Burke's grandfather, was a restless, questing spirit. He was "a man with the bark on," as the pioneers observed when he reached the American West. It was from him that Arleigh was to inherit much of his mercurial temperament, as well as his daring.

In 1844, Anders Petter was apprenticed to a baker in Göteborg. His father, having suffered business reverses, emigrated to the United States with his two daughters, Annicka and Anna Sara Bjorkegren. He was, at that time, a widower, and he left his son behind in Sweden. Report has it that Anders Petter was not included in the family migration because he had run away from home some months before and was not available. Such a performance would have been in character. In any case, Anders Petter got his journeyman's papers as a baker in 1849, moved to Copenhagen, and finally joined his family at Boston, in the New World, in 1857. That same year his father died; the two girls married farmers of Chautauqua County, New York; and Anders Petter, filled with the fire, curiosity, and confidence of twenty three summers, turned his face West, toward adventure and the quest for his fortune. He had little difficulty accommodating his worldly possessions in one carpet bag—all, that is, save his fiddle. From the fiddle he coaxed consolation or merry tunes, as the occasion demanded; and from it he could, under no circumstances, be separated for long. It went West with him and was destined to play a significant role in his future, winning him a home, helping him lose a wife.

Anders Petter Gustafsson Bjorkegren was not a man to stand on formality. He soon discovered that his new-found American friends had one hell of a time trying to pronounce the name Bjorkegren. They made it sound like 'Burke'; so, without the aid of any effete legal flapdoodle, he changed his name to Burke, to accommodate them. This he did unilaterally, without reference to his sisters and, while he was at it, he decided to rid himself of the name Anders (Andrew), for which he had little liking. He preferred the name August and so, in 1857, there fared forth into the pioneer West of a quickening continent not Anders Petter Gustafsson

27

Bjorkegren, but plain Gus Burke. He was well equipped, by temperament and physique, for the easy swing of mountain and prairie and the hard challenge of the pioneers. In due time, and conforming to custom immemorial, he fell in love.

Mary Jane Harding was born near Quincy, Illinois, on April 10, 1841. She came to Denver with a wagon train, met Gus soon after his arrival, and it was love at first sight for both. They were married September 14, 1860.

Gus Burke's Viking spirit sent him restlessly searching for new horizons. He and Mary soon trundled off to the mining camp of Central City. Gus simply had to be near the heart of the gold-fever excitement. Almost immediately, he threw in his lot with two Norwegians (he always sought Scandinavians as partners) and moved his increasing family to Gold Run Gulch, where the three started a mining project. The roseate dreams and expectations failed to materialize. In 1865, Gus and Mary pushed on to Boulder, Colorado where, for a while, Gus worked at various odd jobs. He also applied for his naturalization papers, although he still was having considerable difficulty with the English language. The following year he staked out a homestead, and he and his staunch wife worked from sun to sun in a dogged effort to wrest a subsistence from the wilderness. Finally, through desperate determination and the patient acceptance of crushing hardship, they managed to raise two crops, but they harvested neither. The grasshoppers got there first! As he and Mary watched with unbelieving eyes, the insects stripped the fertile earth bare, leaving it parched and barren. By that time, the substantial stake they had acquired in Denver had been swallowed up in various mine speculations. They were flat broke.

"And now . . . ?" asked Mary. "We haven't even enough money to buy seed grain for another try!"

"I've still got my fiddle," Gus told her. "There's enough food on the place for you and the children for a few weeks. I'm going out and get a new stake."

The next morning, Gus Burke tucked his fiddle under his arm and hit the road. He hadn't a horse, so he walked. Over 190 miles of rocky road, Gus trudged to the frontier community of Julesburg, Colorado. He slept beside the road, or at farms and mining camps along the way paying for his bed and board with lively music which belied his heavy heart. At Julesburg, he played for dances and entertainments; then he moved out to perform in the roaring mining camps of the vicinity. As in all things, Gus Burke was dogged, and he had a singleness of purpose which permitted no deviation from his set goal.

Having acquired a small stake, Gus returned to Boulder. He purchased seed, planted, irrigated, and cultivated, and finally he harvested a crop bountiful beyond his most optimistic hopes. From it he realized two thousand dollars and with this, in 1877, he purchased an additional 130 acres and established one of the most substantial farms in Boulder County. By this time, the Burke family had been increased by six children—Carl, Oscar, Frank, Kate, Maude, and Reuben. Outwardly, Gus and Mary gave the appearance of success and contentment but this appearance was an illusion. A number of serpents were loose in their pioneer Eden and had started mischief making, about the time Gus set out for Julesburg.

Gus Burke was a pioneer, with all of a pioneer's virtues and faults. He was a hard and vigorous man and, like most of his contemporaries, he had a touch of the devil in him. He worked hard and he played hard. And he drank raw, red, likker when the mood was upon him. Certainly, there was nothing to indicate that he was more boisterous than his contemporaries. Certainly, too, he was a builder and a conserver reclaiming barren lands to fruitful husbandry. But, above all else, he was a free spirit and, within the broad interpretation of the time and place, a law unto himself and his family.

Mary Harding, in her way, was as sturdy an individualist as was her husband. She worked at his side, and she conceived and brought forth his children. But she lamented his sprees as they occurred more frequently, and she bridled at his sometimes heavy-handed discipline. For a time, womanlike, she bent to these blasts. Then, one day in the spring of 1878, a new charmer appeared in Boulder. Whence he came, how long he stayed, and whither he went, are considerations beyond the memory of living man. But one thing is a certainty: when he left Boulder, Mary Harding Burke went with him, leaving husband and children flat. One day she was there; the next day she was gone. It was as simple as that.

Oscar Burke, the second of Gus's and Mary's children, was born in the minuscule mining community of Nevadaville, Colorado, on June 2, 1863 —the year made notable in history, on its very first day, by Lincoln's signing of the Emancipation Proclamation. When the fireworks caused by his mother's elopement finally flickered out and his father had remarried, Oscar was a gangling youth of seventeen.

From his father, from his mother, and from the pioneer West, Oscar inherited a substantial legacy, not of treasure but of temperament, character, and capacity. He had something of Gus's enterprising spirit and eagerness to see what lay over the horizon. He had a full measure of the peasant Scandinavian determination to scrupulous honesty, moral rectitude, and the strict apportionment of his hours of labor in relation to present goals for accomplishment. If anything, he had a greater compulsion to hard and sustained work than had his father. But his character did not show his father's overweening predilection for gambling, speculation, and occasional roistering. Oscar Burke was inherently conservative. More, he was the first of the Burke line to absorb fully, and nurture zealously, the typical American mores and superficial stigmata so indelibly stamped upon, and characteristic of, the second generation of Western pioneers. These included a strong dash of roughhewn individualism and an increment of patriotism which had about it no trace of chauvinistic taint. The Fourth of July always was a notable occasion for Oscar Burke, and he taught his children its intrinsic significance.

For Oscar Burke, economic and social freedom came slowly. For a half dozen years he helped his father farm the acres he had homesteaded and purchased at Boulder. Saving his money (Oscar was always to know the value of a penny, but not always the value of a pound), he rented a nearby farm from a family named Pine. Eventually, he purchased the property. Known as the 'Upper Place,' this parcel consisted of 180 acres of rocky land, with only fair soil between the rocks. It was difficult to irrigate, but plenty of water was available, and Oscar was a resourceful as well as a hardworking, stubborn man. He made the farm flower and, after some years, added the 'Lower Place' to his holdings. This was an additional sixty-eight acres of native grass and pasture, about three-quarters of a mile east of the original tract.

Sharing in this constructive adventure with Oscar Burke was Clara (sometimes called Claire) Emogene Mokler. Clara Mokler, one of twelve children, was born March 6, 1878, at Whitefield Corners, Illinois, and was of solid Scotch-Irish ancestry. The family drifted West by way of Kansas eventually coming to Boulder in 1899. At twenty-one, Clara Mokler was a statuesque woman of considerable capacity and determination. She had red hair, was big boned, and scaled about 180 pounds. She had a soft voice and was musically inclined. Most of all, she had a calm, but pervading, presence which commanded instant universal respect. Hard work had been her portion and was to continue to be. But, despite the abrasive impacts of farm labor and the raising of a numerous family, Clara was to preserve that requisite quality of femininity essential to any normal and stable union between man and wife.

When for the first time, Clara Mokler saw Oscar Burke she was favorably impressed. He was a big man, a shade under six feet, and a solid 220 pounds. He was blond, blue eyed, and he wore an attention-arresting moustache with the demanded soupçon of flair. He was jolly, and he enjoyed the dances to which he squired her. Although, certainly, he was not wealthy, Clara guessed that his financial position was about as stable as most in those hectic, scrambling days of the new frontier. He was fifteen years her senior but that was the marriage pattern of the time. Oscar Burke and Clara Mokler became man and wife at Boulder on November 10, 1899.

As had his father before him, Oscar Burke sired six children. The first was Arleigh, born in 1901. Three girls—Ruth, in 1903; May, in 1906;

and Edith, in 1911, followed. Then came another boy, Victor, in 1913, followed by the baby of the family, Barbara Jeanne, born in 1919.

Indelible and of transcendent consequence to his future career were the imprints made upon the character of Arleigh Burke by his life on the farm and the happy felicity of complementary traits and talents exhibited by his parents. It is almost possible, one by one, to chronicle the circumstances and the events which molded the boy's character and inevitably insured his great achievements. For at the core and root of Arleigh Burke lay one value, character—*extraordinary* character—and that value emerged, rough but fully formed, from the stern disciplines of a frontier farm and the preachings and precepts of Oscar and Clara Burke.

The first Burke house had "five rooms and a path." It was a clapboard affair, weatherbeaten and brown. There were two bedrooms, a living room, a dining room, and a kitchen. The house was heated by a coal stove in the dining room, and Clara and the girls cooked on a wood-burning range in the kitchen. As soon as they were old enough the girls chopped and fetched the wood and brought in the coal, but they were not allowed to handle the hot ashes until they reached the age of fourteen. The girls slept in one bedroom, their parents had the other; Arleigh and later, Victor, slept on a folding couch in the living room. On cold nights, they would creep into the dining room and bed down on blankets behind the stove. Kerosene lamps provided the only illumination. The chimneys were washed by the girls with the breakfast dishes each morning, and polished with paper. Despite careful wick trimming, these lamps invariably smoked when first lighted. There were no sanitary facilities in the house, a 'Chic Sales' about a hundred feet from the back door providing that convenience. That accounted for the "path" with the "five rooms." Water had to be carried in from the well. Sometimes, because it was softer, Clara used water from the irrigation ditch for washing. The Burkes were not wealthy but they were happy.

For the most part, the routine of the farm was unvarying. Oscar raised alfalfa, corn, wheat and oats and, on the 'Lower Place,' hay. A couple of hired men, usually, were available to help with the spring plowing, but, through the summer, all of the Burke children had their appointed tasks on the farm. In winter, too, they had their before-school chores, milking and taking care of the stock. The day began at five o'clock, when Oscar and Clara arose and set about the morning milking. In winter, Clara would delay going to the barn until she had kindled the fires. She was the top hand of the tribe at milking, and she enjoyed it because the barn provided temporary sanctuary from the noise and confusion of a houseful of waking children. While one of the girls stayed behind to get breakfast under way, the other children helped with the milking, fed the calves, and assisted their father in cleaning out the barn.

31

After the milking was completed, Clara Burke returned to the house to finish cooking breakfast, which was served promptly at seven o'clock. At breakfast, Oscar assigned each child a task for the day and allotted the time in which it was to be accomplished. It was not enough for the work to be assigned; the time for its completion had to be specified also. This methodical characteristic Oscar Burke transmitted to his son, and its impact was not negligible. All his life, Arleigh Burke's waking hours were bracketed by lists of tasks to be accomplished and checked off at specified intervals. Long before he won the sobriquet "31-Knot Burke," he was widely known in the Navy as "Checkoff-List Burke."

Breakfast over, a Burke child was dispatched to get the teams in, and by eight o'clock, father and children were headed for the fields. One girl always stayed behind to help Clara with the housework.

Nancy, the horse most of them learned to ride, finally grew decrepit with age, and Oscar Burke took her to Denver, to sell her to the circus for meat for the wild animals. But, when the circus people refused to kill Nancy before his eyes, Oscar turned around and brought her back home again, accomplishing the sixty-mile round trip in a day and a night. He refused to leave the horse without positive evidence that she had been humanely destroyed. He could not bring himself to kill Nancy, but hired a neighbor to do it. She was buried on the Burke farm.

The children and their father regarded branding and dehorning the new cattle as the worst job on the farm. Although Arleigh subsequently was to participate in much sanguinary combat, all of the Burkes had weak stomachs in the face of blood and suffering: the spurting blood and odor of scorched flesh and singed hair attendant upon this operation invariably made them sick. Oscar, a stern disciplinarian, would allow no child to quit, under any circumstances, once the work was begun, nor would he allow them to tie a calf. They had to hold the animal down with their hands, steeling themselves as best they could against the blood spattering in their faces and the pitiful bawlings assaulting their ears.

A number of well defined and progressively more difficult tasks marked the ascent of each Burke child upward, through the hierarchy of the farm toward goals of privilege and responsibility. At age ten, a child was promoted to driving a team, raking hay, or harrowing, *if* he or she could perform to Oscar's satisfaction. Next, the candidate graduated to operating the buck rake. This was a job calling for coordination and precision, and it was the end of the line for the girls. For the boys, there lay ahead a real test of manhood: they were challenged to "go on the ditch."

The Burke places were irrigated by three ditches. These would fill up through the summer, fall, and winter seasons, and each spring they had to be cleaned out to insure a free flow of water. This was man's work and was undertaken by the neighbors on a communal basis, one of their number acting as Ditch Superintendent. First, a ditch had to be plowed out. Then, the loose sod had to be pitched out of the ditch, and this was desperately hard labor for man or boy. The Burke boys always took a pitchfork and strove to keep up with their sturdier elders. If their work was satisfactory, the Ditch Superintendent would offer them a bite from his plug of Brown's Mule chewing tobacco. It was a great day in his life when Arleigh Burke "went on the ditch," but he never mastered Brown's Mule.

As on every farm, harvest time for the Burkes was joyous. It was then that the children got their rewards for their summer's work. Oscar believed in teaching his children to work hard, but he also believed in showing suitable recognition for satisfactory endeavor. In the fall, the kids shocked the grain, pretending that the shocks were tepees, and building many an Indian village. On clear, moonlight nights they would return to the fields for an hour or so of work after supper. In time, Oscar Burke got his own threshing machine, and at harvest time the neighbors traded work. There would be a dozen men on a threshing crew; as many as twenty on a silo crew. Clara Burke and her daughters cooked for the lot. All of the farm wives were proud of their cooking and vied with each other in setting elaborate spreads before the hungry men. Clara was a talented cook and met these Gargantuan challenges with no apparent strain. Her special dinner consisted of roast beef with brown gravy, mashed white potatoes, candied sweet potatoes, lima beans, cabbage salad, sliced tomatoes, home-made bread—she habitually baked twenty-two large loaves a week for her family alone—biscuits, jelly, pickles, and lemon pie, the whole washed down with gallons of steaming coffee. Her offerings were many times weighed and never found wanting.

By the second week in September, the silo was full, and the Burke children faced fall and winter routines, including attendance at school. They were never kept out of school to do farm work. During the summer, Oscar and Clara drove to town about once a week to shop for staples. Now, larger quantities of supplies were laid in against the prospect of hard weather—flour in hundred-pound sacks, sugar in hundred pound sacks, slabs of bacon and cases of canned tomatoes, peas, and corn. On balance, Oscar Burke had decided against a garden; it was his conviction that the necessary effort would be more productive if expended on the farm.

Holidays were occasions for lavish celebration in the Burke household. On the Fourth of July, the kids got up early and ran up and down the road, shooting off firecrackers until all neighbors were well awake. Later in the day they would be taken on a picnic or to town, where their father listened intently to the Fourth-of-July oratory in the courthouse square. Homemade icecream was traditional, with willing hands to crank the old-fashioned freezer, and even more willing tongues to lick the dasher. It was a routine as normal and healthy as blueberry pie. Thanksgiving and Christmas saw the Burkes keeping open house, with relatives crowding in for huge dinners, topping breakfasts of outsized pancakes loaded with whipped cream. Clara, laughingly but nonetheless firmly, guarded her recipe for the ginger cookies which graced these occasions and would share it with no one. Not alone on holidays, but throughout the year, dining protocol in the Burke household was strict. Meals were served punctually, and every meal was eaten in the dining room with a white linen cloth on the table.

The elementary school attended by the Burke children was next door to their house and only a few hundred yards away. Named the Baseline School, it was a red brick building built in 1901, the year of Arleigh's birth. It consisted of one big room, divided by a sliding partition, permitting a two-classroom arrangement. One teacher taught all eight grades for a time, and the student body fluctuated between twenty and forty. If the Burke children were in a hurry to get to classes, they crawled through the barbed wire fence separating their property from the school. But if one of the Burke girls had her mind set upon being walked to school by "someone special," she marched sedately out the Burke gate and up the road until the "someone special" came along.

Arleigh Burke's first day at school was sheer disaster, but it taught his mother one of the few lessons she still had to learn. So far as Clara Burke was concerned, young Arleigh, blond and blue-eyed, was an ever livin' doll, and she was determined to do justice to her treasure on this, his first formal public appearance alone. With loving care and many a maternal pat, she tricked him out in a Little Lord Fauntleroy suit—the romantic *ne plus ultra* of the doting mothers of the day—and topped off the rig with a big white embroidered collar. She thought him stunning, but the getup failed to stupefy his schoolmates. They took one look, tore off the collar, and tossed the surprised Arleigh into a muddy ditch. He stuck out the morning session but at noon he arrived home, demanding overalls. Clara Mokler Burke was no fool, nor was she one to buck the odds too vigorously in matters of small consequence. Her son returned for the afternoon session, clad as were the other boys, and in all probability spared a great deal of fighting thenceforward in defense of his masculinity.

The Burke children were no models of brotherly and sisterly love and consideration. They fought vigorously among themselves and occasionally stayed awake of nights, thinking up hateful spites to practice on each other. "Mom! Make them quit picking on me!" was an oft-repeated refrain around the Burke manse. But, woe unto the outsider brash enough to try to take unfair advantage of a Burke. Either he retreated, or he fought the whole tribe!

For all practical purposes, though teachers and pupils continued to go

34

through the motions, the process of learning at Baseline Elementary School ground to a halt about two weeks before each Christmas. Instead, all turned their attention to decorating the schoolhouse and rehearsing the special Christmas program which annually reassured skeptical parents that their little darlings were up to, at least, some good, along with the mischief which was more congenial to them. A few days before the big event, the eighth-grade boys en masse journeyed to the nearby Velie place where, after appropriate comparison and debate, they selected what they agreed to be the finest Douglas spruce in sight. This was chopped down and transported ceremoniously to the schoolhouse, where it became the center-piece for the forthcoming festivities.

The big Christmas program was a mélange of short plays, readings, and song. The singing was loud. The climax of the show was the appearance of Charlie Wilson, a Burke neighbor, who pinch hit for Santa Claus. Charlie had the kids fooled up to about the fourth grade; and the older sophisticates, once in the know, were at great pains not to initiate their younger and more gullible brothers and sisters. At that Mr. Wilson proved to be something of a real-life Santa Claus for Arleigh Burke. Wilson was prominent in the life of the community and had political connections. When the time came, it was he who got young Arleigh the opportunity to compete for an Annapolis appointment through incumbent congressman Charles B. Timberlake.

The school season closed with a fruity bang when all of the parents of the School District (and their cousins and their aunts) assembled to watch the County School Superintendent hand diplomas to the new crop of eighth-grade graduates. This rite, understandably, was concluded only after the assemblage had been drenched in a flood of academic oratory which permitted the Superintendent to exercise his erudition for the edification of his constituents. However, on the last day of school, the weighty memory of these high-toned and cultural doings was balanced for the children by a school picnic on the Chautauqua grounds. Everybody attended, and the jollity was climaxed by a baseball game between the fathers and sons. The kids invariably won.

In casting up and interpreting the enduring values of this Western pastoral—and there were plenty of enduring values in it—three people claim primary attention, if we would measure its impact upon Arleigh Burke. They were Clara Mokler Burke, who might be called the producer; Oscar Burke, who played the role of director; and, of course, Arleigh Burke, the star. Although a host of others contributed, now and again, to the formative processes which went into the development of the traits and character exhibited later by the adult Arleigh, they were, to a large extent, but spear carriers in the Burke drama.

Soft voiced and multi-talented, Clara Mokler Burke was the strong mem-

35

ber of the family. She never yelled at the children, but her tone and address conveyed to them an unmistakable demand for prompt obedience. She encouraged them to individual enterprise, and she allowed them full liberty in the enjoyment of the extra money they earned. When one of the girls bought a fur scarf with money she had earned picking blueberries for a neighbor, Clara observed tartly that the child might better have used the family cat—but the scarf stayed.

Clara Burke had expressive, competent hands, clearly remembered by all the members of her family. Those hands worked with incredible skill and speed; they milked, handled hoe and rake and reins, sewed, canned, cleaned and cooked, and played the pedal-pump organ which eventually graced the Burke living room. And, through some alchemy known to Clara alone, they did not become swollen, rough, or red. Through the school next door, Clara soon became a leader in the distaff activities of the community. She contributed poems to small magazines, wrote plays for the school dramatic programs, and many a Burke sheet did double duty as a stage curtain. She kept a wary eye on the community interest, and more than one county commissioner was called on the carpet through her instigation.

Clara handled the farm finances and did the family purchasing. She was a good manager, and the rule she lived by and taught her children was, "When in doubt, do without." Under her regime the Burkes didn't have everything they wanted, but what they did have they fully owned. The harassments of debt were spared them, and the avoidance of debt was to become a lifelong rule for Arleigh Burke. As a young ensign in New York, he became, by his own admission, a foremost authority on finding free entertainment. What he could not find free he passed by, thus remaining free himself. Perhaps the most striking evidence of Clara Burke's talents as a manager came when she was unexpectedly widowed in 1933. Alone, she managed the two Burke farms through the depths of the depression of that time, and she managed to eke out a small profit when many of her male neighbors were mortgaging their property and losing it.

Clara fled from sham and pretense as she would have the plague. "Powder and paint make you seem what you ain't!" was a scornful admonition oft repeated to her daughters, and all of the Burkes grew up to be uncommonly plain-spoken and without affectation. She had nothing but contempt for what she called "two-bits snobs," and when her son attained the influential office of Chief of Naval Operations, and a few self-nominated "bosom pals" of his boyhood came crawling out of the woodwork, they usually were stopped dead by the coolness of the whole Burke clan.

Clara was the thinker of the family. It was she who encouraged her first-born to break away from the land and seek goals of greater responsibility, achievement and service. Wrote one of her daughters: "Dad may have been the iron of the family, but Mom was the flame that tempered it."

36

Oscar Burke had incredible strength. On one occasion, being in a hurry to make an adjustment, he picked up the whole back end of the threshing machine, to the amazement of his colleagues. But it was Clara Burke who had the vision and the courage. On one occasion, when long past her prime, she found herself face to face with an angry bull in a confined area. She proceeded to back the animal down and put it to flight—her only weapon a buggy whip.

When her active and noisy children started quarreling among themselves, Clara did not shout at them. She removed the cause of the trouble —swiftly and permanently. Among the games the kids received, one Christmas, was a deck of cards for playing "Flinch," a popular pastime in the early 1900's. The young ones soon started fighting over the game. Clara warned them once, quietly, to desist. When the next fight broke out, she calmly picked up the cards and tossed them into the stove. No more "Flinch": no more fights. The lesson may have been a bit severe and dramatic; but it was effective, and it will be remembered so long as a Burke child lives.

Under Clara, religious dogma and ritual played little part in the social organism which was the Burke family. Being farmers, and living at the foot of the snow-capped peaks of the Rocky Mountains, they achieved an intuitive attunement with nature, and they "lifted up their eyes unto the hills" in the certain conviction of the existence of a higher, if somewhat sketchily defined, power. They did not study the Bible at home, however, nor did Oscar Burke say grace at meals.

Clara Burke was an ever-present help to her neighbors in troublous times. She was a friendly woman, but not too friendly. She had a dignity and presence which discouraged too easy familiarity. At her death the community mourned, but they mourned for *Mrs. Burke,* not *Clara.* As they had not been allowed to presume upon her in life—not been allowed to get too close—no more did her friends presume upon her memory at the end. Alive or dead she always was "Mrs. Burke."

Of fundamental and well-nigh incalculable significance were the legacies which Arleigh Burke inherited from his mother. Her steady determination was, many times, for him a sheet anchor to windward. Her strong sense of responsibility, not just to her own but to others, set the pattern for her son's dedicated service to his Navy and his nation as a man. Her spurning of sham and pretense fortified his lifelong quest for real and stable values, and prompted him instinctively to reject the hollow trappings of empty honors achieved without striving and worth less than they cost. As Chief of Naval Operations, Arleigh Burke once gave unequivocable evidence on this point. He was invited to express an official opinion on the desirability of awarding the Legion of Merit to the visiting Chief of Naval Operations of a friendly power. His scathing reply went as follows:

37

"Since Admiral ———, Chief of Naval Operations of the ——— Navy has been invited to this country, and since all other Chiefs of Naval Operations from all other countries, upon visiting the United States have been awarded the Legion of Merit, and since it is proper that he should be awarded the Legion of Merit *in spite of the fact that he is a weak man, has probably had some dealings for his own personal gain with Communist organizations, and probably has conducted unsavory financial transactions in his own Government,* it is felt that the Legion of Merit should be awarded Admiral ——— during his visit. If the award is not given, it would become desirable to curtail or cancel his visit, and as this is now impossible he may as well have the award!"

Clara Mokler Burke's inherent dignity and sense of the appropriate restrained Arleigh, even as a youth, from disturbing excesses and marked him as a suitable repository for the confidence and trust of both his seniors and his juniors. As he rose through the ranks, Burke looked down more often than up, and it was axiomatic with him that "an officer's service reputation is made by those who serve under him." That was a direct reflection of Clara Burke's constant concern with those whom she could help. She was a teacher and a leader. So was her son.

Oscar Burke, Arleigh's father, came very close to being the perfect complement for his strong and stoical wife. He had a hair-trigger temper which could, and did, explode suddenly into a torrent of profanity with matching action. Afterward, he would gasp in incredulity when the children picked up some of his incandescent expletives. All his life, Arleigh Burke was to be a fluent "cusser." He did not indulge in vulgarity. Oscar was methodical, a stern disciplinarian, and dedicated to the principle that, so far as his children were concerned, prompt application of a willow switch or the toe of his boot were salutary remedies for character correction. Impudence or gross misbehavior brought an immediate and well-directed kick or a switching. Shirking or minor offenses were punished by the imposition of extra work. Oscar believed firmly in work as a panacea.

So far as Oscar was concerned, the latchstring always hung on the outside of the Burke door and the pot always was on the fire. He liked to have company for meals and any peddler, tramp, or neighbor who chanced into the Burke front yard at or near the appropriate time was pressed to stay for dinner. Clara took a dim view of this on occasion, but she never quite managed to housebreak her husband so far as openhanded hospitality was concerned. Ruth, the oldest daughter, favored her mother's more conservative approaches. On one occasion, when Clara was in the hospital, Ed Kohler, a neighbor, brought his cutter and silo crew to work on the Burke place. Ruth served them dinner—and charged them for it. When he learned the awful truth Oscar Burke was horrified. Clara was amused.

Oscar liked to sing and dance, and his days as a cowboy remained a verdant memory. Gathering his stair-step brood about him in the evening, he'd tell them stories of those days. Then he'd throw back his head and give tongue:

> *Come along boys and listen to my tale,*
> *I'll tell you of my troubles on the old Chisholm trail.*
> *I started up the trail October twenty-third—*
> *I started up the trail with the Two-U-Herd,*
> *On a ten-dollar horse and a forty-dollar saddle,*
> *And I'm goin' t' punch in Texas cattle!*

Other of the family favorites were the very melodious *Streets of Laredo,* the plaintive *Goodbye Old Paint,* and the rollicking *Rye Whiskey*—"Rye whiskey, rye whiskey, rye whiskey I cry! If I don't get rye whiskey I surely will die!" The children loved it. So did Oscar.

Oscar Burke—his neighbors called him "The Boss"—had one boast and one complaint. The boast was "I've got land, I've got kids, and I owe no man a dime." His perpetual complaint was "Here it is Tuesday morning, half the week gone, and not a damned thing done!"

Oscar was quick in his movements, quick in his judgments, and a fanatic about keeping his word under any and all circumstances. He liked to wrestle, and all of the hired men who worked on the Burke place from time to time were dragooned into tests of strength and dexterity with The Boss. Son Arleigh subsequently won his numerals at the Naval Academy as a wrestler. One day, Oscar went to town and, for the first time, saw girls wearing the forerunners of slacks. He came back, raving about the women wearing "calico pants," and no daughter of his was left in doubt about the prohibition of such revealing attire for the Burke females.

When Arleigh was about six years old, his father gave him a knife. It was rather more expensive a toy than a boy of Arleigh's age normally might expect to own, but the child had only a fuzzy notion of comparative values, and he soon traded the knife to a playmate for a homemade toy. A few days later, Arleigh realized that he had made a bad bargain; so he returned to his pal and raised so much hell that they reversed the swap. Arleigh's argument was that it was not a fair deal.

Oscar Burke heard of this bit of business about a week later. The first thing he did was whale the daylights out his son, just by way of italicizing the importance of prudence. Then, he marched the boy over to call on the playmate and his father. Arleigh was forced to give up the knife and take back the toy. With Oscar Burke, a bargain was a bargain; and it was a long time before Arleigh got another knife.

The worst whipping Arleigh Burke ever got was for lying. When he was ten his father sent him to fetch the cows from a pasture about a mile from the Burke house. The boy rode off on his pony but he dawdled along the way and was late getting back with the cattle. Oscar had the same built-in time sense that subsequently emerged in his son, and the ten-year-old boy feared the consequences of his tardiness. To escape punishment, he told his father that he had been delayed repairing a broken fence—a plausible enough excuse in the circumstances. Oscar accepted the boy's story without question; but a couple of weeks later, when they both were at the pasture, he asked to inspect the repairs. Arleigh was caught in his outright lie. Oscar proceeded to give his son the business, right there and then. That afternoon, Arleigh walked his horse home! Fifty and more years afterward, a dignified Chief of Naval Operations of the U.S. Navy was to remember that prototype of all corrective beatings —and think fondly of his father for it.

Oscar was a devoted reader of the public prints. He kept himself abreast of the times through the columns of the Denver papers (delivered a day late) and the *Boulder County Farmer and Miner,* the *Boulder Tribune,* and the *Daily Camera.* And the recurring annual news which made his eyes light up and his heart leap was the announcement that the circus was coming to town. All of the Burkes were inveterate circus buffs, and Oscar invariably took the whole tribe to town to witness the morning parade and attend the afternoon performance beneath the big top. He was known to threaten the young ones with a withholding of this treat, but he never executed his threats. He would no more miss a circus than he would cheat a neighbor. He remained young at heart.

Arleigh Burke's heritage from his father was both substantial and stern. An abiding and uncompromising honesty—a deep sense of personal honor and integrity—these were a part of it. A physical quickness and sturdiness was a part of it too. And dreams . . . Oscar Burke never lamented his lot; he strove constantly toward the acquisition of more land, and he bequeathed to his son the art of dreaming and the willingness to accept the hard work through which dreams sometimes become attainable. It was a rich legacy that the boy inherited from his father—as rich as that handed down by his mother and, although different, wondrously complementary.

At age four, Arleigh Burke first evidenced the seriousness which was to characterize his approach to life as a man. Curiously, the event which proved revealing involved the same Ollie Stromberg who had indirectly assisted at the child's birth. Ollie forsook single blessedness and was married February 3, 1904. A daughter, Violet, was born January 26, 1905. At a suitable time, Clara Burke took her young son on a visit to see the new baby. Arleigh was deeply impressed.

"May I have her?" he asked hopefully.

"I can't give her to you," said Ollie, "but I'll sell her to you for a dollar."

The visit ended, and nothing further was thought of the matter. An hour later, however, the Strombergs heard unexplained noises on their front porch. They opened the door to see tiny Arleigh standing, patiently, his little baby carriage beside him, and his piggy bank in his right hand. "I've come for the baby," he announced matter of factly. Revelation of the adult flippancy and duplicity brought cruel tears. Clara found him, comforted him, and escorted him home, herself misty-eyed for the tender trust of her first born.

Arleigh Burke started to school at the age of six, and it would be pleasant to report that he developed into an uninhibited young extrovert. But that would not be entirely in accordance with the facts. His teachers found him encouragingly malleable, well behaved, and a good average student. For a time, he and a pal of the same age, Bob Hockaday, dueled to be ranked at the head of the class. A dark horse came from behind, however—a girl named Dora Viele—and showed them both her heels. Competition ceased, and both boys discovered that they weren't so hot for academic honors after all. True, Arleigh Burke got on well with his schoolmates. His participation in group projects was satisfactory, and he achieved an entirely adequate social adjustment. But much of this was objectively and deliberately accomplished, just as, later, he would become a "flamboyant captain" because that quality was necessary to great and inspirational leadership. He had analyzed the challenge, found the answers, and sought their attainment with complete objectivity. In his inner self, Arleigh Burke often responded to the motivations of introversion. He was mercurial, and while he strove to keep this from interfering with his judgment or his actions, he was throughout life subject to recurring fits of depression which temporarily plunged him into the depths. How often these were conditioned by justifiable stimuli and how often they sprang from the deep recesses of his Scandinavian ancestry is moot, but his colleagues soon learned to walk softly when "a mood" was on the Chief.

Work and play—in that order—were the sum of the boy's days into his teens and beyond. His father had respect for both the therapeutic properties of honest labor and an appreciation of the fruits thereof; and these he impressed upon his son early. While yet of tender years, Arleigh started working for the neighbors an hour or so a day to earn nickels and dimes. He suspected, later, that his father may have paid him indirectly through a neighborly understanding, but the lesson sank home nonetheless: *If you want anything badly enough, you'll work for it.*

When the boy had fleshed out a bit and his muscles had hardened from strenuous work on the farm, he got the job of taking care of the schoolhouse furnace, keeping the building warm, and cleaning up the classrooms—in other words, he became the school janitor, although a student as well. One winter evening, someone turned off the steam radiator in the cloakroom, and Arleigh neglected to check it. That night, the pipes froze and burst. Oscar Burke administered the expected licking by way of reminding

41

his son of the demands of responsibility. Then, he paid for the damage. Arleigh was allowed to reimburse his father at the rate of fifty cents a month—exactly one half of his monthly "salary" of a dollar as janitor. The episode, although painful at the time, sharpened the boy's disposition toward responsibility and thoroughness.

Arleigh's talents for earning extra money crystallized rapidly. Soon he was trapping along Bear and Boulder Creeks, using light spring traps to take muskrats. The pelts he cleaned, stretched and dried, and shipped off to furriers in Denver, St. Louis, or Chicago. While a dollar was a big price for a pelt, Arleigh managed, through this endeavor and hiring himself out to the neighbors for farm work, to put by enough money to pay his expenses when, later, he went to Columbia, Missouri and took a special cram course to prepare himself for the Annapolis entry examinations. Not all of these hard-wrought earnings went for the Columbia expedition, however. Some of the money earned when he was younger went for "higher education"—the acquisition of each new book in the lengthening Frank Merriwell, Tom Swift, and Jack Harkaway series. Arleigh was a breathless follower of these tales of derring-do when he was of appropriate age, and, fortunately for him, this conditioning as a reader led to more substantial benefits. Clara Burke saw to it that there was a supply of good books around the house, and, when Arleigh first started to school, she procured a library card for him. When he accompanied his mother and father to town on their Saturday afternoon shopping expeditions, he would visit the town library. His mother made an arrangement with the librarian to permit him to draw three books at a time, and she insisted that he read at least two books a week during the winter months. Because of the increased farm work, this reading requirement was cut down to one book a week in summer. As Arleigh grew older, Clara Burke followed up this regimen by asking his teachers to assign him extra reading—a program in which they were delighted to cooperate. But there was a difference. In the beginning Arleigh had selected his own books. Now, his teachers selected and drew the books from the library, thus guiding the boy's questioning and receptive mind. An early teacher, Miss Maude Morgan, devoted herself enthusiastically to this program, and it was she who kindled the boy's initial interest in attending the Naval Academy. That torch was taken up in high school by another teacher, wife of Dr. T. D. A. Cockerell of the Biology Department of Colorado University, with conclusive results.

In June, 1919, the big day came for Arleigh Burke, but with it came contretemps. As he prepared to leave for the Naval Academy, his father fell ill. Dr. F. H. Farrington, who had replaced Dr. McClory as the Burke physician, was called and, after one look at Oscar Burke, he pronounced the diagnosis: *Smallpox!* Here was a pretty kettle of fish, the implications of which were plain. The family would have to be quarantined. Arleigh would be late reporting to the Academy and, as likely as not, his naval career would be finished before it began.

It took more than smallpox to confound Clara Mokler Burke. She drew the doctor aside for a calm but earnest discussion. Then, she hurriedly packed Arleigh's things. Dr. Farrington himself drove the lad to town and put him on a train headed East. Then, the doctor returned to the Burke home and tacked up the quarantine signs. When he reached Annapolis, Arleigh maintained a discreet silence, and it is not recorded that the Academy administrators ever suspected that, in the Burke boy, they had on their hands a male counterpart for "Typhoid Mary"—in this case "Smallpox Arleigh Burke."

During his Academy years, of which more in the next chapter, Midshipman Burke returned to Boulder from time to time on leave. If the blue and gold of the naval uniform set any local feminine hearts a'flutter, the disturbance was transient. The Burkes gained the prestige of a Dodge sedan in 1919, and senior daughter Ruth became the family chauffeur and custodian of the keys. When Arleigh came home, the family usually met him in Denver and drove him back to Boulder. It took less than five miles of the homeward journey to kindle a loud protest from Midshipman Burke about his sister's driving. He maintained that she was ignorant even of elementary understanding, and when she released a voluble reply, as she always did, he informed her gratuitously, "Oh, I know you can *talk!* You can talk about *anything—intelligently about nothing!*" The thrust was wasted. Ruth, quite undaunted, extracted the maximum enjoyment from her position of power. After all, it was she who had the keys; possession was nine points of the law; and who ever heard of a naval officer, even a midshipman, riding a horse? When Arleigh made his duty calls, Ruth went along, and when he squired a local belle to a Grange dance, she tagged along too. For Arleigh, these affairs—a four-piece orchestra playing for a program of alternate square and 'round' dancing—produced no incalescent glow of romance. His fate lay in the East; he had met it; and he was a gone gosling and knew it. Meanwhile, Oscar Burke and Clara Mokler Burke surveyed their handiwork and found it good. More and more frequently with ill-concealed pride, Oscar referred to "my boy at the Naval Academy" in his casual conversations with friends and neighbors. Clara savored her own quiet satisfactions. Her baby was fast becoming a man, the right kind of man, straight, clean, and purposeful. As for Arleigh, he was aware that he had taken the first halting step on the momentous "journey of a thousand miles"—the allegorical road of life. He was strong, self-reliant, and unafraid.

CHAPTER 3

Midshipman Burke

On Friday, April 21, 1922, Midshipman Arleigh Albert Burke, a member of the Second (next-to-graduating) Class at the U.S. Naval Academy, made a sublime and, so far as he was concerned, an original discovery: *Love is a wonderful thing.*

The sudden, devastating comprehension of this dazzling reality overtook him at a rather awkward moment. Rifle on shoulder, he was trudging across the drill field, manfully playing the part of a private in the rear rank of a squad in one of the companies of the four-battalion Regiment of Midshipmen.

"Squads r-r-r-ight . . ." From afar, the preparatory command beat at, and then penetrated, the consciousness of Midshipman Burke, himself floating placidly along on his own cloud nine. A moment later came the execute signal—"Mar-r-r-ch!"

Midshipman Burke wheeled and marched. He was the only member of his company to do so. For several confused seconds, he strode off across the parade ground in solitary grandeur—a brave, albeit preoccupied, unit of one midshipman. Then the awful truth dawned. The midshipmen were drilling as separate companies, not as a regiment. The command had not been addressed to Burke's company, but to another drilling nearby. His own company was marching purposefully away behind him.

"Inattention at drill" was the citation accompanying the inevitable demerits. Burke minded the demerits less than the embarrassment of having turned in a clownish performance. He was a sensitive young man, although that fact was not superficially observable and it escaped nine tenths of his colleagues.

Roberta Gorsuch—the memory and the mystery of her—lay at the core of Midshipman Burke's black Friday. Scarce a week had passed since he'd spent a three day leave in the nation's capital where she lived. "We sat and looked at the moon ever so long . . ." That was his diary entry upon returning to Annapolis. If there was any question how thoroughly this moon gazing had done the business for brother Burke, just as it has

44

done the business for all young lovers from time out of mind, the itemized score of his otherwise inexplicable conduct on that memorable Friday leaves no room for feckless quibbling:

ITEM: Assigned to work a simple problem in a navigation class he (a) multiplied four by eight and got forty-two for an answer; (b) tried it again on another problem and got twenty-four; (c) subtracted three from six and got five; (d) 'bilged' the navigation work for that day.

ITEM: Choosing a short cut in a panting effort to get to the tailor shop, Midshipman Burke suddenly found himself up to his flaming ears in naked women! He had won his class numerals as a member of the wrestling team just a few days before, and had left his sweater with the Academy seamstress to have the numerals sewn on. Anxious to retrieve and wear the sweater proudly, but with very limited time at his disposal, he took a short cut to the tailor shop through the swimming pool dressing room. Alas, he had forgotten that Friday was ladies' day at the pool. Before he could arrest his headlong dash, he was in the middle of the room.

"When I looked up," he reported afterward, "I saw a woman with one stocking on—and not another damned thing! And all around were others in various stages of nudity."

The seamstress secreted him in an adjoining room until the coast was clear; whereupon he departed in such haste that he forgot his sweater after all.

ITEM: Thinking to find surcease from the hoodoo which obviously overhung the Academy grounds for him that day, Midshipman Burke fled briefly to the small town of Annapolis, Maryland, on the edge of which the Naval Academy is situated. Alas, he chose that ill-starred afternoon to check up on his "grad debts"—charge accounts with the local merchants opened by midshipmen and, by mutual understanding, liquidated upon their graduation. His inquiry produced a shock which his nerves were ill-prepared to accommodate. He recorded the matter thus in his diary:

"I am feeling all faint and dizzy! Went out in town and discovered that my 'grad debts' have reached the enormous total of $462.85! Where in the world will I ever get that much money?"

In point of fact, he didn't get the money in time, and, when young Arleigh graduated the following year, his father settled these accounts. However, upon Oscar's death and the subsequent liquidation of his estate, Arleigh declined to accept his proportionate share of the inheritance. Thus, even though belatedly, he squared this indebtedness of his youth.

The fates gave Midshipman Burke one final shake before freeing him that ill-augured Friday. When the drill period was over, he was detained to listen to a lecture from his superiors on the evil fruits of inattention. It was made clear to him not only that he had been stupid, but that he had disgraced his Company, not to mention the Regiment of Midshipmen. Although he had no acceptable excuse and offered none, this wigging consumed considerable time. When at last he was released, Burke discovered that he had just ten minutes in which to shower, shave, and change clothes for inspection. The bugles blew far too soon, and he was forced to take his place in the ranks disheveled and loosely thrown together. The Commandant surprised everybody by taking the inspection himself, and the fact that Mr. Burke appeared looking like an unmade bed did not escape the official eye. "Put him on report for untidiness in dress!" snapped the Commandant as he flicked an imaginary mote of dust off his own impeccable sleeve before passing down the ranks to scrutinize worthier upholders of the Navy's tradition for smartness. Midshipman Burke's cup of woe brimmed close to running over. But there was still balm in Gilead: Awaiting him in his room was a letter from Bobbie Gorsuch, and in its pages he soon was lost to all the realistic frustrations of his worst day at Annapolis.

What impact did his four years at the U.S. Naval Academy have upon Arleigh Burke, the man who was to make naval history in combat and become the father of the nuclear Navy? It was not at all the impact one might suppose. In many respects, both its significance and its permanence were minor when compared with the formative pressures exerted by the long situation-and-experience sequences of active service which lay ahead. It was Rear Admiral Herald (Correct) F. Stout, USN (Ret.), one of the heroes of the barking Battle of Cape St. George who observed: "The Naval Academy does not brainwash its graduates. Rather, it provides the solid cake of necessary knowledge and information over which the icing of each individual's personality is spread."

This is an extremely apt summation, particularly applicable to Arleigh Burke. The two most striking values which emerge from a study of his Academy years are strong evidences of his developing personality and his desperate fight to acquire that 'solid cake of necessary knowledge and information' to which Stout referred. Burke was not an academically brilliant young man: in his own phrase, he "had to work like hell" to maintain any sort of scholastic standing. That he managed to graduate seventieth in a class of 414—impressive by routine academic standards but only so-so for the Naval Academy—was more a tribute to his tenacity than evidence of a facile talent for academics. Nor is there indication that he absorbed during these years more than the tiniest seeds of the tremendous thrust toward selfless service which he was to evidence fairly early in his career.

The physical plant which swallowed a bewildered Burke upon his initial arrival at Annapolis in 1919 exhibited the following principal features:

Bancroft Hall, where dwelt the midshipmen, was architecturally dominant, along with the armory and gymnasium which flanked it on either side.

46

Next to the gym was the navigation building, complete with a sail loft. Here the most colorful denizens of the Academy—a salty crew of old-time bos'un's mates and signalmen—taught knotting, splicing, signalling, and other lore salvaged from the romantic days of wind ships. Down near the main gate was the academic building—classrooms, physics labs, lecture halls . . . Back of this was the "Steam" building, filled with display models of all the mechanical gadgets the Navy fretted with, and devoted to the teaching of marine engineering in all of its branches. Finally, there was the chapel, notable in a number of particulars.

Rumor had it that the Naval Academy chapel originally had been designed by the celebrated architect Stanford White as a tomb for General Grant. Whether this legend was apocryphal or not, the chapel acoustics were, indeed, suitable for a tomb; the lustiest chaplain alive could not make himself heard. This was accepted by the Regiment of Midshipmen as an act of God aimed squarely at affording them at least one hour's quiet contemplation each Sunday. Mr. Burke used the time to "create poetry." The bones of John Paul Jones repose beneath the chapel. Thus inspired, some merry 'Mids' once generated a song, *Everybody Works Around Here but John Paul Jones*. The ditty was frowned upon and vigorously stamped out by the authorities.

Through these hallowed halls, Arleigh Burke and his mates moved in response to a perpetual, rolling barrage of staccato sound—clanging bells and blaring bugles for the most part. The Academic Department did the teaching; the Discipline Department supervised the rest of the midshipmen's waking hours. Midshipmen officers, selected upon an efficiency basis, supervised the endless formations and marching. It was fundamental midshipman theory that any 'Mids' obviously striving for 'grease marks'—the ratings on which the midshipmen officers were selected by the Academy staff—were "basically low types harboring traitorous inclinations against their own kind." To call a midshipman 'greasy' was the acme of insult. On the other hand, to be 'savvy' was highly honorable. That meant being so naturally (and unobtrusively) smart that one could not be overlooked for selection as a midshipman officer. Arleigh Burke was not a 'striper'; he never attained the distinction of a midshipman officer.

So far as the individual midshipman was concerned, the scores of his derelictions, or shortcomings, or both were inexorably totted up each week in the 'PAP sheet' and on the 'Tree.' The PAP sheet enumerated each delinquency and assessed the prescribed demerits—two demerits for keeping a library book out too long; one hundred demerits for a serious 'Class A' offense. Demerits resulted in loss of privileges. If more than an established number were accumulated, dismissal followed. The 'Tree' was a published list of those midshipmen whose daily average marks for the week in any subject fell below 2.5 on a scale of 4.0 for a perfect record.

To be 'treed' consistently meant inevitable failure. Theoretically the delinquent student might catch up; realistically the academic pace was so rapid and demanding as to make this virtually impossible; and classes were known to lose up to 50 per cent of their members to academics on their first examination.

Outside of a maximum security penal institution, which the Academy was not, life for several thousand high-spirited young men, all of whom had demonstrated superior capacities, could never be wholly grim. At Annapolis there was refreshing relief from monotony in the constant, but sporting, war between the midshipmen and the minions of the Academy's Discipline Department. Many forays in this fight were undertaken purely *pour le sport,* and the game was played according to unwritten, time-honored rules. For example, the Duty Officer was expected to wear hard heels, step heavily, and bang loudly on doors when making a 'surprise' inspection. This gave the 'Mids' fair warning of an imminent visitation, and time to hide their misdeeds. On the other hand, 100 per cent of the midshipmen were suspect of harboring forbidden non-regulation clothing or equipment; and the regular Saturday inspections were battles of wits between the Duty Officers' perspicacity (and divination) in hunting out this forbidden contraband and the midshipmen's cunning in concealing it. Non-reg collars were rolled up in window shades, and non-reg reading lamps dangled down ventilation ducts on four fathoms of light line. But the dice were loaded in favor of the authorities who, through years of accumulated experience, had developed an effective sixth sense with which to anticipate the antics of their charges. It was, at best, a bootless battle, and Arleigh Burke found its attractions nil.

It would be convenient to suggest that Midshipman Burke acquired at the U.S. Naval Academy all of the skills and absorbed all of the doctrine necessary to make him a first-class fighting man. That did not happen to him or any of his mates. The finished naval officer—the superior officer who excels in his profession—may be likened to a finely tempered blade. Such a blade can only be rough-forged at Annapolis. The tempering and the polishing are products of years of experience, association, observation, and study—the experience of increasingly responsible command; association with senior officers; observation and rationalization of worthy precepts set by dedicated colleagues; and endless study of the arts of leadership and combat command. A very fine naval officer, Vice Admiral Bernard L. ('Count') Austin once summed up the Academy's contribution in four words: "We learned to stand." And there you have it. At the Academy Arleigh Burke learned to stand—to face reality honestly and without flinching, to accept responsibility for his acts, to understand discipline and the need for subordination to authority, to glimpse the abstractions of leadership, and to begin to grasp the nature of the Navy *mystique.*

48

And all of that was a great deal indeed, but it was only a rough platform on which to build, not a finished edifice. Even so, young Burke's Academy days were studded with revealing incidents which cast long, long shadows ahead.

The most decisive thing ever to happen to Arleigh Burke—more fundamentally meaningful than his brilliant victory at Cape St. George, his heroism amid the chaos of his blazing and crippled carrier, or his enduring contributions to the U.S. Navy and the Free World—was his chance meeting with five-foot two-inch, ninety-five pound Roberta Gorsuch, whom he was to marry the day he graduated. The meeting happened on a blind date during his first or 'Plebe' year. Burke's roommate, Bernard Duncan, a Pennsylvanian, was 'dragging' Annanora Gorsuch during a social week at the Academy. She had come down from Washington and had brought her younger sister 'Bobbie.' Midshipman Burke, himself without a date, was pressed into service.

Bobbie Gorsuch was a tiny creature, almost birdlike in bone structure, although possessing a pleasingly proportioned figure. She dressed somewhat haphazardly, in a conservative sort of way. She had a symmetrically round face, lightly sprinkled with freckles, and her features were notably balanced. Her eyes were arresting—brown, and almost Oriental in shape, the oval pattern of the lids and sockets accentuated by a fine line extruding from each outward corner. Her carriage, unusually erect, suggested suppleness rather than tautness. She was deliberate of mien and exhibited an economy of gesture and somewhat reserved grace of address which italicized the Dresden-doll quality suggested by her tiny stature.

At their first meeting, although neither Arleigh nor Bobbie was to become conscious of it for a considerable time, a love of tremendous tensile strength was conceived. The corrosive pressures of economic struggle during Arleigh's lean financial years as a junior officer, no less than the violent, disruptive blows of war, were to demonstrate it ductile. Key and clue to this enduring felicity lay, at least partly, in the complementary natures of these two. Arleigh was strong; he led. But, too, he was given to introversion—occasional black moods of depression or quick flashes of blazing impatience and anger. Bobbie also was strong, but hers was the deep running, almost frightening, strength of a dedicated woman who acknowledged no barrier as insurmountable, and who could force herself to objective serenity in the face of any circumstance. While patiently content to follow, she nevertheless exerted a farseeing, subtle guidance over her more precipitate mate.

In ideas, Bobbie was the more steadfast of the two. Her dreams started with the simple determination to provide for and share with her husband, within the framework of their modest circumstances and parochial environment, a useful and mutually rewarding life pattern. But her dreams

49

also soared to the stars. She discerned long-range consequences and goals with instinctive clarity and isolated with precision the objectives she considered worthy of attainment. These she pursued unobtrusively but deftly, with calm resolution. Both strength and purpose flowed to her from her faith. Bobbie Gorsuch—to become Bobbie Burke—was a profoundly convinced Christian Scientist. And, over the years, more than a trace of the cut-glass canon of this dogma was to sink into the soul of the man beside whom she took her place.

When first she laid eyes on Arleigh Burke, Bobbie Gorsuch saw a young midshipman, and not too smooth a one at that. But she also perceived that "he exhibited an unusual capacity to change and to mold himself in terms of higher values and broader perspectives." Higher values . . . broader perspectives . . . the quest for these abstractions was fundamental to Bobbie. In 1945, Burke was a captain fighting the naval war in the Pacific. Many times he wrote Bobbie that he thought he would retire "in about four years," in which event a 'tombstone' promotion would make him a rear admiral (retired), and his assured income would be adequate for the two of them. She did not protest. But neither did he retire . . .

In summary, these two shared a complementary psyche of almost classic perfection. Neither was ambitious in a materialistic sense. But Arleigh had the motivation—the compulsion—and the necessary physical drive to "do something for his Navy." There was no limit to what this something might be; in literal truth, it extended to and embraced the postulate of physical death. Bobbie, keeper of chart and compass, had the vision—the essential appreciation of the need for preparation through the attainment of "higher values . . . broader perspectives." Each shared enough of the other's concepts for their drives to be mutually inclusive; they fed each other, they fed upon each other, and they grew.

Arleigh Burke was to become a staunch and steadfast, but certainly not a demonstrative, lover and husband. He had rough sailor ways, not always tempered to the tenderness of his Dresden-doll wife and, when it came to professing his love for her, he habitually exhibited lingual asceticism. When, during World War II, he took time out to write her between Japanese air attacks and Kamikaze strikes against his ship, he was wont to begin his letters simply "Dear Bob," and to conclude them "Love, Arleigh." Sandwiched between these two restrained clichés, there often were many pages of inconsequential chit-chat—"Old Joe Blow is out here and doing very well"—or trite husbandly warnings as "Don't forget to turn off the outside water connections before cold weather sets in." He never got around to signing himself "Your ever lovin', blue-eyed and adoring husband" or an original version thereof. Sometimes Bobbie wondered why he didn't just sign his letters to her "Very respectfully, Arleigh Burke," which was the way he usually concluded his official correspondence. On one notable occasion he worked up to the yeasty pitch of calling her his "little tomato," but even that lackluster endearment had root in rude, practical association rather than starry-eyed enchantment. Tomatoes were unobtainable at the time and place. Arleigh wanted tomatoes. In somewhat the same frame of reference, he wanted his wife. Not that he didn't love her. He adored her. But always and throughout his criteria were practical and immediate. His was an irresistible compulsion to put first things first; a despotic drive to separate things and place them in the order of their objective consequence. He was fighting a war, and tomatoes as well as wives were remote and relative values—things to be hankered after at odd moments; memories to be cherished with a sort of latent and convenient nostalgia, but not to be admitted to the forefront of consciousness or embroidered by palpable sentiment. Long ago he had written "If it kills Japs, it's important. If it does not kill Japs it's NOT important." Neither wives nor tomatoes killed Japs. When Arleigh Burke wrote "my little tomato," he thought he was being facetious. The probability is that he was being eloquent as well.

Almost any undergraduate, at any large college or university anywhere in the United States, could isolate, in his own career, events and pressures precisely comparable to those which paced Midshipman Burke's progress through the U.S. Naval Academy. He was not a colorful character and the efforts of his classmates to tag him with a nickname—(they tried 'Whitey' and 'Billie')—petered out. For some reason, they did not pick on his middle name and call him 'Al'; he was known simply as Arleigh. He did a little fencing; more wrestling; and was bitterly disappointed and screamed "I've been robbed!" when he was not elected manager of his class wrestling team as he had hoped and expected. When he started a diary in his next-to-last year, he displayed a whimsy not notably characteristic of him and titled it *The Diary of a Well-to-Do Second Classman*—reverse reflection of the fact that he never had much money and considered himself "rich" when he got a five-dollar bill in a letter from home. His diary entries tell a fresh and uninhibited tale of youth burgeoning into young manhood:

"Had an argument with the Ordnance Prof and proved that I was right. *He won!*"

"I have developed a wrestling hold which neither man nor devil can break . . ."

"Created poetry during the sermon at Chapel . . ."

"That wrestling hold of mine has something seriously wrong with it! Nearly failed to get myself out of a fix it placed me in. I'll have to begin looking for another hold . . ."

"Letter from Bobbie today. She is running around with some gink named *Comte Estrilio Pagliano, Conseiller (?) de l'ambassade du roi d'Italie.* How he ever lives with such a name I don't know!"

"I realize now that I love Bobbie more than ever . . ."

"Bilged navigation, juice, and steam!"

"A letter from Bobbie inspired me so that I started a raffle in order to make money for my next leave in Washington. Soon found I couldn't persuade the other fellows that I need their money, so I gave back what little I had collected . . ."

"Ate four bananas; then ate breakfast; then met Bobbie when she arrived at Annapolis. Ate another breakfast with Bobbie . . ."

"At juice 'P' work I ruined a $400 motor *and my grade!*"

"Boxed a while and got all beat up . . ."

"Looked up the pay bill. A married ensign draws $2,271.00. I think I shall wait a year or so after graduation before getting married."

"A letter from Nellie. She seems a little too anxious for my taste . . ."

"Another letter from Nellie. I maintain she is a darned funny girl!"

"Another letter from Nellie in which she acted damned decent. Tonight I'll write my last letter to her . . ."

"Whoops! Another letter from Nellie—a darned good composition on how to bawl a fellow out. I'm not much affected though. Instead I am sending Bobbie a special delivery letter this evening." (NOTE: Nellie seems to have gotten the idea at last; we hear no more about her).

"Ruined another $600 motor in juice 'P' work . . ."

"In navigation the Prof was well stowed with good smelling whiskey, but I missed the problem anyway!"

"I have just discovered how to handle a girl! I told Bobbie not to write, and since then I have been receiving a letter every day!" (NOTE: Has Bobbie gotten a whiff of Nellie?).

"If wrestling is going to interfere with my seeing Bobbie I'll give up wrestling. I may lose my numerals, but they're not worth *that* much!"

"Big day! I got a 4.0 in juice, and a five-dollar bill in a letter from home. I'm rich!"

"My class standing is 284 in Dago (languages), 71 in Steam, 62 in English, and 69 in Math. I'm so bad in Navigation I don't even like to think about it!" (NOTE: Burke never was able to lower his threshold for absorbing languages and remained monolingual throughout life.)

"In preparation for the Class cruise my trunk came up bringing to life many things that had been lost beyond recall including pictures of many girls also lost beyond recall . . ."

The other girls were lost beyond recall all right. Not only had Bobbie won in a walk, but for poor Arleigh the pain of love was so excruciatingly poignant that it attached itself even to inanimate objects associated with his beloved. Bobbie had left her watch to be repaired at Caldwells, an Annapolis jewelry shop, and Arleigh retrieved it. "Oh, what a thrill I experienced when I touched it!" he confided to his Well-to-do Diary. It was high time for him to go to sea, which is what he proceeded to do as a Second Classman in U.S.S. *Michigan,* Captain George W. Laws, commanding.

Two events of note marked Midshipman Burke's second-year voyage in cruiser *Michigan:* (1) He got into serious trouble for the first time during his four years as a midshipman; and (2) Faced with a perplexing challenge, he met it with an audacity which both surprised and amused his superiors.

So far as Burke's deviltry went, both the record and his memory were to become obscure, and details are lacking. It can be reliably concluded, however, that he made the mistake of stepping into too fast company, and it was he who got clipped. His partner in whatever offense took place was one Midshipman Gilbert La Rue ('Tweet-Tweet') Burt—a vertiginously inclined classmate with real talent for daring trouble and eluding the consequences. Mr. Burt was blond, of medium height and build, and gave the impression of being 'twitchy,' from which his sobriquet derived. He was a brilliant student and habitually finished important exams far ahead of his classmates. This left him plenty of time to plan lighthearted departures from the "motonony" of prescribed discipline.

Aboard *Michigan* 'Tweet-Tweet' Burt ran true to form, participating in, but escaping, the consequences of the relatively serious infraction of regulations in which Burke was caught. The penalty for Arleigh was the loss of a sequence of "numbers"—the indices by which a naval officer's relative standing is determined throughout his career. To Arleigh Burke, being thus dropped back was no light matter. For a youth of one-and-twenty, he brought an unwonted maturity to the contemplation of all things having direct influence upon himself and his career. In this early example of crime and punishment, the punishment was painful, but the memory of the dereliction itself was pure anathema. Nearly a half century later, Arleigh Burke could recall clearly many trivialities of his childhood, but he could *not* remember the nature of his difficulties with 'Tweet-Tweet' Burt. The memory simply was too painful and he banished it from his mind.

In the course of her cruise, *Michigan* called at Gibraltar and it was there that Midshipman Burke acted with an audacity which threatened to involve Her Majesty's Navy in as fine a point of protocol as the Admiralty had contemplated since the War of Jenkins' Ear, way back in the mid-1700's. The matter developed thus:

The midshipmen in *Michigan* were avid to go ashore on The Rock and as that was the primary purpose of their visit, matters were so arranged. But they were due back aboard each evening for supper; and to remind them of this stipulation as well as to keep an eye on their general behavior, various of their number were told off for shore patrol duty. Such an assignment befell Midshipman Burke and, while the ship lay offshore at 'Gib' and his fellows shuttled back and forth in small boats, he was denied participation in the fun ashore. He was, so to speak, 'with' the shore party, but not 'of' it. However, Captain Laws had equity at heart, and when the shore-patrol party was mustered the day before the ship's scheduled departure from Gibraltar, the executive officer told them:

"We sail tomorrow morning at 0800. You fellows on shore patrol haven't had much of a liberty, so the captain has arranged a treat for you. You will be allowed to stay ashore overnight tonight. Reservations have been made for you at the Grand Hotel. After you've finished your duty this afternoon you can stay ashore and see Gibraltar tonight if you wish. You'll be on your own. *Dismissed!*"

Midshipman Burke gave a nautical hitch to his trousers, tumbled into a shore boat, and fell to ruminating upon the delights of freedom which would be his to embrace with the evening. Nor, when the time came, did it take much to satisfy his craving for diversion—a stroll through unfamiliar and, hence, glamorous streets, a dinner of his ordered choice, partaken of with all the painfully studied nonchalance of a bored naval officer as a midshipman imagined one, wistful contemplation of a thousand distant, twinkling lights; a lump in the throat induced by thoughts of Bobbie, a whiff of the pungent perfume of empire—and he presented himself at the Grand Hotel, prepared to top off the already overflowing cup of his romantic excitement with the plush luxury of a first-class inn, European style. This Navy life . . . ah, yes, now that he thought of it, the life *did* have its moments . . . and by the way, old boy, call me at six *sharp* . . . Getting under way and all that, you know . . . The soaring moon topping the 1,408-foot 'Rock' to shine impartially upon Europe and Africa alike, shone as well upon a snoring Midshipman Burke, at peace and harmony with the world.

0600 the next morning came and went. At 0730 Mr. Burke opened an eye and allowed it to flicker over the dial of his wristwatch. Then, he sat bolt upright, grabbed the telephone, and demanded to know the time. "It is seven-thirty-two, sir."

Arleigh Burke hit the floor running, but his racing mind was well out ahead of his bounding body. Obviously, something had gone wrong; they'd neglected to call him. The problem which presented itself for resolution had two primary dimensions: (1) he had to get aboard his ship before she sailed, if that could be managed; (2) in any case, he had to secure his rear; the threatened catastrophe was not of his own making, but how to convince his commanding officer of that?

In his gallop through the lobby of the Grand Hotel, Midshipman Burke took precious moments for a strategic move. He cornered the manager and secured a written statement that the hotel was at fault; that he, Burke, had indeed left peremptory orders to be wakened at 0600, and that he had not been so awakened. Shoving this extenuating document into the crown of his cap for safekeeping, he bolted for the waterfront.

The sight which met Burke's eye, as he charged to the end of the pier, set his taut spine twanging like a musical saw. Off across the water lay U.S.S. *Michigan* trig, trim, and purposeful. All of her boats were clustered at her side, preparatory to being hoisted inboard. The anchor chain was being roused out, the crew were lined up at quarters, and heavy black smoke rolled from her stack. She was ready and able for sea, whither she was on the point of proceeding, and the absence of a midshipman or two obviously was not bothering anybody on her bridge.

In sheer panic Midshipman Burke looked about him and saw, bobbing in the water at the end of the stringpiece, the captain's gig of a British warship. The cox'u'n, obviously taking great professional pride in the sleek smartness of his little craft, was wiping beads of morning dew from the mahogany and brightwork.

"Ahoy, the gig!" sang out Mr. Burke. "Can you set me aboard *Michigan* —the U.S. battleship out there?"

55

"Sorry, sir," replied the cox'u'n. "I'm standing by for my captain."

"It'll only take five—maybe ten minutes . . ." coaxed Burke.

"Sorry, sir," repeated the cox'u'n. "Cap'n's orders were to pick him up at eight. He's due any minute now, sir."

Burke turned and took a long look back down the dock. No British captain was in sight. Then the midshipman made an audacious resolve and turned once more to the gig. "Cox'u'n, he said firmly, *"I order you to put me aboard Michigan!"*

Now it was the British seaman's turn to be flustered. He could recall no sanction to govern him in this sort of situation. Plainly the self-possessed youth standing above him on the dock was a junior officer. And an officer was an officer, no matter in what navy he belonged. Discipline in the British Navy was rigid; the cox'u'n had been a part of that discipline for a score of years and more; compliance with orders was bred in his bones. His mental struggle was short; his decision soon reached:

"Why, sir!" he said, "that makes things different! If you make it an order . . . well, tumble in, sir. I'll have you 'longside yon battleship in a shake or two."

Michigan was making way through the water when Midshipman Burke scrambled inboard over the armor belt and headed for the bridge to report to the executive officer. That astonished individual listened stone-faced to the tale, examined the hotel manager's note briefly, and turned to hide a grin as he dismissed Burke. This would, indeed, be a juicy morsel for the captain! As *Michigan* stood out, her yardarm signal lights blinked a half-humorous, half-serious apology from Captain Laws to the British captain, whose gig Mr. Burke had appropriated. The message said something about there being no telling what a crazy blankety-blank of a midshipman might do . . . and please excuse it . . . and rule, Britannia . . . and cheerio, pip, pip, and goodbye . . . ! But Mr. Burke had, by no means, heard the last of his highhanded commandeering of the captain's gig of a friendly naval power. The first night out, he was nonplussed to receive an invitation to join Captain Laws for dinner in his quarters. Stiff in spotless whites, Midshipman Burke presented himself and was seated with the captain and several senior officers of the ship. Step by step and detail by detail, the young man was directed to recount his adventures ashore at Gibraltar, and, when he came to the part about 'ordering' the British cox'u'n to set him aboard *Michigan* Captain Laws and his guests laughed themselves helpless. Night after night, Mr. Burke returned to the captain's table until every senior officer aboard had heard the tale from his lips and savored its peculiarly naval humor and significance. It threatened to be the longest run of a single act since Mae West played the Palace, and the ordeal was almost worse than the formal reprimand which he expected, but did not receive.

The incident of the gig was revelatory of two strong Burke characteristics. The first was a relative value: What *is* important and what is *not* important. "In war," Burke was to write, "it is quite possible to throw yourself away. I do not look upon this with any admiration." Interpreted in terms of his observations as a midshipman, that simply meant that he perceived the need for a constant separation of the significant from the trivial. It was another facet of the 'tomatoes-wives' approach. In Gibraltar, his enjoyment of liberty—the luxury of the hotel and of sleeping late—was a trivial value through which he could "throw himself away," if he accepted it. Rejoining his ship at the appointed time was important, because his failure to do so would place a black mark in his record, which would remain through his entire naval career. He had no desire to throw himself away, so he got the note from the hotel manager and then hurried to the dock to devise ways and means of complying with orders, despite the fact that he had been betrayed by a careless clerk and might have accepted the situation philosophically.

The second characteristic which Arleigh Burke exhibited that fine morning was audacity. Audacity was to become his hallmark in combat, and he was to write:

"You can hurt the enemy only if you hit him, and to do that you must often act with audacity. The audacious commander almost always has a superior force. The dash of the commander is transmitted to those he leads; they become always ready and eager to go; they have a keen fighting edge. That's what wins battles."

For Arleigh Burke, the quality of audacity never was to be different, whether the challenge was one to be met with powder and shot or the pusillanimous pettifogging of politicians to be braved on Capitol Hill.

In 1922, Midshipman Burke was not yet ready to lead men in battle; but he sensed instinctively the need for audacity when the goal was important and the obstacles formidable. He knew what he was doing when he issued 'orders' wholly without validity to the British cox'u'n, and he was prepared to abide by the consequences. Better to be chewed out for overstepping his authority than to have it permanently written into his record that he missed his ship. His was a courageous solution of a sudden and unexpected problem—a sort of table-top exercise in daring and resourcefulness—and, as Captain Laws rightly concluded, even though the event itself was more humorous than important, it set this midshipman apart as a young man to watch.

Clara Mokler Burke journeyed East for her son's graduation, commissioning, and wedding on June 7, 1923, and for the first time, met Roberta Gorsuch. Instinctively, the two women took each other's measure, and their differences were notable. Bobbie observed that her mother-in-law-to-be was no fashion plate: Clara dressed well, but her tastes tended toward the ultra-conservative. The younger woman was prepared to meet a 'big' woman in Clara, but she found the bigness a bit different from what she had visualized. Clara was "not big fat," as Bobbie explained it, "but she gave an impression of solid strength." In other words, Clara's impression of bigness derived as much from the impression of competence which she gave, as from her stature. Also, she radiated a calm serenity which was not lost on Bobbie. With her sandy complexion, erect carriage, and dark, copper-colored hair which she wore long, Arleigh's mother presented a quiet, interesting study in self-confidence. To Bobbie, she seemed almost phlegmatic, and if she had any special emotions at the time—and surely she must have had some—she kept them concealed. Roberta was especially appreciative of the fact that Clara raised no ruckus about losing her son; set up no fuss or yammering of shared joy and personal lament, as some mothers had been known to do in identical circumstances. Bobbie was Arleigh's choice? Very well. He was old enough to know his own mind. The demand that he take full responsibility for his decisions had been bred into him long before he set foot in Annapolis. Clara Burke was content to trust her son. She met the excitements of the Naval Academy commencement and his wedding with the same cordial calm she was accustomed to exhibit at meetings of the Neighborly Circle back in Boulder. Hers was an impressive tranquillity.

Roberta Gorsuch, the younger of the two, was a more complex package. The many-pointed pattern of her life had not impinged too frequently upon the raw challenges of survival. She was impelled to introspection and nourished a strong fantasy life. Her ancestral heritage was one of reserve —an external protective husk provided by the British derivation of her father, Emerson Benjamin Gorsuch. But beneath this outer shell there lay, and she shared in, a whimsical world of leprechauns and good fairies emergent from the genes of her mother, Adolia Moore, the daughter of an Irish carriage maker. Of course she admitted the fairies to none but herself, and, indeed, time was to turn some of them into hobgoblins.

Although also tending Westward, the Gorsuch family had not quested quite so far as had old Anders Petter Bjorkegren and his faithful fiddle. As a young man, Emerson Benjamin sought for a time to till his father's acres in the vicinity of Westminster, Maryland. Differences arose between father and son when the latter sought to introduce modern innovations to the agricultural process, and young Emerson Benjamin pulled stakes and struck Westward on his own. Eventually, he came to Lawrence, Kansas, early hinge of the war between the states, where he set up as a fruit buyer. Here he met and married Adolia Moore. Three girls were born to this union.

The days at Lawrence were relatively brief, but they were days of great malleability for Roberta, and they left a strong impress upon her. Evenings, when work was done and twilight shadows lengthened, Adolia

Gorsuch was fond of gathering her little brood around the piano in the front parlor. Here, while they awaited the return of Emerson Benjamin from business, she would play and all would sing the nostalgic melodies of the period. This musical bent was carried forward in all the girls. Bobbie studied violin, her sisters the harp and flute, and their amateur trio filled a few local engagements. She always sought to deprecate what she referred to as her "slender talent," but she fooled few. Whatever may be said of Roberta Gorsuch Burke, she had a woman's realism, and she always knew the score, whether it was cast up in inches, foot-pounds, volts, range, deflection, or the pretensions of some of Washington's well-heeled hostesses. As her husband progressed from being very, very junior in U.S.S. *Arizona* to being very, very senior in Admiral's House, she kept the score in different symbols, but she always kept the score.

In Kansas, Emerson Benjamin transferred from the fruit business to the grain business but, before long, wistfulness triumphed over wheat; the unpolished rawness of the Western plains made the relative sophistication of the East seem more desirable than ever, and the family retraced its steps, first to Baltimore, then to Washington.

Bobbie's and Arleigh's wedding had a Wagnerian prelude. As the little wedding party—Bobbie's parents and her two sisters; Clara Burke and a sufficient number of Ensign Burke's classmates to provide the traditional arch of swords—gathered in the Naval Academy Chapel, forked lightning flashed and cracked over the little town of Annapolis, and thunder roared. Theirs was a late-afternoon ceremony, and they were lucky in escaping the full fury of the storm which smote other Academy nuptials scheduled earlier. By the time Chaplain Evans faced the young couple at the chancel rail, prepared to tie the knot in nautical as well as ecclesiastic fashion, the lashing rain had subsided. After the benediction, they were able to step forth into a softly sunlit, freshly washed world filled with the felicitations of their friends and their own exclusive bluebirds of happiness.

Ensign and Mrs. Burke went at once to Baltimore—to spend a single night! Then, they entrained for Bremerton, Washington, and here again was exposed the dominating drive of Arleigh Burke. The circumstances were these: He had been ordered to duty aboard U.S.S. *Arizona*—BB-39 now lying at the bottom of Pearl Harbor—a brute commissioned October 17, 1916. *Arizona* was undergoing overhaul in the Navy Yard at Bremerton, and Mr. Burke's orders specifically authorized him to delay thirty days in reporting; the authorities saw no immediate, pressing need for the presence of a buck ensign. But to delay thirty days doing anything, particularly in reporting for duty aboard his first ship, simply wasn't in the character of Arleigh Burke. He was a young man on fire—on fire, specifically, to start serving "his Navy" (for so he was to think of it all his life), and he could not tear West fast enough. There was fire for Bobbie too, of course, but of the conflagrations burning in Burke's breast upon his graduation from the Naval Academy it's a safe bet that the blaze of *Arizona* was by far the more compulsive. This imbalance would be corrected but it would not be dissipated; and Commodore Burke was to mean every word of it when he wrote:

"Basically the primary motive power driving naval officers is the desire to accomplish useful work for the United States and for the Navy. The greatest reward which can be obtained from a naval career is the self-satisfaction and self-respect which result from the knowledge that, because of him, the Navy and the United States are better.

"This satisfaction cannot come about, except through hard, conscientious work."

As a newly commissioned ensign young Burke's thinking had not yet crystallized into such formal statements as the foregoing. Nevertheless, the raw conviction was there; service to Navy and country was the highest virtue—and he was for getting on with it.

In Bremerton, Bobbie found a small furnished apartment near the Navy Yard and thus set a pattern which she was to pursue, up and down the coast of California, for the next five years and more. Understandably, Arleigh liked to live ashore with his wife when *Arizona* was in port. But, also, he damned well wanted to be sure that beloved battleship didn't get out of his sight. After all, who could tell what might happen to a thirty-thousand-ton battleship without a dedicated ensign close by to keep an eye on it?

"I'd get the word when *Arizona* was returning from sea," explained Bobbie, "and find out where she was going to dock. Then I'd start walking . . ." The walking part was very real, and young Mrs. Burke tramped endless miles, seeking acceptable accommodations—both economically acceptable and physically endurable—as close as possible to the waterfronts of a dozen ports from San Diego to Cape Flattery. "Usually, I found something," she concluded, "although now and again Arleigh just had to put up with being out of sight of his big canoe."

Ensign 'Checkoff-List' Burke was a great hand for having everything shipshape and Bristol fashion—for others. "We'll travel light, Bob," he told his wife when their journeying first began. "You will be allowed one household box and your wardrobe trunk. You'll just have to give away or throw away any accumulated excess." Bobbie set her firm little jaw and proceeded to live by this austere dictum. Arleigh? When finally he came ashore permanently from *Arizona,* he brought thirteen boxes of uniforms, books, instruments, and marine curiosities, topped by a specially made container for the old "fore-and-aft," gold-trimmed dress hat which was the glory of the U.S. naval officer, prior to the recent war. Throughout his life, Arleigh Burke was a great squirrel and 'string-saver,' and an inventory of his pockets, at any given moment, might have provided a yard-long list.

Ensign Burke was to spend five years in *Arizona*. During that time, he really met the U.S. Navy on the operating level. The two interacted upon each other to the complete complacency of the Navy and the complete surprise of Ensign Burke. He was to learn, among other things, that girls could, and did, stow away aboard battleships; that loyalty was all very fine, but that it *still* was imprudent to bet all the mess funds on a boat race, particularly at the beginning of the month; that an officer's refund from a 'broke' mess upon transferring to another ship could be paid in pineapples; and that an electrical gunner was apt to be a skilled enough artificer to fashion a ten-gallon copper still which he could be induced to rent to the junior officers on suitable terms 'for the short term.' By the time all the returns were in, Mr. Burke's introduction to the Navy afloat constituted one of the most hilarious stories ever to drift in on a flood tide. That he managed to survive it without being hurt, was at least in some degree attributable to a basic Navy canon: *Ensigns don't know anything; are not expected to know anything; and must be treated accordingly.*

CHAPTER 4

Mr. Burke Meets the Navy

A keening, bone-chilling wind sent riotous gouts of crisp, white, snow crystals whirling up the Hudson River, all but obscuring the massive bulk of U.S.S. *Arizona,* lying to her anchors off the foot of West Ninety-Sixth Street, New York City. It was a bitter January night and seven bells already had been struck—two and two and two, and one . . . In a steady stream pea-jacketed sailors, their collars turned up around their ears and their heads pulled in turtle-fashion for protection against the biting cold, clambered up out of the motor sailers, flashed their liberty cards for inspection by the junior officer of the deck, and scuttled below to the welcome warmth of the crew living spaces. Liberty was up at midnight; *Arizona* was under orders to sail on the morning tide toward the Caribbean.

"Boy, we can't sail out of this stuff soon enough for me!" muttered Ensign Burt Davis to the muffled up 'jimmylegs' standing at his side, as he checked the men aboard mechanically. Mr. Davis would a lot rather have been below in the cabin which he shared with Ensign Arleigh Burke than standing the J.O.O.D. watch that particular night. Not that it was much of a cabin, heaven knows. It was in the lower wardroom, all the way aft over the rudder stocks. It had the disadvantage of being virtually on the water line when *Arizona* was in trim; when the vessel lay at anchor in balmy weather and the two young officers 'cracked a port' for ventilation, a motorboat rounding the stern at any speed would send its wash to flood their quarters and set them bailing. In cold weather, when the ports were closed, that nuisance was eliminated but another was substituted. *Arizona's* chief engineer was hell-bent on winning an 'E' for fuel economy; and when he was aboard, little heat found its way to junior officers' quarters so far aft. No, reflected handsome Ensign Davis, it wasn't much of a deal, winter or summer. But better down there than out here in this damned blizzard! As the last thirty minutes of his watch ticked away with congealed and infuriating hesitation, he checked the latecomers aboard automatically in response to what had become a conditioned reflex for that monotonous, but necessary, chore.

The ghastly fact which Ensign Davis never remotely imagined on that cold and windswept night was that, under his red and unsuspecting nose, an incredible and outrageous breach of Navy traditions, regulations, and disciplines was taking place. For one of the 'men' in the ant-like procession of sailors filing past the J.O.O.D. and being mechanically motioned below was no man or sailor at all. She was a nineteen-year-old girl disguised as a sailor. She answered to the sobriquet of *Blackie;* and before Blackie quit the ship, five weeks and many thousands of salt-water miles later, she was to shake the venerable battleship from trucks to keelson, and cause to be entered upon the official record of one Arleigh Albert Burke the only blemish ever to mar its pristine purity.

There are two versions of the Blackie story: one, her own embroidered confection of sweet innocence; the other, the consequence of a grimly official inquiry. The story told by the girl herself is as follows:

She had seen posters bearing the legend "Join the Navy and See The World" and, on the spur of the moment, she decided to do just that. She had a brother-in-law who had served a hitch in the Navy, and she appropriated his uniform, which was a reasonable fit. Having hidden the uniform behind some bushes in a public park bordering the Hudson River, she then managed to meet a friendly *Arizona* sailor 'on the beach' for his last New York liberty. She stole his liberty card; then managed to lose him in a drugstore with multiple exits. Changing into uniform, her face all but obscured by tilted hat and turned up collar, she boarded the ship, was waved below by Ensign Davis—and the rest was a pleasure cruise during which she found *Arizona's* sailors invariably gallant and attentive to her every need.

In doleful contradiction of this simple saga is the tale told at a court-martial by various of *Arizona's* personnel including twenty-three enlisted men who paid for their participation in the Blackie lark by serving terms of up to ten years at hard labor in the Navy's Portsmouth prison. The official story is indeed well documented; Arleigh Burke—unwittingly and unknowingly—was right in the middle of it, and the facts inch well over toward the incredible and the fabulous.

The girl did indeed board the battleship, using a fake liberty card or a stolen one. Amid a large group of sailors bundled up against the cold, her appearance, in uniform like the rest, excited no suspicion; her credentials were checked perfunctorily as was the custom, and she was waved below.

Friends among *Arizona's* crew hid Blackie—(her proper name was Madeline Blair)—in Number Three turret, where she was supplied with food and drink by a detail of ship's cooks and bakers. An ingenious accommodation was worked out in this regard: The cooks and bakers insisted on charging Blackie ten dollars a day board. So far as is known, she hadn't a dime when she boarded *Arizona,* and Ensign Davis reported that she still didn't have a dime when he set her ashore at the Old French Pier in Panama. But she was a sultry, buxom wench; she imposed her own charges for various diversions in which she participated with an ever-growing group of *Arizona* sailors (as witness a batch of arresting photographs exhibited at the court-martial), and Blackie's maintenance turned out to be a standoff despite the stiff tariff imposed for her food.

Lieutenant (jg) Joe Shaw, a mustang and friend of Rear Admiral W. V. Pratt, who flew his flag in *Arizona,* was Number Three turret officer, and he and Ensign Burke gave the girl enough exercise to keep her figure trim and neat. When Joe Shaw approached the turret, a blue jacket lookout would warn Blackie by sounding three rings on the turret bell. Immediately she would drop down to the lower shell deck, where she could hide effectively behind the fourteen-inch ammunition. So effective was her concealment that she was not even discovered by *Arizona's* commanding officer, Captain P. N. ('Pete') Olmsted and his staff on their periodic and always thorough inspections.

Ensign Burke, of course never aware of what he was doing, frequently chased Blackie from her turret bower as the vessel plowed steadily south, a happy ship under a bright blue sky. Meticulous attention to duty always was a Burke characteristic, and in *Arizona* he brought his wonted thoroughness to a task generally regarded as tiresomely onerous and often neglected by other junior officers. It was the regular inspection of the double bottoms. Burke's enthusiasm for work quickly impressed Lieut. Commander J. H. ('Jimmy') Taylor, *Arizona's* first lieutenant; and before the ship was long out of New York, young Burke found himself assigned to make all double-bottom inspections throughout the vessel rather than just in his own section to which, normally, his responsibility would have been limited. After that, Burke's invasions of turret three, which gave access to the double bottoms, became so frequent that Blackie was forced finally to shift her quarters to number three generator room.

It was Blackie's boldness which proved her undoing and brought confusion, consternation, and temporary disgrace to *Arizona.* The girl rode the battleship to Culebra; idled away three weeks of maneuvers there; enjoyed the transit of the Panama Canal; and was complacently settling into the routine of her curious life in the generator room during the ten days *Arizona* lay at Panama. Continuing security made her contemptuous of discovery, and she took to roaming topside at night, dressed in dungarees provided by her friends, and rarely failing to attend the outdoor movies provided for the crew in fair weather. Her favorite perch for this divertissement was the after searchlight platform, and it was here that the integrity of her masquerade suddenly was breached.

The picture was absorbing. The young sailor sitting next to Blackie

64

was not a party to the plot of her clandestine presence aboard the battleship, and he accepted her as just another silent shipmate absorbed in the drama unfolding on the screen. Pulling out a cigarette he fumbled vainly through his pockets for a match. Not finding one, and without taking his eyes from the screen, he casually reached over to extract a packet of matches from Blackie's jumper pocket. "What I grabbed hold of didn't belong to no man!" was his pungent summation of the matter at a subsequent hearing.

Curiously, this incident did not result at once in Blackie's discovery. Not only was the young sailor shocked, but he was fully aware of the flap which must inevitably attend the discovery of the girl's presence aboard; and he was prudently averse to becoming involved in such an uproar as a principal. He did not report the matter officially, although he discussed it with trusted friends.

Blackie's official discovery—and subsequent events with all the improbable overtones of the most irresponsible slapstick comedy—began at precisely 0430 of a February morning. The Battle Fleet lay at Panama, raising steam for an 0730 departure for San Pedro. Lieutenant (jg) 'Prof' Kelley had the deck and, deep down in the engine room and clad in gaudy pink pyjamas, Lieutenant (jg) N. O. ('Piggy') Schwien was supervising the routine of warming up the main engines in preparation for sailing. At that moment a chief radioman stepped out of the main radio room on the second deck, took the few steps to a nearby scuttlebutt, and stood patiently waiting until another sailor had finished drinking. The other 'sailor' was Blackie, and as she raised her head from the drinking fountain, the radio chief found himself gazing full into her sloe black eyes.

There was no hesitation this time! Startled almost out of his wits, the chief dashed to the bridge and poured out his hair-curling report to Lieut. Kelley. Within minutes *Arizona* was a madhouse! Search parties were organized. Blackie retreated downward deck by deck; and after some minutes the pink-pyjamed and goggle-eyed Lieutenant Schwien caught sight of her, ghosting through the lower engine room spaces. A mighty "Tally-Ho!" went up as the engine room watch, led by the redoubtable "Piggy," took out after Blackie. The hilarious chase led over and around the blower turbine casings, up and down ladders, and over the steel grills of engine room platforms. Finally the quarry was run to earth, and the luckless Ensign Davis himself—(a retired Rear Admiral in 1961)—tells the rest of the story:

"The captain was awakened and informed. God! I'm glad I didn't have *that* job! The language issuing from his cabin was frightful! Anyhow, I was called and told to get ready to take this blankety-blank-blank of a woman and dump her on the dock at the Old French Pier in Panama, and return with all speed. The ship, under orders to sail with the Battle Fleet,

65

would lie to and pick up my motorboat upon our return; then steam after the rest if they'd already sailed.

"It was about forty-five minutes from our anchorage to the French Pier, one way. The girl and I embarked. She had on a pair of dungarees, no baggage, no hat; hair cut like a boy's. And the little darling cussed me for the full forty-five-minute run! It really was something masterful; her profanity shamed eloquence. Of course the commandant of the Fifteenth Naval District (Canal Zone) had been alerted by signal and he had the Canal Zone police waiting on the pier. I told them 'Here's the stowaway; she's all yours!,' and I got th' hell out of there fast.

"When I got back to the anchorage, the rest of the fleet was under way. *Arizona* hooked me aboard, and I sighed with relief. But not for long were we to remain quiet and peaceful. The little so-and-so told the Panama Police that *there were two more women stowaways left aboard* Arizona!

"Well, the commandant, Fifteenth Naval District, radioed this information to the Commander, Battle Fleet—and that's when all hell *really* broke loose! *Arizona* was informed by Commander, Battleship Division (in not very nice language either), that there were two more females aboard, and that we'd better damn sight produce them forthwith. Things were tense. All officers and men not on watch were mustered topside and remained there until a detail of officers had searched *Arizona* from stem to stern and from trucks to keelson. Result: negative! When this was reported, the 'boss man' indicated considerable skepticism, and hinted that there was considerable doubt whether the officers and crew of *Arizona* would be granted liberty upon arrival 'Pedro.' That was one hell of a note, and it produced action.

"At that time the Navy still had the old Chief Master at Arms rating —the old boys who wore a star under their crow. I was junior officer of the deck during the midwatch several days out of Panama; the time was about 12:30—0030 Navy time. It was customary for the J.O.O.D. to make hourly inspections of the below-decks spaces during the night watches. The Chief Master at Arms drew me aside and told me confidentially that if, on my rounds, I saw a light in the sail locker it would be all right; he would be in there doing some *necessary work*. In the circumstances, a house didn't have to fall on young Ensign Davis for him to get the point . . .

"As I neared the sail locker on my rounds I saw the light and heard the sound of many voices. I concluded that the Chief was reading the riot act to his gang of Masters at Arms, and I went quietly on my way. My surmise didn't go quite far enough! I learned later that the senior petty officers had held a kangaroo court in the sail locker that night, and they came up with full and accurate details of the Blackie business, including the names of those who had been in on the plot. There had been only one

66

woman aboard. Captain 'Pete' was informed of the facts; we were granted routine liberty upon arrival 'Pedro'; a score or more sailors eventually were convicted at a court-martial held at Bremerton, Washington, and we all relaxed in the happy delusion that *l'affaire Blackie* was finished and done with. Which simply shows how naive *we* were!

"The little darling was a smart cookie, as I have indicated. After I set her ashore at Panama and thought I'd heard the last of her, I'll be damned if she didn't talk the Grace Line into giving her first-class passage from Panama to New York. She blandly told them that the U.S. Navy would pay the bill—and they fell for it!

"A few months after Blackie's arrival in New York, all hell suddenly broke loose aboard *Arizona* once more and, again, I had the misfortune to be right in the middle of it. The Navy's Bureau of Navigation forwarded to Captain 'Pete' Olmsted the bill for Blackie's first-class passage from Panama to New York.

"Captain 'Pete' sent for me—and I learned things about my ancestors I'd never even suspected! The captain demanded to know what I'd told the Panamanian police when I'd turned Blackie over to them, and it took a bit of doing for me to convince him that all I'd said was 'Here's the stowaway; she's all yours.' Gad, what an ordeal for a lowly, frightened ensign! But he finally subsided, and once more we thought the Blackie business was behind us. Not so! A few days later we were informed by Commander, Battleship Division, that all officers serving in *Arizona* at the time of the Blackie incident would have a black mark—'woman on board' —entered in their fitness reports! This was serious, and there was absolutely nothing we could do about it. But Admiral Pratt could, and he did. When he became Chief of Naval Operations he ordered all those black marks expunged from the records—which is the only reason Arleigh Albert Burke was able, in 1961, to end his naval career with a spotless record!"

It was significant that Arleigh Burke did not allow the Blackie incident, nor any of the other lighthearted nonsense to which he was exposed as a very junior officer in *Arizona,* to divert him from course and speed toward the serious goal of becoming the best possible Navy officer in what he considered the best of all possible navies. Burke was not without humor of a somewhat gusty and rough sort. Once during a wardroom party at Monterey he booted Colonel 'Hap' Hazard, U.S. Army, commanding the Presidio, in the stern sheets for "cluttering up the passageway just like a Marine!" But humor—relaxation—fun were purely secondary values in Burke's thinking; and it is entirely probable that the impress which his five years of service in *Arizona* made upon him was more constructive and abiding than that made by any other single period of his long and distinguished naval service, including his dashing combat performances in the Southwest Pacific and his unprecedented six years of service as Chief of Naval Operations.

At various times young Burke had different jobs aboard *Arizona,* and in each of them he attracted the favorable attention of his superiors through meticulous hard work and, of equal importance, his demonstrated willingness to accept responsibility. Unlike some of his more complex colleagues who, at least in secret, were prone to approach command responsibilities with healthy hesitation, Arleigh Burke not only welcomed command but he demonstrated his command presence almost from the first day he stepped aboard the huge battleship. He evidenced this remarkable command capacity very early in his career, when he saved *Arizona* from what gave every promise of being serious damage, had he not acted promptly and correctly. With other ships nearby, *Arizona* lay at anchor and, despite his youth, Ensign Burke had been entrusted with the heavy responsibilities of the deck watch. Suddenly, with virtually no warning, a Santa Ana— dreaded and violent tropical storm—smote the anchorage, and many ships started dragging their moorings and colliding in the chaotic night. No one would have blamed a very junior officer of the deck if he had sent an emergency call for senior and more experienced help; but that would have taken time, and Ensign Burke instinctively perceived that every moment was vital. He rose to the challenge, ordered a second anchor dropped on his own responsibility, and very possibly saved the ship from severe damage. It was a tough, split-second decision for one of his years to make, and it earned him a 'well done' from his superiors.

As *Arizona* galloped around the Atlantic and Pacific, young Burke— (he was promoted to lieutenant, junior grade, in 1926)—served successively as turret officer, torpedo officer, plotting room officer, and in various engineering divisions. He learned in every job but, being a compulsive perfectionist, he was driven nearly frantic during part of his gunnery service. *Arizona's* gunnery officer (less formally known as 'the gun boss' or just plain 'guns') was dark, heavy-set Lieutenant Commander A. D. Denney. Denney was nearing forty at the time; was married and had a family ashore at Long Beach, California; he and Burke got on well together. As a junior division officer, Burke was in charge of Number One turret handling room, and both he and Denney were optimistic of making high scores when *Arizona* steamed out for a 'shoot.' Alas, their glowing hopes soon turned to seething bitterness and rage, for they discovered that the Navy's Bureau of Ordnance had sent *Arizona* the wrong powder charge for her triple fourteen-inch, forty-five-caliber Number One turret guns. The guns had been bored out to large chamber size which called for a fourteen-inch projectile and four bags of powder per round. The Bureau of Ordnance had sent powder charges for guns with small powder chambers and in consequence, at long range practice, *Arizona's* guns couldn't even reach the target at maximum elevation! Mr. Burke swore loud and long, and so did gunnery officer Denney!

Among the several characteristics which marked Arleigh Burke as a young officer to watch was his almost larger-than-life sense of loyalty. The Navy did not give it to him. It was a basic family legacy. But the Navy provided a precise frame of reference for Arleigh's loyalty, and crystalized the abstraction into a white-hot flame which never faltered and which illuminated his entire career. It was an across-the-board kind of faithfulness. He was fiercely loyal to individual comrades; he was loyal to his ship; he was dedicatedly loyal to the Navy as an institution and, during the latter phases of his career, he was to demonstrate this same almost super-loyalty to the concept of his country and its well-being, as differentiated from individual loyalty to those set immediately over him in the chain of command. Interestingly, when he was a young officer in *Arizona,* it was this same quality of all-out loyalty which impelled Mr. Burke to a rash action, precipitated an epidemic of wrinkled bellies in the junior officers mess and, perchance, taught him the virtues of tempering impetuosity with prudence.

Arizona, a taut and happy ship, lay at Panama, and the battleship was buzzing with appreciative laughter over Captain 'Pete' Olmsted's recent handling of a bit of official business. Two weeks before, a young ensign had requested and received ten days special leave to get married and enjoy a honeymoon. He had departed with the best wishes of his shipmates; the ceremony had been duly performed, and the young couple had retired to a tranquil tropic bower to enjoy their honeymoon. In fact, they enjoyed their idyl so much that, as the day for his return to *Arizona* drew near, the groom decided to request an extension of leave. He messaged Captain Olmsted: "Request five days extension of leave. It's wonderful here."

The Captain's reply ever since has been a Navy classic: "It's wonderful anywhere. Request refused. Rejoin the ship." *

Having rejoined the ship, the new husband still was being twitted about his pithy exchange of messages with Captain 'Pete' when cruiser *Concord* steamed in, dropped her hook, and *Arizona's* junior officers suddenly found themselves absorbed in a new diversion. The challenge was at once simple and, to a loyal Navy man, fundamental: *Concord* had the champion pulling boat crew of the Atlantic Fleet. *Arizona* had the champion pulling boat crew of the Pacific Fleet. Obviously and inescapably, an immediate race for the two-ocean championship was demanded. But, unfortunately, along with the excitement there was no little dolor among the junior officers of *Arizona*. They were, in a word, *broke*. Yet, traditionally, in the Navy large

* While this anecdote since has been variously attributed, diligent research and the memories of those who were serving aboard at the time offer sound confirmation that it originated in *Arizona* as set forth above.

69

sums were bet on these whaleboat races—even the destroyers had crews, and good ones—and it was unthinkable that *Arizona's* crew, coached by Ensign M. K. (Pug) Kirkpatrick, a classmate of Arleigh's and member of a former Annapolis Olympics winning crew, should not be suitably supported by a solid wager representing the junior officers. What to do? The challenge to *Concord* had been issued and accepted; the race had been scheduled, but the inhabitants of *Arizona's* junior officers mess simply didn't have any money.

Arleigh Burke was president of the junior officers mess aboard the battleship, and he found himself facing an absorbing problem. 'Biddle' Ball, the outgoing mess treasurer, recently had left the ship. His legacy to the junior officers was a rich one: A single barrel of mushrooms!

"Well," said Ensign Burt Davis crisply, "we sure as hell can't bet a barrel of mushrooms!"

"No," said mess president Burke thoughtfully, "but look. Each of you guys has chipped in twenty-five bucks to cover your mess bills for the next thirty days . . ."

"And we've still got that in *cash?*" asked Ensign Bertrand B. Cassels.

"We have," said president Burke, "and so far as I'm concerned, loyalty absolutely demands that we back our boat crew by betting the works; the whole mess treasury is what I mean."

"Do we know anything about the *Concord's* crew?" asked Davis cautiously.

"Nothing to it!" Burke reassured him airily. "We've scouted 'em; they've got a little short stroke—no real power; we're a shoo-in to win."

Not only was it voted accordingly to bet the entire liquid assets of *Arizona's* junior officers mess on the boat race, but those few individual officers who had a cash buck or two tossed everything they had into the pot. There may possibly have been those who perceived the shade of future hunger hovering in the background, but if there were they kept their peace. The demands of loyalty were that they bet their last bottom dollar, and that's exactly what they did.

The race was rowed. The 'little, short stroke' developed amazing power, and *Arizona's* crew came in a poor, bitter, and beaten second. President Burke and his messmates faced the facts: So far as money was concerned, they were broke in the most literal sense of the word. And so far as food was concerned, they had a few pounds of coffee, a bag or two of rice, and a barrel of mushrooms on which to live for a month.

Each junior officer in *Arizona* met the calamity in his own fashion. For one thing, there suddenly developed a marked eagerness on the part of the juniors to draw watch officer duty. This arose logically from the fact that it was the junior watch officer's responsibility to inspect and sample the crew's meals. The 'samples' those husky youngsters permitted themselves were Gargantuan. Nor were the consequences of the lost whaleboat race confined to those immediately aboard the battleship. Along with his equity in the mess funds, Ensign Burke had supported *Arizona's* boat crew by betting the special fund set aside for Bobbie's living expenses, and now he had no money to send her. Characteristically, he faced this problem forthrightly; wrote her explaining what had happened, and ended with the tentative query "Do you suppose you could get a job somewhere until we can get straightened out again . . . ?" She could and did. More, she wrote that she fully approved his action.

While the incident of the boat race was lighthearted and its impact transient, it was highly revelatory of several abiding Burke qualities, one of which was to undergo considerable refinement and achieve a certain subtlety during his long climb up the Navy's twin ladders of service and promotion. First, it was characteristic of Burke to "shoot the works" and to urge the same course upon his colleagues. In every situation he ever faced in life, this all-out impulsiveness was dominant. He not only invariably gave everything he had and was to the Navy, but he imperiously demanded that every man serving under him do the same. As to the motivation behind his wagering of his last dollar, no one who really knew Arleigh Burke confused it for a moment with cupidity. Of course it would have been pleasant to win, but Burke did not bet with that objective primarily in mind. His *first* motivation was the loyal and unreserved support of his shipmates which, he considered, the situation absolutely demanded. It was this concept of loyalty which, over the years, was to undergo a considerable development and refinement, achieving a highly personal and deeply perceptive and courageous form by the time he became Chief of Naval Operations and found the demands of loyalty far more complex and subtle than he'd thought them to be as a junior officer. In 1961, after his four-star flag finally had been hauled down for good and he had time to look back on a number of things, Admiral Burke wrote the authors as follows:

"I don't have any real definition of loyalty. I just have a feeling about it. Perhaps the best definition of loyalty is the oath which an officer swears when first he comes into the service—to support and defend the Constitution of the United States. You don't swear loyalty or fealty to an individual or group or to a party or anything else. You swear to defend the United States against all enemies, foreign and domestic. But how to defend the United States in the right way and to the fullest measure? Sometimes this is a pretty difficult judgment to make. For example, there are some people who come into the Armed Services and who think that because they are military men they should owe absolute and eternal loyalty to the individual who is Secretary of Defense. Well, I'll go along with that, so long as the Secretary of Defense is doing everything he can to protect the United States. But all Secretaries of Defense are human, and all Secretaries of Defense make mistakes. When they do, it's a man's absolute and inherent duty to call the attention of the Secretary of Defense to those mistakes . . ."

Arleigh Burke then went on to correlate loyalty with duty. If you think any man is doing something that might jeopardize the security of the United States, it's your duty to try to convince him that he's wrong. If you can't convince him, then you're faced with a difficult choice: You can either carry the disagreement higher, or let it go. But if you let it go, you haven't done your duty. There are laws, he pointed out, which confer on a military man the right to go over the head of his superior either to the President or the Congress. "But," he pointed out, "a military man should have the integrity to do that without the necessity for a law. Not that it's easy. In any military organization the subordinates naturally want to do what their seniors want them to do. It's a natural thing. It takes a very good man indeed not to do what his senior wants him to do. It takes great stamina; it takes a lot of guts—and if people don't have guts, then you have a flock of 'yes men.' But men who always 'yes' their superiors will also 'yes' an enemy. A man who doesn't have the courage to stand up for what he believes to be right in his own friendly councils, will not stand up on the battlefield for what he deems to be right. In other words, a man will not fight for principles unless he fights for principles in all arenas, friendly as well as unfriendly."

As Burke finally saw it, loyalty to an individual, at least for a military man, is part and parcel of this somewhat complex or at least exacting conception of loyalty to the State. He wrote:

"There is such a thing as loyalty to an individual. Take my relationships with Admiral Marc Mitscher in Task Force 58/38. I didn't agree with everything that Admiral Mitscher did. But I fully realized that everything he did, he did because he thought it was best for his country. I had great personal affection for the man and great personal loyalty to him. I would do anything and everything that he wanted me to do. But I did it not because I felt that it was *my* duty to do it, but because I felt that he was doing *his* duty, and I wanted to help him do his duty. That's a very fine distinction indeed."

In the long view and in summary, Burke finally concluded that, while the captain of a ship might earn a high degree of loyalty from those who served under him, loyalty really is not a personal matter: the *cause* demands loyalty; the individual may be the complement through which that loyalty is expressed. He concluded:

"I would like to emphasize that I don't think loyalty is a personal matter. It's a matter of a man's own belief in a cause—his own support of a cause."

As contemporary history amply shows, in this discussion of loyalty Burke

72

was not simply paying lip service to a fancy notion. His official conduct always reflected these convictions, and his determination to live by them not only brought him into many bitter battles but, on one occasion when he had achieved senior rank, resulted in his being held overnight incommunicado in the Pentagon, along with his staff, by the Inspector General of the Navy acting upon the orders of the Secretary of the Navy. (As Burke was not required to turn over his sword, he was not technically under arrest as was widely assumed at the time.) It resulted, too, in his name being stricken temporarily from the Navy's promotion list by President Truman.

Long after it was over, the disastrous business of the boat race plagued the junior officers mess in *Arizona*. "Any mess Arleigh presided over was bound to be one hell of a broke outfit anyway," reminisced one member of the mess long after he had attained the rank of Rear Admiral, "and the thing finally came to a head in the sad and sorry saga of Ensign 'Reiny' Day.

"His real name was Dwight Harvey Day, but we called him 'Reiny' because, during his days as a midshipman at the Naval Academy, he spent most of his so-called 'leisure' time under hack and aboard the prison ship *Reina Mercedes*. 'Reiny' was smart, bordering on brilliance, but he was an eccentric; a real screwball. He was generous to a fault; would give you the shirt off his back; and he was a magnificent shipmate to go ashore with. There never was a dull moment when you were with 'Reiny,' but he and the duty officer rarely saw eye to eye. He belonged in Greenwich Village, not the U.S. Navy.

"Well, the mess still was struggling to recover from that boat race disaster, and we were still broke. 'Reiny' was mess caterer, and he knew our desperate situation very well. And then, suddenly, there came an order from on high: We were to stock up on a lot of horrible foodstuffs to simulate war cruising. We took a very dim view of this order and complied with it only superficially. We did, however, lay in a supply of canned pineapple, which was one of the items on the 'war cruising' list, but there wasn't much else around. We figured we could rely on the largess of our good friend the Supply Officer to see us through until our finances could be brought into some sort of equilibrium.

"We were sadly mistaken! The Supply Officer shut down and wouldn't give us credit. He advanced just enough food to keep the junior officer of the deck on his feet (along with sampling the crew's chow). Then, out of a clear sky, came a new emergency: Ensign 'Reiny' Day was abruptly transferred to another ship and, as he pointedly and insistently reminded us, he had a mess refund of $4.50 coming!

"Arleigh immediately convened an extraordinary meeting of a few key members of our group—Burt Davis, 'Pug' Kirkpatrick, 'Jenks' Longfellow,

Murray Tichenor, George Phelan, 'T' Benson, and a few others—and we faced the facts of life. 'Reiny' was thundering demands for his mess refund, but we couldn't raise four dollars and fifty cents cash among the lot of us! What to do?

" 'Pineapples . . . ?' The idea was advanced hesitantly by Arleigh, but it won instantaneous and unanimous approval. And so, when Ensign 'Reiny' Day went over the side to transfer to his new ship there went along with him in the boat $4.50 worth of canned pineapple. (We were generous and let him have it wholesale.) He was so damned mad he could have chewed the cans open, especially after he found out that his new ship was bound for Hawaii where, in all probability, the pineapple had come from in the first place. But he managed to get even. We were all pretty proud of the pictures we had on our messroom bulkhead. When nobody was looking, 'Reiny' snatched a couple of these, and they went along with the pineapple. We deplored the loss of the pictures but, before his new ship sailed, we managed to get a message to 'Reiny' specifically suggesting what he might do with the pineapple!"

Arizona was known as a party ship—the junior officers usually conned the wardroom into throwing the parties—and for many of Arleigh Burke's shipmates duty aboard was one great lark. Of some thirty-five juniors, only three were married and had family responsibilities which tended to restrain them from participating in the all-night crap and poker games invariably attendant upon pay days. 'Jenks' Longfellow and Murray Tichenor usually ended up with the loot, and became filthy rich by junior officers' standards. Longfellow and George Phelan rented a series of apartments at successive locations in Long Beach—(recurring 'landlord trouble' made frequent changes of location not only prudent but often necessary)—and *Arizona's* electrical gunner provided the magnet which drew the junior officers to these hideouts like iron filings. The 'magnet' was a fine ten-gallon copper still, and the gunner rotated its rental among the junior officers, collecting his liquid fee weekly and converting it into cash in other quarters. At that time the fare from Long Beach into Los Angeles via the Pacific Electric System was only fifty cents, and the uninhibited youngsters of *Arizona* quickly discovered that they could make a memorable liberty in Hollywood for about five dollars. The mantle of officer responsibility rested lightly upon most of them, and fight or frolic were equally welcome.

Arleigh Burke's participation in this razzle-dazzle was restrained. In perspective, it seems a singular tribute to the young man's presence that he was able to maintain very serious course and speed toward professional goals and still hold the admiration and affection of his more boisterous colleagues. Although he rarely participated in their gusty goings on, they still regarded him as a 'splendid shipmate,' a 'likable fellow,' and 'a very able young officer.' In other words, he managed to be with but not of the

74

sophomoric side of *Arizona's* junior officer group and to retain full acceptance while pursuing patterns of conduct rather more conservative than
those adopted by many of his colleagues.

It was during this formative period that young Burke learned a basic
lesson which he never was to forget, and the fruits of which he was to
apply again and again throughout his career. It was, in a sentence, that
an attitude of *laissez faire* was or could be a treacherous trap. If he expected to gain stature and competence in his profession, he would have to
act positively and on his own responsibility, leaving nothing to chance or
someone else's good intentions.

The anecdote is a mellow and meaningful one. Burke had achieved the
heady rank of lieutenant, junior grade. *Arizona* was participating in maneuvers in the Caribbean, and Lieutenant (jg) Burke was going in for
gunnery with the same obsessive passion which he brought later to chasing and sinking important units of the Imperial Japanese Navy. By chance
he happened to hear that the Navy was starting a new school in New York,
to which young officers could be ordered. The school was concerned with
a new type of director-controlled antiaircraft gun system. Up until that
time all antiaircraft fire had been barrage fire using three-inch guns, and
Mr. Burke immediately decided that he must learn this new and improved
gunnery system. He asked the captain if he might attend the school; the
captain consented, and Burke submitted the necessary formal request
through channels. However, because of delays in the captain's office,
Burke's request did not reach the flagship until the quota of officers designated for the school had been filled. It was then that he realized that
he would have to take matters into his own hands if he was to gain his
objective.

Burke asked the captain if, in view of the circumstances, he could go
over and see the flag and try to talk them into increasing the quota by
one. The captain was not especially perturbed. He said he'd send a dispatch explaining to the flag that Burke's request was due to a clerical delay, and that would be enough. But he did not specifically forbid Burke
to visit the flag himself.

Burke wasted no time in visiting the cruiser *Raleigh,* which was the
vessel designated to take the young officers back to the States. He told
his tale of woe to the executive officer, but met with little encouragement.
"We're full up," said the Exec. "There's no more room."

"Look, sir," said Burke, "I won't even need a bunk. I'll sleep in a
passageway and keep well out of the road."

"Will you stand watches?" asked the Exec, cocking his head on one
side and eyeing the eager beaver before him quizzically.

"Yes, sir!"

"Will you eat in the third mess . . . ?"

"Yes, sir!"

The Exec then piled on a number of other onerous provisions, all of which Burke enthusiastically accepted. Finally, the three-striper capitulated. "All right. If you can get clearance from the flag I'll take you." Burke immediately boarded the flagship; explained that the *Raleigh's* executive officer would give him transportation to New York if the flag would clear him; and won his point.

The denouement of the episode came when Mr. Burke returned to *Arizona*. Almost immediately, he was ordered to report to the captain (who knew nothing of the young man's visits to *Raleigh* and the flag).

"Burke," said the captain sententiously, "I have good news for you. I've received a dispatch from the flag that your request to attend that New York school has been granted. You've got to learn patience, young man; you can't go around trying to force things. A little while back you wanted to go over to the flag and do a lot of things that were entirely unnecessary. This dispatch proves that they were unnecessary. Now get your gear together and shove off—and in future don't be in such an all-fired hurry to take matters into your own hands!"

"Yes, *sir!*" said Lieutenant (jg) Arleigh Burke—and he never did tell the captain the facts of the matter.

Burke's attendance at the gunnery school developed an unexpected side effect: it made him and Bobbie experts on finding free entertainment in New York. It was the old question of money—or of the lack of it—and Burke himself tells the story:

"I thought I would surprise my wife and not tell her I was coming— which shows not only that I was immature, but inexperienced as well! In due course, *Raleigh* reached Norfolk, I took a train for Washington, and called Bobbie from the station with the news that we were going to New York. I caught her just in time: she was on the point of leaving to visit an uncle. She met me at the station and we got under way for New York. On the trip up I told her I had $100 which, I hoped, would last for the duration of the school, which was six weeks. She looked at me with amusement and said she had exactly twenty dollars, which was why she'd planned to visit her uncle. It looked like rough sledding ahead! Could two people live in New York for six weeks on $120?

"Neither Bobbie nor I knew anything about New York, but we'd heard about Greenwich Village and thought we might find cheap quarters in that area. I had to report to the Ford Instrument Company, where the school was to be held, so I dropped Bobbie off in the vicinity of Fifth Avenue and Twenty-fifth Street with instructions to call me at the Ford Company when she'd found a place for us to live. I waited five hours for her call, and when she did call she sounded a bit distressed. She hadn't been able to find any place that would give us room and board within our budget, but she'd talked a landlady into renting us a very small room on Thirty-third Street near Fifth Avenue at ten dollars a week. The room wasn't even big enough to have a chair!

"Well, we worked things out satisfactorily. We lived principally on day-old doughnuts from a nearby bakery, visited the aquarium, all the art galleries, free exhibits, and took lovely walks. We learned to avoid the days when admission was charged at various places, and we had a wonderful time.

"The manager of a Knox hatstore—a widower and a very understanding man—had a room in the same house with us. He was amused and intrigued by our efforts to see the sights of New York without spending any money, and immediately offered to take us to all sorts of places. We had to decline however, because we couldn't repay him. Then he hit on a very happy scheme, which enabled him to entertain us and still didn't cost him anything. Because of the location of his store, he received a good many complimentary tickets to shows. He insisted that we share these with him, and we saw lots of shows, although some we had to pass up because we couldn't afford the twenty cents round-trip subway fare. As a matter of fact, we had many serious conferences to determine which show really was worth the sacrifice of twenty cents.

"When the course was over and the fleet came in, Bobbie had all of our money except thirty cents which I'd held out for emergency transportation. She had less than two dollars. The fleet arrived just in time!"

CHAPTER 5

Promotion—Command—Combat

Between World Wars I and II the promotion escalator of the U.S. Navy was a slow-moving lift. Detached from U.S.S. *Arizona,* young Arleigh Burke stood at the bottom of the promotion ladder, looked upward, and was daunted—probably for the first and only time in his life. He summed up his feelings in an observation at once philosophical and bitter: "Any man who expects to make captain in this man's Navy just isn't modest!" He would have been greatly surprised had he known that, at about this same time, one of his shipmates had made the sage observation, "Either Arleigh Burke will be dead before he's fifty, or he'll be the Chief of Naval Operations!"

While the term is not apt in the military sense, it is realistic: Leaving *Arizona,* Mr. Burke found himself adrift in the U.S. Navy. The training and development of a young officer present diversified demands. He must attend various technical schools to gain heightened insight into various technical matters. His duties must prompt him to expanding mastery of navigation, gunnery, and seamanship; understanding of the fundamental considerations underlying Navy disciplines; a glimmering of apprehension with regard to the intricacies of leadership. Arleigh Burke now embarked upon this formidable obstacle course. Trying to relate his successive assignments one to the other in terms of a rational close-up continuity may have eluded him but, at long range, the purpose to be achieved, and the method of approaching that achievement, were extremely rational. It was essential that Burke learn by doing every aspect of Navy functioning. The particular duty of the moment might seem inconsequential, but its contribution to the over-all objective of producing a wholly competent officer was incontrovertible. Burke fussed, and he fumed. But, also, he worked, and he learned.

Having a natural interest in gunnery, young Burke applied for and was granted permission to undertake a year's postgraduate work in this subject at the Naval Academy. Following this, he was posted to the University of Michigan for work leading to a master-of-science degree in chemical (explosives) engineering. He had a rough time at Michigan. His math and science background at the Academy was average, but it was slender support for the more complex demands now made upon his intellect. He studied every night until midnight, six nights a week, and he managed to squeak by.

It was characteristic of Burke that, while absorbed in the hard demands of learning the higher technics of explosives, he did not for a moment lose sight of the broader picture. In "Chemical Engineering Nine"—a course involving the solution of engineering problems in fluid flow, evaporation, filtration, etc., he was teamed with a colleague—a civilian—named Alvin J. Herzig, from Detroit. They spent much time in each other's offices, and Herzig noted with some puzzlement that Burke had plastered the walls of his office with *National Geographic* maps of the Far East and the South Pacific. These maps not only lined the walls of Burke's office, but from time to time he entered personal notations upon them in colored pencil.

"Why do you pay so much attention to those maps, Arleigh?" asked Herzig.

"One day, my friend," replied Burke prophetically, "our country will be at war with Japan. In that conflict it will be my mission to do my bit for my country in that theater of operations. When that time comes I intend to know that area of the world as intimately as possible."

Thinking ahead—reasoning, and casting up probabilities in an almost global dimension—was a Burke characteristic as early as 1930. Not that he was exclusive in this; many other Navy officers thought likewise. But it was a Burke hallmark that he implemented his thinking and his conclusions by daily reference to maps and the entering of data thereon. Considering the weight of the academic demands upon him it was an extra, added, and self-assumed chore, and he stood to gain nothing immediately from its accomplishment. But he considered it his duty, and he did it.

With two stripes, Arleigh Burke had what long has been known as "the most comfortable rank in the Navy." His responsibilities were minimal; his privileges were maximal. Sea duty alternated with the hard grind of technical study ashore, and it was a full life. Most important to Burke, during this period he was offered his first opportunity to win a Navy decoration. (Most times, Burke sought opportunities for extra service. When they were offered for free, it was, in his terms, 'Katy, bar the door!')

The occasion was a December morning, and Burke was a watch keeping officer in U.S.S. *Procyon*. *Procyon* wore the flag of the Fleet Base Force, Pacific, and she was a tender. She stood to sea that morning from a California port, and shortly after daylight a lookout spotted what seemed to be wreckage off their starboard bow. A Santa Ana had hit, and the ship was laboring. Binocular inspection showed that there were men on the wreckage. Rescue obviously was demanded.

79

Putting his ship on a course to windward of the floating wreckage, the commanding officer of *Procyon* called for volunteers to man a whaleboat to take off the survivors, if any. Burke stepped forward, as did an adequate crew for a whaleboat. *Procyon* dropped them in a turbulent sea, and they were on their own.

As the whaleboat approached the wreckage, Burke carefully appraised the situation. One man was standing upright, waving. What he was standing on, Burke couldn't tell; the man seemed to be standing on the top of the sea. Other figures were huddled nearby, secured by ropes to the erect man. As Burke's whaleboat drew near, he determind that there were five men in all on the wreckage. He took them all off, returned to *Procyon,* and the ship was put on a course for San Diego at flank speed.

When the realities were sorted out, they turned out to be: The rescued party had set out in a fishing barge the day before, headed by Harlan Major, an internationally famous fisherman. At about 2200 the Santa Ana had struck them, and the barge broke up. The roof of the cabin broke loose, and all the men tried to climb upon it. Again and again, they were washed off. In the whole party, Major was the only man who could swim, and each time he went after the man adrift and brought him back. Finally he roped the party together. They sighted some passing vessels, but had no means to signal save for waving, and were not sighted until *Procyon* came along. Although he had a broken elbow, Major waved and attracted the attention of *Procyon's* lookout. Two of the fishermen had died during the night and, when Burke took them all off, two more seemed on the point of death. Prompt medical attention saved them, however, and the net score was the rescue of three out of five "distressed mariners." For this exploit—and at a relatively very early age—Arleigh Burke received his first Navy decoration. Subsequently, he was to go on to win every decoration it is within the competence of the Navy Department to award.

Detached from *Procyon,* Arleigh Burke found himself participating in a course of "practical gunnery instruction" at the Naval Proving Grounds, Dahlgren, Virginia, and the Naval Powder Factory, in the dismal reaches of Maryland at Indian Head. His contribution during this period was typically Burke, although not necessarily champion.

There is an apocryphal story that he invented or designed a fuze for naval ordnance so sensitive—so fast and volatile—that even Navy gunners were afraid to handle it. That would have been quite in character for the impetuous Burke, but the facts lie elsewhere. He didn't invent or design a new fuze; he modified an existing one. The facts were given the authors by Rear Admiral R. H. 'Bob' Speck, who had official cognizance at the time, which was between 1936 and 1938. Admiral Speck recounts:

"Arleigh Burke was in the Ammunition Section of the Bureau of Ordnance, and became involved in consideration and design of this fuze. However, the design of the fuze already existed, so his concern was with corrective measures.

"The design he finally came up with suffered from two aspects, which only experience could indicate. It had an insufficient degree of safe features, and it was too sensitive and could be upset at the wrong times. The fuze was amenable to design correction, and this was reasonably well accomplished. When the matter shook itself down—and without injury to any Navy personnel—Arleigh admitted that his performance was less than complete and corrected his mistakes by turning in a final fuze design which retained the essential characteristics of simplicity, but still achieved adequate sensitivity. The point is that he recognized and admitted his mistakes, and went on to correct them."

Back afloat at the latter part of 1937, and serving as Executive Officer of U.S.S. *Craven,* a DD, Lieutenant Arleigh A. Burke found himself in the sternest trouble which can overtake a mariner. On October 21 of that year, *Craven* crossed The Line, and Lieutenant Burke was served with a subpoena issued from the Domain of Neptunus Rex, and signed by Davy Jones. The Bill of Particulars charged him with:

"Mopery on the High Seas" in that he so annoyed Old Sol, the Sun God, by taking observations every half hour, that he drove Ol' Sol off his rocker, resulting in three consecutive weeks of stormy weather.

"Aiding and abetting the promulgation of seditious literature" in that he permitted to be displayed on the ship's bulletin board the writings of a Pollywog.*

"Assuming the responsibilities of the commanding officer, and the duties of trusted Shellback † Division Officers while himself not yet a Pollywog."

Properly humbled, the haughty Exec of *Craven* was shaved, hazed, and became himself a Shellback. The incident has this significance: Few Navy officers responded more sincerely than Arleigh Burke to the traditions, pomp, and panoply of the Navy and the sea. Later in his career, as commander of his own ship, he slowed to minimum speed while crossing The Line and afforded the ship's company every opportunity to enjoy to the full the horseplay of Neptune's visit and the acid wit of his minion, Davy Jones.

Destroyers and Arleigh Burke went together like ham and eggs. From the moment he set foot aboard *Craven,* he fell in love with destroyers— the swift greyhounds of the sea—and although he attained and retained top naval rank, four stars as Chief of Naval Operations, for an unprecedented six-year term, he remained a 'tin can' sailor until the hot, soggy,

* A sailor who has not previously crossed the equator.

† A sailor who has already crossed The Line and been initiated into the fraternity of the sea by King Neptune and his Scribe, Davy Jones.

and sorry August day in 1961 when, with a near-sob in his voice, he concluded his Navy career by requesting the Commandant of the Naval Academy, "Please have my flag hauled down!"

By 1939, Burke had attained the rank of Lieutenant Commander, and in that year he achieved the goal of every Navy officer since Noah: A command of his own! She was U.S.S. *Mugford,* and a more gallant ship never fired a gun. Mercifully, the clouded crystal ball of 1939 gave no glimpse of *Mugford's* future, but she was to steam bravely out of Pearl Harbor during the Japanese surprise attack, participate as a unit of Des-Ron Five in the New Guinea campaign, follow up in the Northern New Britain and Marianas operations, and finally be put out of action in December, 1944, when a Japanese *kamikaze* plane crashed into her port side, killing ten men and inflicting agonizing burns on sixteen more. *Mugford* was all steel and guts, and so was her new skipper, Lieut. Commander Arleigh Burke.

Mugford was a new design built at the Navy shipyard, Boston, and Burke was her third skipper. She had four 5" thirty-eight single guns, with automatic train and elevation to the director, a modern fire control system, and four quadruple torpedo mounts. Burke took command at San Diego, relieving Lieutenant Commander Marcy M. Dupree, who was an able captain and had the vessel in top shape. *Mugford's* number was DD-389.

It is improbable that any single event in Arleigh Burke's life achieved the impact and the significance of his first command. Here was a young Navy officer of high talent, tremendous thrust, and almost a demonic devotion to detail. Always, before, he had been under wraps—smothered by an immediate command presence. Now, in *Mugford,* although still under command, he was the immediate boss, with full opportunity to implement the enormous drives toward technical perfection which were his dominant characteristic.

Burke's outstanding performance in *Mugford* began in a very low key and on a gently humorous, southern note. His inherited Executive Officer was Gelzer Sims, a thoughtful, meticulous officer from South Carolina. Intellectually and technically, Sims was well able to keep up with his fiery new captain, but personality-wise the two were as different as night and day. Burke was obviously vigorous, impetuous, thinking ahead, and dreaming big dreams with a very realistic reference. Gelzer was slow, nostalgic, mellow—but none-the-less perceptive.

After the change-of-command ceremonies on the fantail of *Mugford,* Burke and Sims retired to the wardroom. It was essential that they get acquainted, and quickly. Burke gauged his man. Some men must be led. Others must be driven. Still others should be taken into partnership to get the best out of them. Gelzer Sims was of the latter type. Arleigh

Burke lighted his pipe, sat back, relaxed, and permitted himself the small talk which eventually, he knew, would give him the requisite insight into the character of his Exec. He waited, and in due time Sims laid it straight on the line:

"You know, Captain," he began, "you remind me of a little thing that happened down in my home town of Orangeburg, South Carolina. It's just a wide place in the road, you might say, but it's comfortable, and quiet, and lazy, and we like it. Well, sir, for years we had a character around the town—old Negro name of Sam. Everybody loved Sam; they'd go out of their way to help him, although Sam never got into any serious trouble. The thing was, Sam was what you might call shiftless. He didn't seem to like hard work, and people got concerned about keepin' Sam in greens an' grits. Not, of course, that you're lazy or shiftless, captain; that's not the point.

"Well, came the time when the business men of the town got together and decided that something must be done about Sam. They didn't want him to starve. They didn't want him to suffer. But on the other hand they were perceptive enough to realize that Sam shouldn't be driven to hard, regular work. How to help Sam became the burnin' question.

"Well, sir, I think it was Melton Melton—an improbable name, but he had it—who came up with the righteous idea. He was a young lawyer, an' sharp as a tack. His idea was this: We had an ol' brass cannon on the lawn in front of the City Hall. It probably came from the Spanish-American War. An' it was pretty green an' dingy. This thing is a disgrace to the town, said Melton. Why don't we all chip in, and we'll engage Sam, on a monthly basis, to shine that cannon an' keep it bright so it's an ornament to the town.

"Everybody agreed; everybody chipped in; Sam was engaged for this light work—and for two years he really put his heart in it. Captain, I'm telling you, you never saw a prettier cannon in your life. Sam got so fond of that cannon, he took to sleepin' under it on fair spring an' summer nights. An' then, all of a sudden, after two years, Sam showed up at Melton Melton's office. He waited patiently until Melton could receive him and then, hat in hand, he announced: 'Mr. Melton, I sure appreciate all you folks have did for me. I jes' came in t' tell you I'm resignin'.'

"Well, Melton Melton was struck full a'back, captain. But he didn't panic. He played it soft and easy; he told Sam what a good job he'd done keeping that ol' cannon sparklin', and, finally, he got around to the point. 'What are you going to do, Sam?'

" 'Well, Boss,' said Sam, 'I'm goin' in business for myself. Yes, sir! I've been savin' m' money, Mr. Melton. I been very particular. I been schoochin' meals here an' there, an' it don't cost me much t' live, an' I done bought my *own* cannon! Yes, sah, soon's you can fin' somebody t' take over mah work, I'm goin' in business f' myself, shinin' m' very *own* cannon!' "

"I remind you of *that* story?" asked Arleigh Burke incredulously.

"Yes, captain," said Gelzer Sims. "I figure you're th' kind of man who's got to have his *own* cannon!"

In that little session Gelzer Sims found out more about Arleigh Burke than Arleigh Burke found out about Gelzer Sims. He tried artfully, and often successfully, to cover it up, but Burke always was the kind of guy who had to have his own cannon. The reaches of his mind were deep and devious, and he did not admit strangers to those reaches with enthusiasm. Even so, he fooled few. By his middle years as CNO, he had fallen back upon elementary psychological compensation. Those who really were performing were *with* him. Those who were *not* with him were *not* performing. He couldn't tolerate the idea that there were loyal, efficient, and sincere officers in the U.S. Navy who hated his guts. The reason is not far to seek, and it reflects no lack of sincerity on Burke's part. From the moment he walked into the Naval Academy, he made a cult of the Navy and of loyalty to the United States. For a layman the equivalent would be a reverence for home and mother. You can't go wrong. Nobody throws rocks at Santa Claus. But a great many good and loyal and sincere people have their *own* ideas about home, and mother, and Santa Claus too . . .

Arleigh Burke's work as commanding officer of U.S.S. *Mugford* was outstanding by any standard. He ran a taut but happy ship. Everybody aboard sensed the peremptory demand upon the vessel and her captain: *To break all records, and capture all honors.* And she did nearly that.

Vice Admiral F. E. M. (Red) Whiting had DesRon-8, to which *Mugford* was attached. His comments:

"*Mugford* fired short-range practice, every gun an 'E' * including the officer's string.† In other words, thirty-six shots and thirty-six hits. It did not require any imagination to know that Burke had cleaned up the fleet. Accordingly, as we entered San Diego harbor, I directed Burke to hoist brooms, indicating a clean sweep. So on this occasion, we entered the harbor with brooms at every yardarm.

"It was my practice, when we were a scouting division, to head directly

* The Navy 'E' stands for 'excellence,' and translates to perfect. Admiral Whiting means to indicate that every gun hit the target.

† The *'officer's string'* was the first four salvos from a ship at short-range battle practice. The officers acted as the pointers, both for train and elevation, and as sight setter. The procedure was established for the purpose of testing the ballistic computations and the gun-powder performance when those things were less well defined and manufacturing processes were less well controlled than they are today.

84

for a contact at the highest available speed. I do not think that Arleigh liked it too much at first, but if this had anything to do with his training, it stood him in good stead in the war when he became known as '31-Knot-Burke.' "

Whether 'Red' Whiting was the father of Burke's daring destroyer doctrine may well remain moot in the U.S. Navy for a long time. Perhaps they may share the honors of conception, but to Burke must go the top honor of implementation in battle.

When he took command of *Mugford,* and looking ahead, as he always did, Arleigh Burke saw the shape of things to come and, characteristically, applied his interpretation immediately to the job in hand. It was an uneasy period. Germany already had invaded Poland. With war clouds on the horizon, the U.S. Navy had begun to train around the clock. Lieutenant Commander Burke's idea was to make *Mugford* the most efficient tin can afloat, and to that end he bent his energies. At the end of Burke's first year in command, *Mugford* won the fleet trophy for gunnery, ranked third in engineering, and also placed high in the communications competition.

Burke drove his ship. He drove his officers. But, most of all, he drove himself. Many of the officers who served under Arleigh Burke in *Mugford* went on to achieve exalted rank in the Navy. But none of them forgot the experience of sailing with Burke in his first ship. The following comments by former *Mugford* officers clearly indicate the impress he made upon his subordinates:

"In gunnery he had thorough and complete understanding of both the equipment and the methods of attaining outstanding performances during the conduct of gunnery practices, as well as the ultimate purpose, i.e., battle readiness . . ."

"I will always remember the speed with which he did things, and expected other people to do their assigned tasks. His instruction to us, as officers of the deck, was to take action on a signal and *then* call him. If we received a signal and he didn't happen to be on the bridge, we were to two-block instantly the signal signifying understanding, and that the ship was ready to carry out the order. We were not to wait for him to come to the bridge and give orders. The idea was to *do* something, even though it might not be *exactly* right. He would try, he told us, to get to the bridge before we had gone too far wrong. And he always did!"

Another former *Mugford* officer wrote the authors:

"I particularly recall one night during darken ship exercises. I was O.O.D. The ship ahead in column formation broke down. Before I realized the rapid closing of the two ships, Arleigh had taken the conn, turned, and avoided the danger."

As commander of DesRon-8, 'Red' Whiting observed of Burke to a colleague: "This is a tremendous officer. He does all my work for me, and probably does yours as well!"

Burke's compulsion to perfection didn't embrace only major considerations. It extended to minuscule points of protocol as well. After twenty years, one former *Mugford* officer remembered keenly his humiliation at Burke's hands. When getting under way, it was standard practice to sound the ship's siren three times; then test the whistle. This particular officer, who had the deck, did this routine exercise in reverse. Burke immediately fixed him with such a blazing, angry glare that the junior was forced to seek sanctuary by turning his back, and would have fled the bridge in disgrace, had that not been an even more formidable crime!

Although a perfectionist, Arleigh Burke also was a ready man to admit his mistakes, and one of his earlier bungles caught up with him in *Mugford*. He was present at a heated discussion in the wardroom over the 1.1 gun, which then was their newest weapon, and quite controversial. The Gunnery Officer, later to become Rear Admiral R. H. 'Bob' Speck, held forth vehemently and at length on the faulty design and impracticality of the fuzes for the gun. Burke listened, and then laughed a little hollowly. "I designed that fuze!" he admitted, "and what you say is absolutely right. The design *is* faulty!"

Burke's brand of leadership aroused enthusiastic response in *Mugford's* crew, and he was careful to nurture this priceless abstraction and lead them gently on toward ever higher accomplishment. He frequently addressed his men at length, and the following excerpt from one such address is typical:

"I couldn't wish for a better ship's company. I have been particularly well pleased by two things—two indispensable attributes for a man-of-war: Your loyalty to the ship; and your hard work. I have seen many ships, but I've never seen one that could excel the *Mugford* in these two characteristics. I have utmost faith in you. I believe you'll do your best in any situation in which we may find ourselves. *But that best must be good enough to be successful.*

"A ship can be compared to a good boxer. A boxer is light on his feet. He uses his legs to get in close when he wants to, and to get clear if he must. A boxer with candy legs soon goes out. The legs of a ship are its engines. They must get us in, and get us out. They must be reliable.

"A boxer uses his left to hit. It's his striking arm. A ship's striking arm is its guns, torpedoes, and depth charges. It can deliver a terrific blow, if it can get to a position through its engines, where that blow is effective. No boxer can win unless he can deliver. We've got to be able to deliver blows which are hard and accurate. If a boxer misses, he loses an opportunity, he wastes his strength, and he loses confidence. So does a ship. *We must hit early, often, and hard!"*

Arleigh Albert Burke as a Midshipman at the U.S. Naval Academy. He had trouble with mathematics and languages; was good at history, gunnery, and seamanship. It was about this time that he gave Bobbie his class ring and "she thought they were engaged." They were, and they were married the day Burke was graduated.

Arleigh Burke (*second from right, first row*) when he was an officer in U.S.S. *Procyon*. It was while serving in *Procyon* that Burke won his first Navy decoration for "rescuing distressed mariners."

A portrait of Arleigh Burke. The artist has caught him immediately upon coming topside as the crew of U.S.S. *Charles Ausburne* went to general quarters during the campaign in the Solomons. Burke, at the time, was Commodore of DesRon-23, the famous "Little Beaver" destroyer Squadron. He rode in *Charlie Ausburne*, which was his flagship. *Ausburne* was commanded by Lieutenant Commander Luther K. (Brute) Reynolds.

Official U.S. Navy photograph.

Ships of the Fast Carrier Task Force, of which Burke served as Chief of Staff, at their anchorage at Ulithi Atoll in 1944. The carriers, foreground to background: *Wasp, Yorktown, Hornet, Hancock, Ticonderoga,* and *Lexington,* the first flagship in which Burke served.

Official U.S. Navy photograph.

Task Force 58 proved that it had a sting off Saipan on June 19, 1944, in the Battle of the Philippine Sea. Here a large Japanese carrier burns from bombs dropped by carrier-based aircraft and turns sharply to starboard while near-misses land off her bow and stern. Japanese destroyers are maneuvering in the foreground.

Official U.S. Navy photograph.

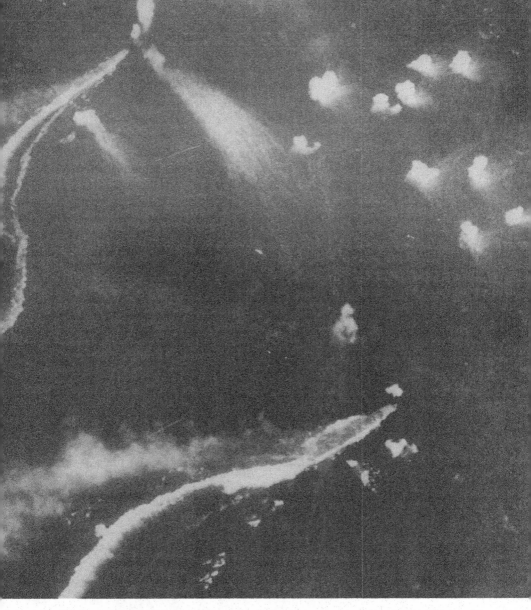

Two enemy carriers attempt unsuccessfully to elude planes from Task Force 38's *Enterprise* on October 25, 1944, during the Battle for Leyte Gulf, the world's greatest naval engagement.

Official U.S. Navy photograph.

After World War II, Admiral Marc Mitscher and Burke were teamed again, as Mitscher took command of the Atlantic Fleet, with Burke as his Chief of Staff.

Major General Henry I. Hodes and Burke leave the conference site at Kaesong, Korea, after another fruitless round of negotiations with the North Koreans and the Chinese Reds.

For a time, Burke was a dry-land sailor as he took command of the negotiators' camp during the Communist-inspired "recesses" in the armistice talks. The Army men called him "General."

Official U.S. Navy photograph.

Armistice conference sub-delegates Burke and Hodes were near the end of their tenure (and patience) as negotiators with the Communists, as they worked on the traditional Thanksgiving turkey in Korea in 1951.

Official U.S. Navy photograph.

"Why can't these recruits at San Diego Naval Training Center learn to march at 31 knots?" yells a hopping CNO Burke in a cartoon presented to the Admiral during a California reception.

Burke as a Commodore in the Atlantic, in 1946, after World War II. The officer standing with him is not identified, but considering the stack of file folders he's holding, he must have been devoted to paper work!

In 1957, Arleigh and Bobbie took an extended world tour on official Navy business—cementing relations with friendly nations. This picture shows them upon arrival by air at London. *Left to right*: Earl Mountbatten, the Countess Mountbatten, Admiral Burke, Bobbie, and Vice Admiral Walter F. Boone.

Submarine *Shark*, nuclear powered, is launched March 16, 1960, at the plant of the Newport News Shipbuilding & Drydock Company, Newport News, Va., where she was built. *Shark* was commissioned February 9, 1961, and commanded by Lieutenant Commander John F. Fagan. She was assigned to SubRon-6, and her first deployment was with the Sixth Fleet, in the Mediterranean. *Shark* was the first nuclear submarine to be so deployed.

Official U.S. Navy photograph.

In May, 1960, Burke returned to Sweden, the homeland of his ancestors. He is shown here immediately after placing a wreath on the grave of his great-great-grandfather, Olaus Bjorkegren, in the churchyard at Hudene. Having left Sweden for the United States, Burke's grandfather changed the family name to Burke, because his colleagues in America had difficulty in pronouncing the Swedish original.

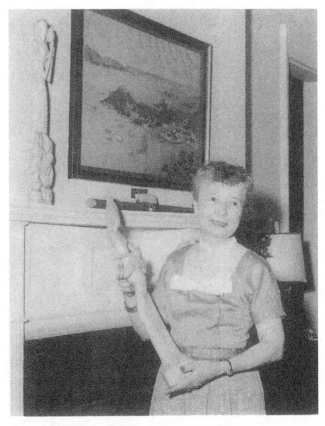

Bobbie Burke, as mistress of Admiral's House, on Observatory Hill, Washington—quarters provided by the Navy for the Chief of Naval Operations. She holds an ivory statue, one of the many curios presented to the Burkes by admirers all over the world.

Official U.S. Navy photograph.

Nuclear submarine *Ethan Allen* can fire the Polaris missile, stay under water for weeks, even months, at a time. It is designed to evade detection.

Official U.S. Navy photograph.

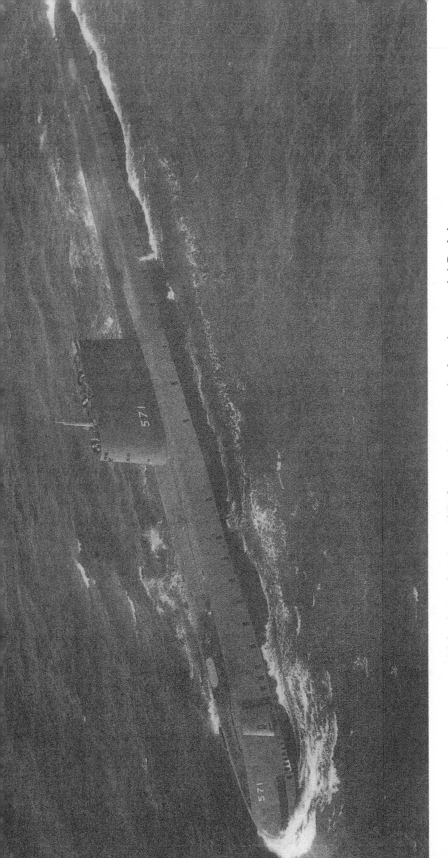

Trials of *Nautilus*, the world's first nuclear-powered submarine, preceded Burke's tenure as CNO, but he pushed development of *Polaris*, the solid-fuel IRBM which gave new strategic significance to the atomic sub.

Official U.S. Navy photograph.

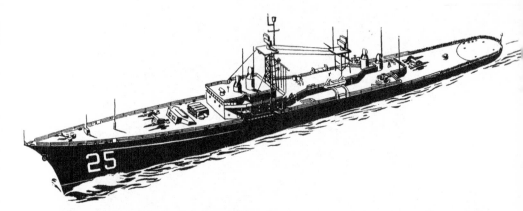

First nuclear frigate (and first frigate in many a year) is *Bainbridge,* designed to work hard on duty with carriers or to operate alone. She is larger than a destroyer and better able to handle herself in the North Atlantic. As are destroyers, she too is armed with missiles.

Official U.S. Navy photograph.

First atomic-powered cruiser is *Long Beach,* with its unfamiliar superstructure. She bristles with destructive weapons.

Official U.S. Navy photograph.

Pride of the modern nuclear Navy, over the birth of which CNO Burke presided, is *Enterprise*, the first nuclear-powered aircraft carrier. President Kennedy boarded *Enterprise* in 1962 to watch modern naval maneuvers.

Official U.S. Navy photograph.

End of the Line! Burke's official Navy career came to an end with his retirement on August 1, 1961. The impressive ceremonies marking his retirement after an unprecedented six years as Chief of Naval Operations were held at the Naval Academy at Annapolis, and he and other top-ranking Navy officers stood at rigid attention as a parting 19-gun salute was rendered. Burke (*left*) is shown here receiving his four-star flag from Rear Admiral John F. Davidson, at that time Superintendent of the Naval Academy. The occasion was a difficult one for Burke, and his voice broke when the time came for him to request Admiral Davidson, "Will you please have my flag hauled down." As the flag fluttered down—and after nearly 40 years as a Navy officer—Arleigh Burke became a civilian.

Official U.S. Navy photograph.

Using this same colloquial approach, which he shrewdly perceived would get through to every man in the ship, Burke proceeded to explain the whole complicated ship's functioning in terms of boxing. He demanded that every Chief Petty Officer under his command fit himself to take over the bridge, if necessary. He told the men that there would not be time to learn by doing; that they would have to teach themselves. But always and always, his emphasis was upon fighting and sinking the enemy—in his thinking the ultimate and only real purpose of the Navy. He even reminded the ship's cooks that, while their job was to obtain stores that would take up little room "but still be good to eat, and enable the ship to go for months, if we have to, without seeing a grocery store," they'd also best learn to handle machine guns. He wanted no man in *Mugford* who wasn't ready and able to *fight,* regardless of the nature of his routine duties.

Mugford was a *top* ship when Burke assumed command. She was an *outstanding* ship when he was relieved and headed for Washington to serve a hitch as an inspector at the Naval Gun Factory.

Prior to joining *Mugford,* while serving in U.S.S. *Chester,* Burke had had a frustrating experience which throws amusing light upon his dedication to the Navy, and the interests of the Navy, above all else. It was during Prohibition, and *Chester* lay at New Orleans. Two of Burke's colleagues —Hall Hanlon, and 'Buddy' Kraker—were poison to each other. Burke didn't know the origin of the feud, but it had been going on for a long time, and he figured it was not in the best interests of the U.S. Navy. So, Burke-like, he decided to do something about it.

Hanlon was a great big bruiser; Kraker was a little bit of a fellow; they both had explosive tempers. As Burke tells the story:

"I had to work with both of them. They soon got to the point where they wouldn't speak to each other—and that put me in the middle. It was an intolerable situation. So I arranged a little dinner party ashore. It was a party for three, but they both thought there would be others present, and they both accepted my invitation. We met at Antoine's, and we had a wonderful dinner, but it didn't do any good. They were both ornery as hell. There was a little bar in the back, and we each had one drink, but that didn't help either.

"On the way back to the ship, I steered them into a little grog shop I knew that sold liquor—just a little hole in the wall. Curiously, the only thing the proprietor had for sale was a bottle of Benedictine. I bought it, and that bottle and the dinner took all my money.

"Well, I wasn't drinking anything much those days, but Hanlon and Kraker sure were! We sat there in the grog shop, and they drank the whole bottle of Benedictine between 'em. Then the *real* trouble began! As the golden liquid slipped down their gullets, their orneriness disappeared like melting snow. First, they became good friends. Three more drinks, and they were BIG BUDDIES! They wanted more to drink, but I didn't have any more money, and the man said he didn't have any more liquor. So I suggested that we return to the ship. No, sir! Neither of them would leave without his 'ol' buddy,' and neither 'ol' buddy' had any notion of leaving! I couldn't handle 'em both, and I was really stuck. I suppose we spent four—five hours in that grog shop before they finally agreed that it might be a good idea to return to *Chester*. But by that time they were mad at me! I did my best to herd 'em along—they were reeling all over the street—and we finally made it. I missed getting into real trouble by a very narrow margin. But the end result was okeh. The feud was forgotten and, so far as I know, they remained friends from there on out. It was a good night's work for the Navy!"

Burke may have thought he was frustrated in the Hanlon-Kraker imbroglio, but when the Japs jumped Pearl Harbor he was to learn that there were depths of frustration which he never had imagined. On December 7, 1941, Arleigh Burke was inspecting gun mounts at the Naval Gun Factory, Washington. His boss was a brittle Captain, who had his own ideas about the war. These ideas were perfectly sound. He figured that, eventually, the war had to be won by throwing rocks at the enemy. But he figured, also, that somebody had to make the rocks, and his job, and Burke's job, was to make those rocks. This philosophy did not at all suit Arleigh Albert Burke. He was a warrior at heart. For nearly two decades, now, he had honed his fighting spirit and technical capabilities to scalpel sharpness, in the hope of getting at the enemy or enemies of his country. He was ready; he was willing; he was able; and he was determined. He wanted to get out there and throw the rocks; let some lesser man do the inspecting, that had to be done.

"Captain," said Burke, "I'd like to be released to sea duty."

"Fine, Arleigh," replied the Captain. "But suppose you train a relief first."

"Aye, aye, sir!" replied Burke—and he *did*. He trained three men to relieve him. But each time the Captain said "Arleigh, you've done such a good job of training that I am forced to use these men for other and more important duties. Train somebody else."

Finally, Burke taxed the Captain with having a ghoulish sense of humor. The song and dance had been going on for ten months—ten months, and Burke was out of the fighting war! Outraged, Burke demanded a show-down with his superior. He got it. Said the Captain:

"Arleigh, you're just too good. I can't spare you. But I'll tell you what I *will* do. You may have a standing appointment with me for 1600 hours every Friday afternoon to renew your request for sea duty. How's *that* for handsome?"

It wasn't good enough, of course, but Burke gritted his teeth and requested permission to take his request directly to the Assistant Chief of the Bureau of Ordnance. Permission was granted. There followed, then, a revelatory sequence which shows how women run the world, despite the warrior instincts and capabilities of the male. The Ordnance Admiral rebuffed Burke; said he was "too busy" to be bothered. But the Admiral's secretary, Delores, had her own ideas. "Look, Commander Burke," she said, "if you will give me a telephone number through which I can reach you at any time, and if you'll promise to do *exactly* as I tell you, I'll get you to sea." Her eyes were sloe and dreamy, and had Burke been human he might have been a little disturbed. But Burke wasn't human at that time; he was consumed with desperation to get into combat, and he seized on Delores' promise with alacrity and without thinking the thing through.

How Delores managed it Burke never asked, and Delores never told him. But two days later Burke received a peremptory summons to the Admiral's office. "I have considered your request for sea duty," said the Assistant Chief of the Bureau of Ordnance. "Your request is granted."

Burke emerged from the sanctum sanctorum in a roseate glow. This was IT! But Delores soon cut him down to size. "Look, Commander," she said, "if you don't move fast you're going to be a dead duck! When news of the Admiral's softheartedness—some will call it softheadedness—gets around, there are going to be a lot of people trying to change his mind . . ."

"What do you suggest?" asked bewildered Burke.

"Three things," Delores told him crisply. "First, get your assignment to sea duty . . ."

"I've already got it! I'm being given command of Destroyer Division 43, in the Pacific."

"Good!" said Delores. "Now, can you operate a typewriter?"

"Sure. But what's that got to do with it?"

"Just this. It takes the Bureau of Navigation an average of four days to cut and process a set of orders. You can't afford to hang around Washington that long. Get over to BuNav and cut the stencil for your *own* orders—at once!"

"That figures," said the now alert Burke. "What else?"

"Get lost!" said Delores firmly. "As soon as your orders are processed, get out of town, and don't leave a forwarding address—because they're going to be looking for you!"

"Honey, I'm on my way—and I don't know how to tell you how much I appreciate . . ."

"Skip it, Commander. You've got a job to do. I'll try to hold the home front meanwhile . . ." Burke bolted through the door. Delores looked after him with a long, steady gaze. "And a fair breeze to you, Arleigh," she added under her breath. She'd never dare call him 'Arleigh' to his face but then—just this once—what th' hell . . . ?

The last thing Arleigh Burke did before grabbing commercial air for San Francisco was to order two dozen long-stemmed roses sent to a certain lady—Government gal type—named Delores. Then Commander Burke, latter-day combination of Lochinvar, Sir Launcelot, and Eric-the-Red, took off for the wars.

Burke's way to the war was bumpy, but not especially significant. He rode a troop transport to Noumea. As Commodore of a destroyer division, he rode briefly in U.S.S. *Waller,* commanded by Larry (Jack) Frost. Burke had many disagreements with Frost, who finally ended up as head of the Bureau of Naval Intelligence.

Burke also sailed briefly in U.S.S. *Conway,* and it was in *Conway,* that, probably for the first and last time in his life, he met his match. Burke tells the story:

"We were lying in Havannah Harbor. This man came aboard and said 'I want to be your signalman.' I said where are you now? He said U.S.S. *Dixie* (a tender). Why do you want to come over here, I asked. The *Dixie's* here, and it's a good job. 'Hell,' said the signalman, 'all I do over there is exchange a few messages—not very much work—and it's dull.' You'd better stay where it's dull, I told him. 'No,' said the man, 'I'm going to come over here to *Conway.'* You don't know about my signalman, I told him. I've only got room for one head signalman, and I've got a good one. 'Your signalman wants to go,' he told me. How do you know, I asked. 'Because I talked with him,' the man told me.

"All right," I said. "But you've got to be damned good. I don't know whether you're any good or not."

'I'm good,' said the man, confidently. 'And if I'm not good enough, I soon will be.'

"You'll have to make arrangements . . ."

'I've already made arrangements.'

"When are you going to get your gear . . . ?"

'My gear's on board . . .'

"I got to thinking about it," concluded Arleigh Burke, "and it all made me sort of proud. So I pushed my luck. Why do you want to serve with me, I asked."

'Well,' said the signalman, 'I figure the best way to learn your job is to serve with the biggest son of a bitch in the harbor . . .'

"And . . . ?"

'And from all reports,' said the man complacently, 'you're the biggest son of a bitch in the anchorage!'

As the man had said, his gear was on board, and he stayed in *Conway.* He was as good as he said he was, and Burke was sorry to lose him upon being transferred to command of Destroyer Squadron Twenty-Three.

90

DesRon-23 was something pretty special when Burke took command as Commodore. Under his leadership, it became the most outstanding destroyer Squadron in the history of the U.S. Navy. A good many of the vessels were 'Bath boats,' which means the finest in destroyers. They were commanded by a group of junior officers of rare talent. These *Fletcher* class DDs, and their commanding officers were:

U.S.S. *Charles Ausburne;* Luther K. Reynolds.

U.S.S. *Dyson;* Roy Alexander Gano.

U.S.S. *Stanley;* Robert W. Cavenagh.

U.S.S. *Claxton;* Herald Franklin Stout.

These four vessels comprised DesDiv 45.

U.S.S. *Spence;* Henry Jacques Armstrong.

U.S.S. *Thatcher;* Ralph Lampman.

U.S.S. *Converse;* DeWitt Clinton Ellis Hamberger.

U.S.S. *Foote;* Alston Ramsay.

The last four ships were the 'off' Division commanded by Commodore Bernard L. Austin. Their designation was DesDiv-46. Burke rode in *Charlie Ausburne;* 'Count' Austin, for the most part, in *Foote.* Burke assumed command of '23' in October, 1943, and the little ships immediately got busy. Their missions up The Slot were interminable. They ran the mail, lobbed shells at enemy shore installations, and their personnel learned to do without sleep. Reflecting their Commodore's impetuosity they did everything at high speed, and this inevitably brought a howl from the Army. With shore positions around Hathorn Sound, the Army had erected a line of privies on stilts at the water's edge. DesRon-23, sweeping back into Hathorn at high speed after a mission, sent a wake shoreward which was death on privies. They were knocked down like ninepins, and the situation finally got so bad that Burke was cornered on the beach by a senior Admiral who said: "Burke, if your ships don't stop knocking down those Godam privies, I'll have your stripes!" Appropriate orders were issued by the Commodore of DesRon-23, but not before an Army wight immortalized the business in the following lines:

When a soldier sits out here with the water lapping near
And dreams of pulley chains and apparatus,
He doesn't want to worry, and he doesn't want to hurry.
And most surely doesn't want to get a wetass!
So any proposition that will introduce Marines
Can be naught but anathema to the soldiers in latrines,
And the aggravating splatter from any passing 'can'
Will run him whacky-wacky; he'll forget that he's a man!
If 'cans' must keep on running through Blackett's gory Strait
And they cannot make the passage unless the tide's in spate

'Twould be well to mind the moon's effect, and time dear nature's urge
To synchronize with ebbing tide, and get a better purge!
DD's high-speed maneuvers should be in open water
And they shouldn't pass through Blackett Strait no faster than they orter,
But perfect peace will never be for any GI jerk
Who's subject to a sortie by 31-Knot Burke!

Along with slowing the Squadron down in its passages through Blackett Strait, Commodore Burke ordered painted out the small privy symbols which some of the ships were displaying on their bridge superstructures, attesting their 'kills'!

Although each unit of DesRon-23 had had its own trial by combat, the Squadron was not welded together as a perfect fighting unit until November 2, 1943. That was the date of the Battle of Empress Augusta Bay in which, for the first and last time, DesRon-23—all eight ships—performed as a unit, and it welded the Squadron into an implacable naval fighting machine.

CHAPTER 6

Burke's Finest Hours

Impetuous by nature, Captain Arleigh Burke was by no means a man to act without careful reasoning. As Commodore of DesRon-23—the 'Little Beaver' Squadron—his thinking, his planning, and his actions reflected three well-thought-out values, which he had worked out to his own satisfaction, and two of which he had written down.

First, there was his doctrine of faith. He had worked that out in *Waller,* after study of the Battle of Tassafaronga—"The Night of the Long Lances." At Tassafaronga a cautious U.S. cruiser task force commander, for four fatal minutes after contact with the enemy, withheld permission for his destroyers to launch torpedoes. The battle was fought on the night of November 30–December 1, 1942. In consequence of the task force commander's indecision—or so Arleigh Burke saw it—in the twenty or thirty minutes of lurid action which followed contact with the enemy, a resolute and skillful Japanese officer, Rear Admiral Raizo Tanaka, grudgingly dubbed 'Tenacious Tanaka' by his U.S. opponents, administered to the U.S. Navy one of the most humiliating defeats in its history. In sum, with a handful of destroyers, Tanaka tore a U.S. cruiser task force to pieces.

Working steadily away at a drop-leaf desk in the appalling below-decks heat aboard *Waller* as she swung obediently around her anchor in Havannah Channel off the island of Efate at the bottom end of the New Hebrides group, 18 degrees south of the equator, Burke concluded his new destroyer doctrine with these words:

"When contact with an enemy force is made, destroyers in the van should initiate a coordinated torpedo attack WITHOUT ORDERS."

Then he added (for he was fully aware of the sensitive ground upon which he intruded):

"This last recommendation is the most difficult. The delegation of authority (by a task force commander) is always hard and . . . where such delegation of authority may result in disastrous consequences if any subordinate commander makes an error, it requires more than what usually is meant by confidence. IT REQUIRES FAITH."

For a very subordinate commander, which Burke was at the time, to enunciate such a ringing demand for faith, was unorthodox. But to Burke it seemed wholly logical. He was calling for faith in himself, and as he *had* full faith in himself, why shouldn't others? As events were to prove, such faith reposed in Burke, would not be misplaced.

Commodore Burke's second enunciation of policy also was typical. Soon after assuming command of DesRon-23, he issued the following statement of squadron policy to his eight captains:

DESTROYER SQUADRON TWENTY-THREE
DOCTRINE

If it will help kill Japs—it's important.
If it will not help kill Japs—it's not important.
Keep your ship trained for battle!
Keep your material ready for battle!
Keep your boss informed concerning your readiness for battle!

Burke's full doctrine for DesRon-23 ran to twelve mimeographed pages, but he directed his captains' especial attention to the twelfth page. Set forth thereon, in capital letters, was the simple legend:

NON-BATTLE ORDERS: *NONE.* CORRECTIONS TO THIS SECTION WILL NOT BE PERMITTED!

Burke revealed the third value in his thinking to Rear Admiral Aaron S. (Tip) Merrill, at a shore-side conference:

"Tip, this morning I'm a salesman, and this is what I've got in my sample case . . ."

From an envelope Burke produced a sheaf of diagrams which he spread on the table.

"In my opinion we haven't been making the most of destroyers operating with cruiser task forces, Tip. I've got a one-two punch doctrine worked out with my boys and they understand it and are capable of executing it."

"I don't doubt that in the least, Arleigh," said Merrill. "How does it work?"

"Simple! On contact with an enemy force, DesDiv-45, which always is the leading Division, takes off instantly to mount a surprise torpedo attack. DesDiv-46 . . ."

"Just a minute, Arleigh," the Admiral interrupted. "You say '45' always is the leading Division. How come?"

"Aw, for God's sake, Tippy! Look, I've got a year's seniority over 'Count' Austin. Isn't that worth a ten-degree advantage?"

Merrill burst into throaty laughter. "Sure—sure, Arleigh! I was just kidding! So what happens next?"

"Well, while I'm attacking with DesDiv-45, DesDiv-46 moves into position to cover us with gunfire if we are discovered by the enemy. Should that happen, the fire of '46' is calculated to draw the fire of the enemy to that Division long enough to allow me to complete my attack with '45.' Once '45' has launched torpedoes, we haul out of the way and '46' maneuvers into position to launch a second torpedo strike. This time we cover them the same way they did us on the first go-round. Get it?"

"It sounds reasonable enough to me but, after all, you run your cans, and how you fight them is your business."

"I know, Tip . . . I know . . . but here's the point: With DDs positioned 6,000 yards ahead of the main body—and that's where we're usually stationed—we'll make contact by radar with an enemy force at between 20,000 and 25,000 yards and at about the same time that the cruisers do. The rate of change of range, Tip, with formations approaching each other, may be between 600 and 1,700 yards a minute, depending upon their respective speeds. Now, before I fire torpedoes from DesDiv-45 I want to come to the reciprocal of the enemy's course, and get in closer than 6,000 yards if I can. That's the only way I can hope to achieve maximum results.

"As you'll recall, it takes a DD about three minutes to make a 180-degree turn with hard rudder. Aside from the obvious fact that TBS or visual traffic probably would betray our presence to the enemy and spoil the party if I had to wait for signalled permission from the Task Force Commander before I could take off with Division 45 to launch my torps, the chances are that the enemy would be long gone before I could get to a fitting point and reverse course." Burke looked at Merrill with wide blue eyes in which there flashed the flinty highlights of a zealot. He was leading up to his Sunday punch, and he was about to throw it.

"Well, what do you want from me, Arleigh?"

"*I want you to have faith in me and my boys,* Tip. I want you to have *enough* faith to let me get going on doctrine the moment I make enemy contact, and without first getting permission from you. I know it's hard, Tippy—but try. *Please* try!"

Arleigh Burke was a good salesman that morning. But, then, he had a good product. Cruiser Task Force Commander Merrill agreed to let the DDs of DesRon-23 get going "on doctrine" and without releasing orders from the task force commander upon enemy contact. The stage was set for U.S. naval maneuvers at the Battle of Empress Augusta Bay.

The antecedents of the Battle of Empress Augusta Bay, as well as U.S. Navy plans for the maneuvers which produced that battle, were pulled together at a high-level conference held at Koli Point on October 24, 1943, at which ComSoPac himself—Admiral William F. Halsey—presided. The plan was a bold Allies bid to roll the Japs right up out of the Central Solomons and bring heavy and constant pressure to bear on major enemy concentrations at Rabaul and Truck. A prerequisite of the plan was to neutralize the Japanese garrison on Bougainville. The enemy's estimated ground strength in the Bougainville area was 100,000 men. In Japanese hands, Bougainville inhibited the final Allied drive to the north and west. Conversely, Allied air strips in that locus would provide convenient points of departure for powerful strikes against enemy targets of major stature and importance.

To knock the Japs out of Bougainville, a landing at Empress Augusta Bay on the southwest coast of the Island, in the vicinity of Cape Torokina, was settled upon. Diversionary feints were planned to cover the main strategy. Rear Admiral T. S. Wilkinson was given responsibility for the transports which would land Allied troops. Rear Admiral George H. Fort, was assigned command of a force to make diversionary attacks. 'Tip' Merrill, commanding Task Force 39, with DesRon-23 attached, was given the job of protecting the landings and meeting and defeating any counter-thrust by the enemy. D Day and H hour were dawn on Monday, November first. But *Task Force Merrill* also mounted diversionary attacks, including a gunstrike at Skunk Hollow which resulted in damage to U.S.S. *Foote,* 'Count' Austin's flag boat.

On November 1, 1943, the torrid sun of noon riding high over the North Central Solomons shone down upon a lot of little men desperately engaged in differing but not disparate activities. Stretching northwest from the bight of Empress Augusta Bay, a double line of U.S. transports and cargo ships lay hove-to, while small craft of all sorts shuttled between them and the beaches, landing troops and supplies. There was a distance of 750 yards between ships, with an interval of 500 yards between the two files. The landings were being effected under intermittent air bombardment and torpedo plane attacks. These strikes by the enemy, partially parried by the planes from the carrier task force commanded by Rear Admiral Frederick C. Sherman and built around *Saratoga* and *Princeton,* several times drove the transports and cargo ships seaward, maneuvering radically. They returned doggedly to their stations, however, and although, by nightfall, sixty-four LCVPs and twenty-two LCMs were to end up forlorn and stranded derelicts—coffins for many gallant U.S. Marines—a lodgment on Bougainville had been secured.

Up north, at Imperial Japanese Navy Headquarters at Rabaul, Admiral Tomoshige Samejima was trying to fit together the pieces of this fascinating puzzle—and he managed to do it all wrong! Admiral Sentaro Omori had been out scouting with a cruiser task force. At the time, the Allies had mounted a bombardment of the Buka-Bonis area, and it is highly probable that the two opposing forces were proximate, but they failed to make contact, and Omori returned to Rabaul.

Omori returned to Rabaul to find Samejima jubilant. "This time," said the senior Admiral genially, "we've *got* them!"

"Ah, so . . . ?"

"Look, this is the way it appears to me," continued Samejima. "There's only one U.S. cruiser task force left in the South Pacific. That task force bombarded Buka at midnight last night, and our installations in the Short-lands this morning. Then, doubtless, it steamed back up the Bougainville coast to protect the landings now in progress at Empress Augusta Bay.

"It's inevitable, Sentaro. Their cruisers and destroyers will pull out of Bougainville at dusk tonight. They've *got* to! All those ships must be low on fuel and ammunition, and the crews must be fatigued after the work they've done. You'll see; they'll leave Empress Augusta Bay early this evening and retire south for rest and replenishment."

"Ah, so . . . !"

"Well, this means that tonight is our great opportunity . . ."

"What do you want me to do, Tomoshige?"

"Primarily, get going as fast as you can. I'll give you Ijuin and Osugi. You'll have two heavy cruisers—the Americans don't have any, so far as we know—two light cruisers, and six destroyers. In addition, five attack transports will be available. Get to Cape Torokina, smash any enemy ships you find there, land your troops, and throw the white bastards back into the sea! If you're *really* lucky you may catch their cruiser task force and tear it to pieces. That, of course, should be your principal mission, should it prove possible."

This unaccountably wrong appreciation of the situation by the Japanese was the prelude to the Battle of Empress Augusta Bay, which was a mixed up thing, at best. Omori thought he was going in to tear up a bunch of transports off the beaches. Instead, he ran directly into Tip Merrill and his task force.

As the clocks turned 0231 on the morning of November 2, 1943, *Task Force Merrill* was steaming toward the enemy. Rear Admiral Sentaro Omori, flying his flag in heavy cruiser *Myoko,* and standing almost due southeast through the thick night, was not the least bit worried. He had two fewer ships, but tremendously more power than Merrill. Omori's dispositions reflected the curious astigmatism which so often seemed to inhibit both the strategic and the tactical vision of the Imperial Japanese Navy command in the sea war in the South Pacific. The ships were in a simple formation and not one designed to deal effectively with a United States battle formation of light cruisers and destroyers.

Omori's two heavy cruisers, *Myoko,* and *Haguro,* steaming in that order, comprised the center column of a three-column pattern. On the left steamed light cruiser *Sendai,* followed by destroyers *Shigure, Samidare,* and *Shiratsuyu,* in that order. On Omori's right steamed light cruiser *Agano* followed by destroyers *Naganami, Hatsukaze,* and *Wakatsuki,* in that order. It was a good enough formation to attack and break up a formation of defenseless transports, which is what Omori thought he was about to do; it was a weak formation to meet a determined enemy formation, which 'Tip' Merrill soon convinced Omori he was.

At precisely 0231 the opposing formations made contact. At that precise moment the word came from *Charlie Ausburne's* Sugar George radar "Contact bearing 291 degrees true at 30,000 yards. Believe this is what we want!"

The bearing was off *Ausburne's* port bow; it *had* to be Omori!

Burke's action was now instinctive, as he knew it would have to be. The collision course was 311 degrees, and he put DesDiv-45 on that course without a moment's hesitation. Following doctrine, he did not increase speed, for that might have led to detection. But he grabbed the TBS transmitter and yelped "Contact bearing two-nine-one, 30,000 yards. I'm heading in!" He did not say "What are your orders?" or "By your leave." He simply said "I'm heading in!"

That moment—that fragment in the undeviating march of the seconds and the minutes and the hours which measure men's lives and establish fixed and immutable points for the orientation of their accomplishments in the broad tapestry of history—marked the first fulfillment of Arleigh Burke's doctrine of faith. Tip Merrill had accepted that doctrine. Division 45 suddenly became the pledge of the Admiral's faith, and dashed to the attack without formal release by higher authority. At long last, the superb weapon which is the modern destroyer was exploiting fully its inherent offensive role with a cruiser task force.

Omori's Division 5—cruisers—and Burke's Division 45—destroyers —were closing each other at a speed of the order of fifty knots. Burke estimated that it would take fourteen minutes before he would be in position to launch torpedoes. And in fourteen minutes, a man with an agile mind can do a deal of thinking. Burke did, and he instantly noticed the relatively weak formation of the Japanese ships. At first, he feared a trap but, failing to detect one, he decided to fire torpedoes on the enemy's starboard bow and, if necessary, pass down between the enemy's leading and center columns. It was, characteristically, an audacious maneuver. It would place *Ausburne, Dyson, Stanley* and *Claxton* within point-blank range of heavy cruisers *Myoko* and *Haguro* to starboard as well as light cruiser *Agano* and her accompanying destroyers to port.

Without even knowing he was there, however, Admiral Omori took the initiative away from Captain Burke. At 0236, with the formations still 18,000 yards apart, Omori made a routine course correction sufficiently far to the right to defeat Burke's intentions.

"That's all right, Brute," Burke told Reynolds—whose birdlike build had earned him the nickname of 'Brute' at the Naval Academy—"we'll fire on his port bow, and retire toward the north. After all, that's the direction he'll have to take if he hopes to get home, and if we don't get him this time, maybe we'll get another crack at him!"

Burke launched torps with six minutes to run to target. At 0248.30 —3½ minutes after the torps had left the tubes of DesDiv-45, Omori spotted the destroyer Division on his rudimentary radar, and instantly altered course to the south. He knew full well that torpedoes were on their way!

When word of this maneuver by the enemy came to *Charlie Ausburne's* bridge from CIC, 'Brute' Reynolds observed, drily, "That, Commodore, is what comes of a Swede expecting to have the luck of the Irish!"

The battle which now blossomed at forty-five miles west of Empress Augusta Bay lasted more than four hours, which is an uncommonly long time, as such things go. Twenty-four ships were maneuvering at high speed —a dangerous situation in itself. Tip Merrill's fundamental strategy was to push Omori to the westward, while keeping him at arm's length, thus preventing him from pinning the task force against the offshore reefs and shoals off Bougainville Island. At 0249, having noted Omori's turn away, and knowing that Burke's torps would run for Sweeney, Merrill opened gunfire on Omori's northern column of *Sendai, Shigure, Samidare,* and *Shiratsuyu.*

First hit was cruiser *Sendai*. The U.S. shell walked right into her across the ocean, and by 0252 she lay dead in the water, her guts torn out by an explosion of her magazines. Still and all, crippled as she was, and with dead strewn on her decks, she continued to return the U.S. fire. There was nothing chicken about the Japanese naval fighting men.

Maneuvering problems brought Japanese destroyers *Samidare* and *Shiratsuyu* into a high-speed collision and both, damaged, went reeling off north, out of the battle.

Omori maneuvered frantically. He sent *Myoko* and *Haguro* into a looping evolution, and upon coming out of the loop, the lumbering *Myoko* speared into destroyer *Hatsukaze,* slicing through her hull as if it were so much prime Wisconsin cheese, and picking up part of her forward section, which *Myoko* wore on her bow through the rest of the battle.

The mixups were not all on one side. *Stanley* and *Claxton* managed to misread a signal; got separated from the formation; sideswiped each other at high speed on reciprocal courses, and Burke, ignorant of what was happening, took them both under fire! They happened, at the end of their trouble, to be headed for the U.S. cruiser line, and Burke figured only enemy DDs would be headed for the U.S. cruiser line.

At 0253 Omori ordered "Offset your five-inch battery from the firing solution and illuminate!" Throughout the Pacific war, the Japanese pyro-

99

technics were greatly superior to the U.S. pyrotechnics, and now the night blazed into white-hot brilliance. Merrill ordered counter illumination, but it was short, weak, and ineffective. He finally took refuge in chemical and funnel smoke, as the Japanese eight-inch salvos walked accurately across the ocean toward his flagship and his task force.

At 0301 U.S.S. *Foote* (*Foote,* the Unfortunate)—was under 25 degrees left rudder. She was trying to rejoin, with her polished shafts spinning at 374 rpm. That's when one or more of Omori's Long Lances reached out and cut her down. She took the torpedo hit aft, at the turn of the bilge. Her mast whipped fore-and-aft in an egg-shaped arc of about ten feet diameter at the top; a thick column of seawater shot up 75 feet, and then crashed down on her after deck; in seconds she was, so far as the fight was concerned, a derelict. 'Count' Austin, ComDesDiv-46 stormed and swore—but there was nothing he could do about it. (If ever there was a warrior in the U.S. Navy who deserved a better fate—a better opportunity to *fight*—it was Bernard L. Austin!)

Sometime after 0310, the battle stood on the threshold. *Montpelier* (the flag), *Cleveland,* and *Denver,* lying behind their smoke screen and on a 000 heading, were pumping out shell at the enemy. At 0320, *Spence* took a solid hit from cruiser *Myoko,* and was knocked out of effective action. Between 0320 and 0325, *Denver* took three eight-inch hits from *Myoko* and *Haguro.* Captain Briscoe was forced to sheer out of formation on the disengaged side, but he continued to fire and, later, was to rejoin the formation. About this time, too, *Columbia* took a freak hit. The base plug from an eight-inch shell ripped through her relatively light plating above the waterline and ended harmlessly in the sail locker.

Then the ultimate happened. *Spence* (to which ship Austin had transferred his flag) was a smoking target. Burke figured *Spence* for a Japanese DD. He opened up with all he had. Within sixty seconds, a dozen or more five-inch shells slammed into the sea close aboard *Spence.*

Austin was imperturbable. He grabbed TBS and said, "We've just had a bad close miss. I hope you're not shooting at us!"

"Are you hit?" asked Burke, anxiously.

"Negative!" replied Austin.

"Well," said Burke, in what has become a Navy classic, "you'll have to excuse the next four salvos. They're already on their way!"—which offered an excellent measure of the rate of gunfire of the DDs at the Battle of Empress Augusta Bay!

Before 0400, the Japanese force, badly battered but intact, made a 180 and started to retire. His lust for battle insatiable, Burke had arrowed northward with the idea of intercepting the retirement. But Merrill had problems on his hands. *Foote* needed help. Also, the commander of the

100

task force was mindful of the additional transports about to unload at Cape Torokina. So to Burke's message that he was pursuing the enemy, Merrill replied: "Arleigh, this is Tip! For God's sake come home! We're lonesome!" The cruisers badly needed the protection of the DDs.

Task Force Merrill subsequently weathered Japanese air attacks, and got back to Purvis in one piece—their job done. The landings on Bougainville went as scheduled. Merrill was not unappreciative of Burke's role in the battle. He messaged:

"Thanks for a job BETTER THAN WELL DONE!"

There is no higher praise in the U.S. Navy.

On November 24, with the Squadron once more at Hathorn Sound, jovial Dr. Hollis Garrard, *Dyson's* medico, was in the act of handing a thin box of suppositories to a pot-bellied bos'un. They both were startled by the insistent hooting of the ship's siren and the bos'un, emerging on deck, found the recall signal "Roger" two-blocked at the signal yard and activity preparatory to getting under way going forward on the foc's'le head. The Squadron had received top priority orders, the general import of which was to get gone from Hathorn Sound, *but right now!* They were tired. They were falling down tired! But sail they must, and sail they would, and if a ship was shorthanded, that was just too bad! Not all of *Dyson's* crew got the word, nor did many ashore from the other ships of Des-Ron-23.

When Commodore Burke sortied from Hathorn Sound at 1405 that afternoon, only five ships of his Squadron were operational. They were *Charles Ausburne, Dyson, Claxton, Converse,* and *Spence. Foote* and *Thatcher* were en route to Pearl, and then the Navy Yard at Bremerton, Washington, for overhaul; and *Stanley* was undergoing imperatively necessary engineering availability alongside U.S.S. *Whitney.*

As was not unusual at the time and place, the orders which sent Burke racing north told him nothing of what he was to look for or what his mission was to be. He was simply ordered to take his squadron to Point Uncle—latitude 06°, 47' south; longitude 154°, 46' east—as quickly as possible. Further orders would be enunciated while he was on the way.

By 1730, the squadron was rounding Vella La Vella, but there was some confusion back at Admiral Halsey's headquarters as to how many ships Burke had with him. Because of this confusion, an officer on Halsey's staff —Ray Thurber—messaged Burke "Report ships with you; your speed; and your ETA Point Uncle."

Burke messaged back the ships with him, his position, and his speed as thirty-one knots. Actually he should have been doing thirty-four knots. But some lubber had jammed a tube brush into a boiler tube aboard *Spence.* It had caused all sorts of complications, and upon receiving orders for his high-speed sortie, Burke had asked Heinie Armstrong, commanding *Spence,* "Do you want to go along, or do you want to stay back and have your boiler fixed?"

"Please, Arleigh!" said Armstrong, "we want to *go!* With our plant cross-connected we can do thirty-one knots!"

"Okeh," said Burke. *"Get going!"*

In the Navy's engineering rules and regulations, a ship standing into battle, with a plant cross-connected, was in violation. The *Fletcher*-class DDs were capable of *thirty-four* knots, and Ray Thurber well knew it. Therefore, when Burke reported his speed at thirty-one knots, and his ETA Point Uncle as 2200, Thurber was amused. He directed his next message to DesRon-23 to *'31-Knot Burke.'* It was, actually, a sardonic 'rib' because Burke was going so slow, having vessels capable of thirty-four knots —but it has stuck with Burke all his life, and has been interpreted as an indication of great speed. Actually, of course, Burke would have been making thirty-four knots, had he not been under the necessity for waiting for *Spence,* with her power plant cross-connected, and her top speed thirty-one knots.

The next message to Burke was meaningful:

"Get athwart the Buka-Rabaul evacuation line about 35 miles West of Buka. If no enemy contact by 0300 love (local time) 25th come south to refuel same place. If enemy contact, you know what to do! For ComTaskForce 33: Get this word to your B-24s and Black Cats. Add a night fighter for Burke from 0330 to sunrise, and give him day air cover."

Early that evening, Burke went on TBS to his captains. "Gentlemen," he said, "this is lovely work if you can get it—*and we've got it!"* By that time he knew that his mission was to intercept a Japanese force which had landed one thousand soldiers on Buka, and picked up seven hundred air personnel no longer needed there. Captain Kiyoto Kagawa was in command of the enemy force, and the number of ships was exactly equal. The Japanese DDs were 2,000-ton new destroyers, and, if anything, outmatched Burke's force, although not on the books.

At 0140, DesRon-23 came to a 000 heading, with DesDiv-46 on a 225-degree true line of bearing. "It was," Burke said afterward, "an ideal night for a nice, quiet torpedo attack." The night was very dark, with no moon; the wind from the east at force one; and the sea tranquil.

Completely unaware of Burke's presence, Captain Kagawa, of the Imperial Japanese Navy, took his DDs to sea. They were: *Amigiri, Yugiri,* and *Uzuki,* transport destroyers. Screening them were destroyers *Onami* and *Makanami.*

Welcoming the challenge, Arleigh Burke stood north until his squadron was deeper into enemy territory than any U.S. surface force had dared go since the beginning of the bitter Solomons Campaign. Stealthily, DesRon-

23 came to a 000 heading. The barometer stood at 29.86 inches; the air temperature was 85 degrees, and the water temperature a degree warmer. The sky was overcast with frequent rainsqualls moving over the area, and the visibility, with binoculars, was about three thousand yards. It was the night before Thanksgiving Day, and aboard *Claxton* that merry warrior Heraldo Stout strode from bridge wing to bridge wing, sending sulphurous clouds of smoke skyward from his very ripe pipe, and murmuring to himself *"Wonderful! Just wonderful!* If the bastards will just show up, we'll *take* 'em!" Below decks, the duty cook had other ideas. He shoved the first batch of his Thanksgiving turkeys into the pre-heated oven, checked the temperature at 325 degrees, and turned to assembling of the ingredients for pumpkin pie. And as he did so, he whispered a pious prayer that the squadron wouldn't open with the damned guns for at least a few hours. Every time the guns fired, his oven doors flew open, and he had a hell of a time. In *Converse*, 'Ham' Hamberger, the philosopher of the squadron, many years later to become greatly intrigued by the notion of Moral Rearmament, was tranquil and alert. Ensign Ray Peet had the deck. Peet later was to command the first nuclear U.S. frigate. Aboard *Charlie Ausburne*, 'Brute' Reynolds helped himself to a ham sandwich from the steward's tray, and munched away in sour satisfaction. Burke, who loathed ham sandwiches, took one too. After all, ham sandwiches were Reynolds' idea of the most appetizing form of human food—and who was the Commodore to question the choice of the skipper of his flag boat? They gnawed away in silence, the one savoring a morsel which he was certain rated a *cordon bleu*—the other disgusted with the whole thing, but knowing that he needed food.

In *Dyson*, Roy Gano stood calmly on the port wing of the bridge, looked intently ahead, and waited. Gano was a tall, reedy, sturdy type. He was to survive to make Vice Admiral, head the Military Sea Transport Service, and be betrayed by subordinates, although the lustre of his character and reputation never was to come into question.

All these men—those on the bridges, those in the engine rooms, and the dungaree-clad sailors and chiefs about the decks—shared in a *mystique* which was peculiar to DesRon-23. It emerged from Arleigh Burke's challenging brand of leadership. But, also, it abided in the hearts of his men who knew, with quiet pride, that they were a little better than the best. That was Burke's criterion: *Be a little better than the best.*

Disregarding official admonitions, Arleigh Burke held to the north for ten minutes more than the quarterbacks back at base thought he should. It was his way to follow the book when he must, but when a fight was brewing he followed his instincts. And in this instance, his instincts were precisely right. At 0141 on that Thanksgiving morning of November 25, 1943, Roy Gano's ship messaged:

"Please check bearing zero-eight-five, distance 22,000. We have a target!"

Seconds later Heraldo Stout crowed, from *Claxton's* position immediately behind *Charlie Ausburne*, "We have two applegadgets (enemy ships) at zero-seven-five, distance 22,000 yards. We have course 280, twenty knots for applegadgets. Hello, DesRon-23! Hang onto your hats, boys! Here we go!"

On course 280 degrees true, Kagawa's leading ships, *Onami* and *Makanami*, were headed almost due west. They were the only two targets Burke could see on his radar screen. He immediately swung his Division to a collision course, and warned 'Count' Austin, "Hold your Division back until you get your proper bearing, which is 225 degrees."

While the squadron still was in its turn, Burke messaged his headquarters, "Enemy vessels, strength unknown, at latitude 05°, 16' south; longitude 153°, 44' east. I am attacking. This is my first report this force."

At 0150, slicing toward his torpedo launching position, the Commodore messaged the Squadron, "We think he is on course 290 degrees, speed 20. We will fire on his port bow. We will fire to port—*I hope!*"

This again was a warning to Austin to stay out of Burke's torpedo water, and Austin wasn't the least bit happy with it! He wanted to get in there and heave some rocks of his own, so he immediately messaged the Commodore "Suggest that I cross under your stern and cover your other side!" *"Stay where you are!"* snapped Burke, in the shortest TBS transmission of the entire battle.

By 0156, Burke had closed the range to 4,500 yards which, he figured, was as close as he could get and still have any hope of surprise. *"Execute William!"* he ordered—which meant fire torpedoes—and, almost before the torps had left the tubes, Burke turned nine, and rang up thirty knots, to be clear of the enemy's torpedo water, should he have fired.

The next 100 seconds brought surprises for Arleigh Burke. Following along behind their leaders, Japanese destroyers *Amigiri, Yugiri,* and *Uzuki* came into view on *Charlie Ausburne's* radar. Burke did some rapid calculating. His fifteen torps were due to detonate, or reveal themselves by passing wakes, at 0159:30. Whatever happened, it was certain that any undamaged enemy ships would take evasive action. Therefore Arleigh Burke once more swung Division 45 onto a collision course with the enemy and messaged Austin "We have second target bearing east from us. Polish off the first targets fired upon. Watch yourself now; don't get separated from one another, and don't get too far away. We're going after new targets."

Onami took the first hit. The darkness was ripped to shreds by broad sheets of flame leaping skyward hundreds of feet and raping the velvet blackness of the night with swift, insensate fury. Few aboard *Onami,* including echelon commander Kiyoto Kagawa, knew more than a few moments of horror and agony. Hissing upward from gigantic whirling spheres of blazing vapor at the base, thick fiery fingers three hundred feet tall clawed spasmodically at the night for an awful thirty seconds. Then suddenly, at 0200, and as if someone had turned a switch, they disappeared. With them, into oblivion, went Imperial Japanese Navy destroyer *Onami*, her captain, and her crew.

Moments after Burke's torpedoes hit, *Makanami* presented the aspect of a grotesque mirage. Her bow and stern appeared to be raised islands of billowing fire laced with dark patches of shapeless debris hurled high into the air by successive explosions. There was relatively little fire between bow and stern, which gave the ship the appearance of having broken in half. But she had not. She floated stubbornly, although not firing, and at 0202 Austin twitted Burke with the edged message, "I'm coming north to finish off what you didn't finish." "Keep your transmissions short, please!" snapped the Commodore.

In *Amigiri*, Captain Katsumori Yamashiro showed no disposition whatever to pit his three DDs against the matching ships of Division 45. At the first sign of the U.S. force, Yamashiro wheeled by ship's turn movement to a course a little east of north, and backed his throttles wide open. Burke streaked in behind him "with the safety valves tied down, and the Chief Engineer's cap hung over the steam gauge!" For a few tense minutes the two formations greyhounded north in silence, the deep plunging DDs sending up huge semicircular sheets of spume to be shredded on the wind and disappear in trailing veils of twinkling iridescence.

Could *Charlie Ausburne, Dyson,* and *Claxton* catch *Amigiri, Yugiri,* and *Uzuki?* That was the question. The Japanese formation had a head start of about seven miles; the distance between Yamashiro's ships was one thousand yards, and he was building up speed rapidly from thirty-one knots. Warrior Burke watched through slitted eyes; all other emotions swept forever away in the climactic joy of combat. Even so, he did not neglect his duty to his superiors. As the ships raced north, Burke messaged Halsey: "Have made contact with two groups of enemy ships. The first group consisted of two ships destroyed by torpedo; the second group consists of three ships. I am attacking the second group."

At 0212, with the chase little more than ten minutes old, Burke had a hunch that torpedoes were headed his way. He swung his formation sharply through a 45-degree turnaway, to course 060 degrees true. He held this course for sixty seconds, then returned to his base course. Sure enough, a thunderous detonation shortly shook *Charlie Ausburne.* "Is our bow still there, 'Brute'?" asked Burke. *Charlie Ausburne's* bow was still there. The Jap torps had detonated in the turbulent wake of DesDiv-45. But Burke's hunch, and his radical turn, had saved his ships.

105

A stern chase is a long chase. Burke appraised the situation, and said to Reynolds: "We'll never reach them with torpedoes, now. As a matter of fact, the range is opening; we'll never reach them at all unless we slow them down. So let's see if we still know how to shoot!"

The Commodore of DesRon-23 grabbed TBS, pressed the button, and after a wonderfully salty preface, ordered the ships of his leading Division: "Take station left echelon. We can't catch these rabbits, so we'll open gunfire as soon as you're in position. Our target is on course 005 degrees true, speed 31. *Claxton* and *Dyson* report when you are on echelon so we can open fire!"

At 0220, Heraldo Stout reported, "On echelon, and ready!" Seconds later Roy Gano echoed him. At 0224, Burke ordered "Commence firing with guns. Start fishtailing—not too much; just enough to confuse the range." Instantly, every ship in the Division began hurling five-inch salvos at the scurrying enemy. The Japanese reaction to being taken under fire was not long delayed. Within seconds, Japanese salvos, their patterns small and well grouped, were falling around Division 45. Meanwhile, of course, Yamashiro started taking radical evasive action. The Japanese might be running, but the sting in their tails was lethal. On *Claxton's* bridge, two inches of water sloshed around, thrown on board by near misses, and only dextrous darting around saved the U.S. DDs from solid, crippling hits. The men of Nippon were warriors all the way, and they knew their business and were good at it.

Whether his captains knew it or not, Arleigh Burke knew that he was playing a sticky wicket. He watched the Japanese force ahead for just one thing: A 90-degree turn, left or right, by Yamashiro, could signal the beginning of the end for DesDiv-45! Such a turn would place the fleeing Japanese destroyers on a course at right angle to the course of *Ausburne*, *Dyson*, and *Claxton*, and constitute an effective capping of Burke's 'T.' In such circumstances *Amigiri*, *Yugiri*, and *Uzuki* would have only to fire a barrage of torpedoes at the U.S. ships, which would be rushing to their own destruction. Masters of the Long Lance, there was not apt to be much fumbling on the part of the Japanese warriors, should they undertake such a maneuver, and well Arleigh Burke knew it!

On *Amigiri's* bridge, Yamashiro studied the situation intently for a minute or two. Then he came to a quick decision. It was not to attempt to cap Burke's 'T,' as the Commodore feared, but rather to offer him a much more subtle gambit. Yamashiro's orders were issued quickly: *"Amigiri* and *Uzuki*, come left to course 305 degrees true, by ship's turn movement. *Yugiri* continue on course 350 degrees true!"* If the American commander wanted a fight, Yamashiro-san would separate his formation and invite Burke to continue the battle in a pattern of individual combat, ship against ship! Thus, a somewhat surprised Arleigh Burke saw the enemy ships before him opening out like shoots from the main stalk of their base course, *Yugiri* continuing to race almost due north, while *Amigiri* and *Uzuki* peeled off to the left on a course diverging 45 degrees from the original direction of their flight.

Burke took time to check the 'off' Division. He messaged Austin "Have you finished your job, and are you closing?"

"Negative!" came the reply. "Many explosions on target, but he's still afloat!"

31-Knot-Burke now faced a decision which racked his aggressive soul. Would he play Yamashiro's game—or would he not? One of Burke's favorite maxims was "ship against ship is a good battle in *any* language." And, seemingly, that was the kind of battle Yamashiro was offering him. But Burke was smart enough to know that the offer was spurious. It was of the order of the childhood jingle "Will you step into my parlor, said the spider to the fly . . ." And aggressive Arleigh Burke knew, instantly, that he had *other fish to fry!* The fundamental values which Burke knew he must resolve were these:

The chase had carried the ships of DesRon-23 far north, and they were very close to the principal Japanese base at Rabaul. There were several strong air installations there. For that matter, there also were enemy air installations behind Burke, between him and his own base at Purvis Bay. DesRon-23 was far beyond the reach of friendly air, and could expect no support or defense from the skies. Dawn was short hours away, and if the squadron stayed where it was, or went further north, it could confidently expect to be jumped by Japanese bombers and torpedo planes, once the black sky brightened. Still and all, warrior Burke was by no means ready to give up. He declined Yamashiro's invitation to step into his parlor, but he picked his target. He ordered *Dyson* to fire on *Uzuki*. But *Ausburne* and *Claxton* were ordered to concentrate their fire on *Yugiri*, still arrowing north.

At 0254, Burke received a message from Austin which went largely unheeded: "One more rising sun has set! We are joining you now." Finally *Converse* and *Spence* had polished off *Makanami*.

The thirteen minutes between 0247 and 0300 were a form of crucifixion for Arleigh Burke. *Dyson* was pouring shell after *Uzuki* and thought she was registering, but *Uzuki* didn't slow. *Claxton* and *Ausburne* were concentrating on *Yugiri*, but with similarly disappointing results.

Beside himself with frustration, Burke messaged *Claxton*, "I simply don't understand why you're not firing to the north! That fellow's getting away!" Heraldo Stout came back instantly: "We're firing with all guns that will bear!" "Well, dammit," exploded Burke, "*somebody* ought to be able to slow this target down!"

Burke, keeping his ships together, had worked his speed up to thirty-three knots, and he knew his shells were registering on *Yugiri*. Almost with awe in his voice, he said to Reynolds, "That guy up ahead *can't* take much more of the kind of punishment we're giving him, Brute."

"Well," replied Reynolds, "don't look now, but I think he's slowing down!"

It was true! By 0256, *Ausburne* had closed the range to *Yugiri* to 8,800 yards. Four minutes later the Japanese destroyer seemed to get her second wind and went surging off, this time at thirty-four knots. But Burke was not fooled. "That's just his dying gasp!" he exulted. "That guy's number definitely has been posted!"

As the chase continued, Burke took time to send his third report to base: "The gun battle continues. The enemy has scattered. Some may get away. These are tough babies to sink!"

In her last minutes of life, *Yugiri* knew all the frantic desperation of a hare run to ground by a pack of relentless hounds. In just ninety seconds, the symbols of her death were graved at evenly spaced intervals upon the endless dial of time by the stylus of destiny:

0305:30:	Speed 22 knots.
0306:	Speed 10 knots.
0306:30:	Speed 5 knots.
0307:	Dead in the water.

For 21½ minutes longer, helpless, blazing *Yugiri* defied her executioners. At a range of four thousand yards, all ships of Division 45 poured shell into her, but she refused to sink. Burke countermarched and closed the range to three thousand yards, but the result was the same. "I guess you'll have to put a fish into her, Brute," he told Reynolds. But this time *Ausburne* couldn't oblige. Blast damage and near misses had fouled her torpedo battery and she couldn't fire torps. Burke then ordered Stout to administer the *coup de grâce,* but before the order could be executed it was belayed. *Yugiri* capsized to starboard, but she continued to float. So *Dyson* moved in at 0328 and fired torpedoes. They were wasted. At 0328:30, before *Dyson's* torps had time to arm and run to target, *Yugiri* disappeared silently beneath the surface of the tranquil sea.

Burke grabbed TBS: "Roy," he messaged Gano, "you must have fired your torpedoes at too much altitude!" It was a grim jest, but then, killing is a grim business . . .

Turning toward Purvis, the little ships of DesRon-23 stormed home. They got air cover, after a time. And Burke messaged Halsey: "On this Thanksgiving Day we are grateful to ComAirSols for cover! At 0410 love, in latitude 04°, 55′; longitude 153°, 38′." Halsey replied:

"31-Knot-Burke: Return to refuel at Purvis. Your Thanksgiving rendezvous with the enemy was a very excellent one, conceived by the creator, and directed by Commander, Destroyer Squadron 23!"

When Burke got back to Purvis, he pulled all the ships of the Squadron which were there together, their bows nesting. A foot-pumped organ was set up on *Charlie Ausburne's* bridge; a chaplain from one of the cruisers directed the Thanksgiving service; officers and men attended; and together they raised their voices: "When through fiery trials thy pathway shall lie; My grace, all-sufficient, shall be thy supply; The flame shall not hurt thee; I only design Thy doss to consume, and thy gold to refine."

Ordered to duty as Chief of Staff to Admiral Marc Mitscher, commanding Carrier Division 3, Arleigh Burke was devastated. "Somebody's trying to railroad me out of these lovely destroyers," he exploded. But, as always, he obeyed orders—a promotion, of course—with a cheery *aye-aye*. He sent a parting message to the officers and men of DesRon-23:

"No Squadron in any navy has won more battle honors in less time than the fighting, chasing Twenty-Third! There are no ships which have delivered more devastating blows to the enemy than those of this Squadron. Your heroic conduct and magnificent ability will make your families and your country proud of you. May God continue to bless you!"

Officers and men manned the rails when Arleigh Burke left. He, himself, had a struggle with his emotions. Finally, as he took his seat in the chair for transfer by high line to the *Lexington*, he growled to Reynolds:

"I don't want any cheers, Brute. I'll always keep track of *Ausburne*. Tell the boys, if any of them ever is in Washington where I live, to look me up; they'll be welcome! Goodbye, now—and for God's sake don't drop me in the drink when you transfer me by high line to the *Lex!*"

Captain Reynolds stepped back and signalled. The bos'un waved a weary hand—and Arleigh Burke was on his way to challenges more complex than he'd ever contemplated.

CHAPTER 7

The Bee Hive

The immense and magnificent Task Force 58 which Burke joined late in March 1944 was a comparatively recent creation. Its commander, Vice Admiral Marc A. ("Oklahoma Pete") Mitscher, a former aviator, had been handed his new assignment only two months earlier, following a reorganization of Admiral Chester A. Nimitz's Pacific Fleet into two striking teams.

One new team, the Fifth Fleet, was headed by intelligent, conservative Admiral Raymond A. Spruance; the Third Fleet was under the command of Admiral William F. Halsey, the scrappy hero of Midway. Mitscher, in command of four carrier Task Groups, was to work continuously for both Fleets, wherever there was critical action, wherever Navy planes were needed. And that was to be nearly every major battle of the Pacific war, for "Pete" Mitscher's armada of floating airfields and their one thousand fighters, torpedo planes, and bombers were the weapon that would carry the war to the Japanese home islands.

Mitscher's force was to bear several names before World War II ended, but it is most properly referred to as Task Force 58/38, indicating that its official designation was TF 58 while serving as part of Admiral Spruance's Fifth Fleet and TF 38 while part of Admiral Halsey's Third Fleet. Variously it was called the Fast Carrier Task Force and First Carrier Task Force. The multiplicity of nomenclatures was confusing to the enemy as well as to modern readers; for a time, the Japanese thought that the U.S. Navy boasted *two* carrier task forces of the size of TF 58/38.

Eventually, the Japanese were going to come to know TF 58/38 very well. After the war, General Hideki Tojo, the ex-Premier of Japan, who was later hanged as a war criminal, told General MacArthur that he attributed the defeat of his country to three principal causes: (1) the "leap-frog" strategy employed by the Navy in bypassing important Japanese military strongholds; (2) the toll of Japanese merchant ships exacted by American submarines, and (3) the deadly work of Task Force 58/38, the Navy's floating "bee hive."

It was to assume his duties as Chief of Staff of this redoubtable Task Force that Captain Arleigh A. Burke swung aboard the carrier *Lexington* that March day and confronted his new boss, Admiral Mitscher, a man he had never happened to meet. Burke would always recall that encounter vividly. It was a far-from-propitious moment, for Mitscher was no happier to see Captain Burke than Burke was to leave his beloved destroyers. The two men had been brought together forcibly, as it were, following a decision by Admiral King that every former aviator serving as a commander would have to have a surface sailor as his Chief of Staff. Conversely, every non-flying commander who dealt with aviation at all would have to have an aviator as his Chief of Staff. As far as CNO King was concerned, there had been too many mistakes on both sides, and he hoped that his new order would mean greater surface-air cooperation and greater understanding.

But while Admiral King may have had good reason for his decision, the whole business rankled Mitscher, who believed that a Task Force commander should have the privilege of selecting his own Chief of Staff. Furthermore, he was well satisfied with his present Chief of Staff, a tall, easygoing flyer named Truman J. Hedding. The Admiral liked Captain Hedding and trusted him, and he was angry when Hedding showed him the list of names from which he was to select Hedding's replacement. Burke believed that the Admiral picked him because he didn't even know him —and because Burke had seen plenty of combat.

Captain Burke looked like a destroyer sailor when he reported to Admiral Mitscher on the flag bridge of the *Lexington*. He was rumpled. He was weary. He had lost all of his clothes except those on his back.

The Admiral was formal and very considerate—almost too considerate, it seemed to the matter-of-fact "tin can" sailor. The Admiral also was cold, cold as an iceberg. Icily, he told Burke that he realized Burke was a destroyer captain and that he had not been aboard carriers before.

"You probably are tired and sleepy," he added softly, staring at his new Chief of Staff. Then he added ominously, "There's nothing for you to do here. Why don't you go below to my cabin and get a good bath and turn in and get slept out. Then come back here and see if you can't find something to do."

Burke went to the Admiral's big cabin (Mitscher never used it, but slept in a small sea cabin aft of Flag Plot). He took a hot shower, then stood for five minutes staring at the big bed that Mitscher had invited him to use. Suddenly Burke felt strongly that if he took advantage of the Admiral's offer, he was finished with Task Force 58 before he started. He shook off his weariness, did an about face, and sought out the ship's Supply Officer to get some clothes. Spic and span in a new set of khakis, Burke hustled back to the flag bridge and reported once more to the Ad-

111

miral, who was sitting in his famous swivel chair on the port wing, squinting out to sea from beneath the visor of his lobsterman's cap. Mitscher didn't even reply to Burke. Finally he grunted and swiveled away. It was obvious that he had nothing to say to his new Chief of Staff.

After a moment, Burke walked into Flag Plot and introduced himself around. Unfortunately for him, the man he was replacing, Captain Hedding, was on another ship, substituting for an officer who had been killed in an airplane accident. Burke began asking questions to try to find out what a Task Force Chief of Staff was supposed to do.

Flag Plot, which was to be Burke's office for the next fourteen months, was a crowded room in the island of the *Lexington,* jam-packed with an array of humming, chattering, and squawking equipment. In the center of the room was a gigantic chart table, surrounded by a variety of tracking and communications devices. Radar repeaters, ship and aircraft status boards, the short-wave radio called TBS (for Talk Between Ships), and almost every kind of device imaginable for keeping tabs on a large and complex operation were ranged about the room. The only sign of comfort was a leather couch for the Admiral.

This was the province of the Task Force Commander and his flag staff of 140 officers and enlisted men. Their working space, their quarters, even their dining areas, were kept separate from those of the officers and crew of the *Lexington.* The *Lexington* had its own skipper; he sailed his ship, and Admiral Mitscher commanded his Task Force. Years later, in a paper on the art of combat command, Burke wrote: "It is well for the men on the staff of a flag officer to lean over backwards to act as if they were guests on the flagship, even though they can obtain all the services which they demand by the mere demanding of them." Admiral Mitscher, Burke, and the staff were riding on the *Lexington;* they were not running it.

There was plenty for the Admiral's staff to do without worrying about sailing the *Lexington.* The four carrier Task Groups which comprised Task Force 58 soon would include seven large carriers—*Hornet, Yorktown, Bunker Hill, Wasp, Enterprise, Lexington,* and *Essex.* It would include eight light carriers—*Belleau Wood, Bataan, Monterey, Cabot, San Jacinto, Langley, Cowpens,* and the ill-starred *Princeton.* It would have one thousand planes; one hundred thousand officers and men; cruisers and destroyers in each carrier group. It would include a battle line of seven battleships, four more cruisers, and three destroyer divisions under command of Vice Admiral Willis A. Lee. Burke remarked in awe, as he first saw TF 58 from the flag bridge, "She sure takes up a lot of ocean." There had been nothing quite like it in the history of the world.

As Captain Burke began to orient himself for the stupendous task ahead, he quickly sensed that he would get little assistance from Admiral Mitscher. But he was too busy to find time for anger. Indeed, Commander J. Robert

North, the fleet gunnery officer who saw much of Burke, was not even aware of the tension which existed between the flying Admiral and his surface-sailing Chief of Staff.

But another staff officer, Lieutenant F. W. Pennoyer, III, aide and flag lieutenant, realized that Burke might be in for some stormy sailing. Pennoyer was the son of a retired vice admiral, and his personal radar was excellent for spotting points of strain. He considered Hedding a razor-keen Chief of Staff, and he thought privately that Burke was taking quite a step for a dyed-in-the-wool destroyer sailor. Lieutenant Pennoyer kept an eye on the new man, but he soon lost visual contact as Burke disappeared behind a rising mountain of textbooks, tactical doctrines, technical publications, and everything else he could find aboard which had to do with naval aviation. Burke worked "furiously," Pennoyer observed with interest, and he began a practice (which soon turned into a habit) of rising two hours earlier than the Admiral to study the weather and get a start on his work.

After several days of intensive reading, listening, and questioning, a period marked by the total absence of communication to Burke from the Admiral he served, the new Chief of Staff suddenly gave his first combat order to TF 58. It was the day before an air strike against the Palau Islands, and the Task Force was attacked by enemy aircraft. At one point, the Japanese launched a low-level torpedo attack that looked "very good" to Burke. He noted that the planes were coming in about 45 degrees off the port bow of the *Lexington,* and he realized that something had to be done in a hurry. Strangely, nobody gave an order. Nobody appeared to be concerned. Burke wheeled, grabbed a TBS and ordered the Fleet to come to course 45 degrees to the left, head into the torpedoes, increase speed, and open fire. The attack soon ended, with several enemy planes shot down, the rest routed, and no torpedo hits on any of the ships.

After the action, Burke went to the port wing and told the Admiral what he had done. Mitscher turned and stared at his Chief of Staff for a long time. Finally he said, "Well, Captain, it's about time." That is all he had to say on the subject.

Burke went back to Flag Plot in confusion. "About time for what?" he thought heatedly. As the months passed, however, and relations slowly improved between Burke and the Admiral, the Chief of Staff eventually decided that Mitscher had been testing him to find out whether he would take charge in a crisis. If Burke wasn't the man for the job, the Admiral wanted to find out in a hurry. If he could handle the job, Mitscher felt that he needed no special instructions from him.

It seemed to Burke a hard, hard test, and he was grateful when his predecessor Captain Hedding returned to the *Lexington* to help him take hold. Hedding also helped Burke to hold his temper in check, as the Admiral's chilliness pushed him to the boiling point. Hedding insisted that

113

Mitscher was a great man and that if Burke could hang on, he would grow to appreciate the Admiral. Burke hung on, but it was midsummer before the Admiral finally became reconciled to a Chief of Staff who didn't even know how to fly an airplane.

A principal task of the Chief of Staff was to prepare the operational plans for battles and air strikes, and Burke and the other officers had their hands full from the start. Just before Burke's arrival, the Joint Chiefs of Staff had endorsed a dual advance across the Pacific by the Army and the Navy. MacArthur's Southwest Pacific forces were to continue to move up along the northern shore of New Guinea and invade the island of Mindanao in the Philippines in the fall.

The Navy, under Admiral Nimitz, was to make a daring invasion of Saipan, Tinian, and Guam in the Marianas during June, bypassing a number of enemy strongholds. In September, the Navy was to swing south from the Marianas and attack the Palaus, working their way down to converge on Mindanao to support MacArthur's landings. The general strategy was to be followed with only one major alteration in plans; Mindanao, the southernmost island of the Philippines, was to be bypassed, and the invasion eventually was to take place on a beach in the island of Leyte.

As Burke joined TF 58, it was speeding toward the Palau Islands, where the Japanese reportedly had important air bases and strong garrisons. The Navy had little trustworthy information about these islands and wanted Mitscher to raid them and get photographs. The day after Burke's first combat order aboard the *Lexington,* TF 58 struck the Palaus. By April 2, it had shot down most of the enemy's planes and sunk practically all ships that were still there. During this successful raid, Burke was involved with the first carrier mine laying operation in history, as three squadrons of Avenger torpedo bombers mined the harbors of the Palaus in full view of the enemy.

With his penchant for analysis, Burke considered this operation years later in writing about the adoption of new weapons and the division of opinion which inevitably occurs over their application.

"During the last war," he stated, "mines became most important." New mines were developed which could be profitably laid by carrier aircraft. But mines do not show immediate results, like bombs and torpedoes, and besides, carrier aircraft are most efficient pinpoint attacks. Mining is really an area operation.

"It was with great reluctance that Commander Task Force 58 agreed to use mines in the Palau operation. It was agreed to then because it was a tactical use for mines; that is, the mines could be laid in the channels and, thereby, prevent the Japanese ships in the harbor from escaping. The results were immediate and satisfactory."

"Another reason for reluctance in laying mines was that it placed pilots

114

in danger of being shot down. Mines were generally looked upon with disfavor as a carrier weapon, and were finally sold to B-29's as an area weapon. Here was one new weapon which achieved marvelous results, but proved more suitable for use by aircraft which could lay large numbers of them. Therefore, it is important, not only to evaluate a new weapon, but to evaluate the methods of using the new weapon."

After the Palaus came quick raids on Yap and Woleai, and TF 58 hurried back to the Marshalls. Burke was getting a front-row education on the formidable power of the air arm of the Navy, an education that would make this erstwhile destroyer squadron commander one of the leading proponents of carriers in the United States.

The orders came thick and fast. In mid-April the Task Force supported MacArthur's invasion of Hollandia, on the northern coast of New Guinea, by hitting targets a hundred miles or so on either side of the landing to destroy enemy air power. Admiral Mitscher sent Burke aloft in a dive bomber to reconnoiter the lines and positions ashore and to report on damage inflicted. He returned with his starboard wing full of flak holes to discover all hands aboard the *Lexington* grinning mysteriously. At that moment, a message which originated with Captain Hedding, was being transmitted visually to every ship in the Task Force: "Today 31-Knot Burke rode in an airplane. He was interviewed on landing and stated QUOTE The airplane is here to stay UNQUOTE." Captain Burke, not above a bit of horseplay himself when the occasion demanded, was unruffled by the flyboy's barb. Making no reference to the damage to his plane, he gave a full and complete report to Mitscher on the results of his reconaissance mission.

On the way back from the Hollandia mission, the Task Force slammed the island of Truk in the Carolines, a target which Mitscher's planes had devastated before Burke's arrival. This time, TF 58 took the starch out of Truk for good. Task Force cruisers shelled another Caroline island, Satawan, and Admiral Lee's battleships bombarded Ponape. In all these thrusts, not a single American ship was damaged.

Now Burke was handed his most stupendous operational assignment to date. In May, as the Allies in Europe made final preparations for the invasion of France at Normandy, Admiral Spruance of the Fifth Fleet was putting the finishing touches on another invasion plan, a plan so audacious that it would leave the Japanese High Command gasping and reeling. The Navy would reach out and invade Saipan, in the Marianas, more than three thousand miles west of Hawaii and one thousand miles from Eniwetok, our most westerly anchorage in the Central Pacific. The vast operation involved transporting more than 127,000 troops, two-thirds of them Marines, in 535 different combat ships and auxiliary craft, including landing craft.

The Joint Expeditionary Force was under command of Vice Admiral Richmond Kelly Turner, with the expeditionary troops under direction of Lieutenant General Holland M. Smith, USMC. Admiral Spruance's mission for the Fifth Fleet still has a clear ring to it after two decades:

"This force will capture, occupy, and defend SAIPAN, TINIAN, and GUAM, will develop airfields on those islands, and will gain control of the remaining MARIANAS, in order to operate long-range aircraft against JAPAN, secure control of the central PACIFIC, and isolate and neutralize the central CAROLINES."

Admiral Mitscher's mission for Task Force 58 was:

"Prevent interference by enemy air action with the capture of SAIPAN, TINIAN, and GUAM.

"Protect the JOINT EXPEDITIONARY FORCE and island positions, after occupation, from attack by enemy surface forces."

From the first, the morning of June 15 had been picked by the planners as D-Day, and they stuck to it. Burke had never before been involved in such high-level planning, and he and his staff took little note of the clock during May. While Captain Hedding rejoined the Task Force as Assistant Chief of Staff and gave Burke valuable help in drafting operational plans for the Marianas invasion, the major responsibility for the plan fell on the shoulders of the ex-destroyer commander. Just before the Task Force sortied from Majuro on June 6, Burke handed the finished plan to Admiral Mitscher, requesting that he read and sign it. To Burke's astonishment, the Admiral declined to look at it.

"I am going to rely on you to tell me all that I need to know," he told his Chief of Staff. He was beginning to have confidence in Burke.

The Force began refueling on June 8 as the ships sailed west toward the Marianas and battle. Three days later, when Mitscher was only two hundred miles away from Guam, his planes roared off the carrier decks to strike the southern Marianas. Most enemy planes were in New Guinea, working over MacArthur's forces, and the pilots of Task Force 58 met light opposition. More than one hundred enemy planes were destroyed. On June 13, Admiral Lee's battleships were detached from TF 58 to begin the bombardment of Saipan and Tinian, and the following day, two carrier task groups under Rear Admiral J. J. "Jocko" Clark turned northward to attack air fields on Iwo Jima and Chichi Jima to sever air communications from Japan and stop air reinforcements. Mitscher, in tactical command of the two remaining carrier groups in his Force, sailed west to support the invasion of Saipan directly, as ordered by Admiral Spruance.

But during the invasion preparations in May, the Japanese Navy had not been idle. Admiral Soemu Toyoda had taken command of the Combined Fleet and hastened to produce a Japanese carbon copy of Task Force

58. This imitation was dubbed the First Mobile Fleet, and it was under command of Vice Admiral Jisaburo Ozawa, the enemy's leading naval air officer. All of Japan's aircraft carriers were concentrated in Ozawa's smaller but still wicked fleet.

Admiral Toyoda mistakenly assumed, however, that TF 58 would continue to support MacArthur in his march toward Japan and that the Allies would continue to follow the single New Guinea track northward. Proceeding on that assumption, he ordered Ozawa's First Mobile Fleet to Tawi Tawi, between Borneo and the Philippine Islands, so that the Japanese ships would be in a position to try to halt MacArthur's northward advance. At the same time, Ozawa hoped to lure Mitscher into a fight. On June 11, the Admiral was surprised to learn that TF 58 planes were many miles away, striking the Marianas.

Upon receiving news of the air strike, Admiral Ozawa sortied from Tawi Tawi and ordered a force of battleships steaming toward MacArthur's forces to turn around and join him. Unfortunately for the Japanese, however, neither of these forthright moves was going to come as any surprise to the American forces. A U.S. submarine, *Redfin*, which had the job of watching Tawi Tawi, saw and reported Ozawa's departure on June 13. The fleet was spotted several more times from the coast as it sailed among the Philippine Islands. Submarine *Flying Fish* saw it leave San Bernardino Strait, near Leyte, on June 15, the same day that the Marines invaded Saipan, and a short time later submarine *Seahorse* spotted the battleships which had been withdrawn from the attack on MacArthur. The only information which the Fifth Fleet still lacked was whether or not the carrier force would rendezvous with the battleship force. Submarine *Cavalla*, which sighted the Japanese ships twice on June 17, and knew that they were heading directly for the Marianas, couldn't see enough ships to tell whether the rendezvous had taken place.

After receiving the submarine reports, Admiral Spruance recalled "Jocko" Clark from Chichi Jima and Iwo Jima, and the two carrier groups rejoined TF 58 at 1200 on June 18. It was obvious to all that the First Mobile Fleet of the Imperial Japanese Navy and the Fast Carrier Task Force of the Pacific Fleet were going to collide in battle, and that the battle would be a major test, perhaps the major test of the war.

Burke estimated that if the two opposing fleets sailed toward one another, they would make contact during the night of the 18th. Mitscher sent the following message to Admiral Lee: "Do you desire night engagement? It may be we can make air contact late this afternoon and attack tonight. Otherwise, we should retire to the eastward tonight . . ."

Lee replied: "Do not believe we should seek night engagement. Would press pursuit of damaged or fleeing enemy, however, at any time." Burke was astonished.

117

The Task Force then took a defensive position. The battleships, cruisers, and destroyers formed a battle line under Lee, and all five task groups—the four carrier groups and the surface vessels—assumed formations not unlike those taken by covered wagons to repel Indian attacks. In each carrier group, the flattops were toward the center of the ring, surrounded by a screen of cruisers and destroyers. Admiral Lee's flag was flying on the *Indiana,* which lay in the center of a formidable circle of six other battleships and four heavy cruisers. Spruance was in *Indianapolis,* one of the ships surrounding carriers, *Princeton, Enterprise, San Jacinto,* and *Lexington.*

All day on June 18, TF 58 covered the Marine beachhead on Saipan, probing to the west with search planes. That night, the Force headed back east to prevent any enemy force from slipping past. But before midnight, Pearl Harbor notified Mitscher that the enemy fleet was 355 miles from his own position.

What happened after this bit of intelligence reached TF 58 has already been the subject of brisk and heated debate wherever Navy men gather, and it is likely to be debated as long as there are men interested in the sea and ships. It is the opinion of Arleigh Burke which is of moment in this narrative, and Burke sided with Mitscher in the disagreement which followed.

Admiral Mitscher proposed, as every Navy buff knows, to alter his course on the night of the eighteenth and to sail west toward the enemy fleet. He had good reasons. If he remained close to Japanese airfields on Guam, Ozawa's planes could fly to TF 58, drop their bombs, fly on to Guam, refuel and rearm, and hit TF 58 again on their way back to the Mobile Fleet. Furthermore, carriers must sail into the wind in order for planes to take off, and the wind was easterly. Ozawa was sailing into the wind as he approached Mitscher; Mitscher would be backing away from Ozawa as his planes took off. That was still another reason why Mitscher and Burke wanted to close the distance between themselves and the enemy fleet. By the morning of June 19, the Task Force commander declared, he could launch an air attack against Ozawa.

On the evening of June 18, Admiral Spruance talked over the Mitscher proposal with his staff for more than one hour before he rejected it. He took the course which he believed to be the more prudent. As far as he was concerned, TF 58 had a defensive mission, and Spruance wanted to make sure that no enemy ships slipped by the Fifth Fleet to hit the invading Marines on Saipan.

Burke felt, as did Mitscher, that it would be next to impossible for the enemy to slip around carrier forces and search planes, but Spruance was not convinced. He still didn't know whether Ozawa had rendezvoused with the enemy battleships. And after all, he claimed, it was submarines which

118

had spotted the enemy fleet so far; Mitscher's planes had not found Ozawa's ships. (Ozawa's ships were out of range of the carrier-based craft.) Task Force 58 bitterly began preparations for the attack which they knew would commence in the morning. "We can't go west; we have to go east," said Burke, when he heard the Spruance decision. "So we might as well stay up all night and work on the problem. We'll have hell slugged out of us in the morning." And attack the Japanese would, for their planes had located TF 58 the preceding afternoon some two hundred miles west of Saipan.

While he mentioned no particular battle, Burke wrote later: "The quality of dash seemed to be lacking, or at least restrained, in too many of the senior officers during the Pacific War."

As probable causes, he suggested the natural effects of age; the lack of serious naval combat for eighty years; the effect of Pearl Harbor and of operating on a shoestring during the months that followed, and the "conservative effect of peacetime training, with its tendency to punish mistakes instead of rewarding brilliance."

Whatever the causes, Burke wrote that the effect was damaging.

"The effect on the enemy is obvious: we missed opportunity after opportunity to damage him, discourage him, throw him off-balance and bypass him. We failed to take full advantage of the opportunities we did seize. The effect on our own forces was somewhat less obvious, but possibly it was even more profound.

"The audacious commander almost automatically has a superior force. The dash of the commander is transmitted to the force; they become always ready and eager to go; they have a fighting edge. The conservative commander, whose tendency is to be sure before he strikes, breeds that same spirit in his force. His command rapidly reaches a point of reluctance to fight."

What occurred the following day, of course, was not an American defeat; it was an important American victory in the air. The correct command decision can be important to the outcome of an engagement; sometimes it is the vital factor. But sometimes a multiplicity of factors destine one particular side to triumph.

"Production, strategy, and logistics determine the conditions under which the fighting is done," wrote Burke, "and may set it up so you can't win, as in Bataan, or can't lose, as during the Battle of the Philippine Sea . . . much depends on the skill of the fighters."

This day, June 19, 1944, was to be entered in official records as the date of the Battle of the Philippine Sea, and the skill of the fighting men was indeed going to be an important factor. Admiral Ozawa's Mobile Fleet included nine carriers with 430 carrier aircraft and forty-three float planes, but his aviators had experienced only a minimum of training, and they had had no training at all while the fleet was based at Tawi Tawi. Mitscher's pilots were superbly trained, with a fine edge. It was noted that coordination that day between American fighter-directors and fighters was practically perfect and that interceptions were made like clockwork.

The land-based aircraft which had been one of Mitscher's chief worries soon were neutralized. Carrier-based Hellcats ran into the enemy as they were taking off from Guam early in the morning, shot down several, and sent the rest scurrying for cover. Reinforcements arriving from Truk also were intercepted. In all, thirty-three Hellcats annihilated thirty enemy fighters and five dive bombers.

Task Force 58 detected no carrier-based bogeys until 1000. At that point, American radar reported that the first wave was on its way from the Japanese Mobile Fleet. With a yell of "Hey, Rube," Mitscher launched more than 450 fighters and ordered all bombers and torpedo planes into the air to remain clear of the carriers so that fighters could land, rearm, and refuel. The Hellcats were stacked at high altitudes and they spotted the enemy planes about seventy miles from the Task Force. Dropping down from the sky, they swarmed like bees all over the ill-trained Japanese, shooting down some twenty-five. A few of the enemy got through to TF 58, but they ran into Admiral Lee's deadly battle line. Out of sixty-nine planes in Ozawa's first raid, only twenty-seven returned to their carriers. The Americans lost only one plane.

Ozawa made three more raids, and the Hellcats continued to intercept his pilots and shoot them down. One American dubbed the battle the "Marianas Turkey Shoot" and the name stuck. By the end of the day, Ozawa's 430 carrier planes numbered only one hundred. Meanwhile, American submarines had located the Mobile Fleet, and their torpedoes blew up the *Shokaku* and Ozawa's flagship, *Taiho*. Despite these crushing blows, Admiral Ozawa did not despair, for his returning aviators assured him that they had crippled TF 58. Actually, not a single American vessel had been sunk. Damage was relatively light. Ozawa nevertheless retired to the northwest to refuel, intending to attack TF 58 again on June 21.

On the night of June 19, Spruance finally unleashed Mitscher, but TF 58 miscalculated the position of the enemy and failed to gain on Ozawa. It was 1600 the following day before an American search plane located the Japanese fleet, and it was nearly sunset when Mitscher's fighters, dive bombers and torpedo bombers struck Ozawa. Bombers set two carriers on fire and inflicted damage on a battleship and a cruiser; torpedo planes sunk the carrier *Hiyo*. The enemy put seventy-five of its remaining one hundred planes into the air and shot down twenty American planes, but the enemy lost even more. When the fighting ended on June 20, Ozawa's original 430 carrier planes had been reduced to only thirty-five. There was nothing for him to do but run.

120

It was after dark when the planes of TF 58 returned from their successful sunset raid, and Mitscher ordered Burke to turn on the lights. Burke gave the order to all carriers to switch on running lights and truck lights to outline flight decks. Searchlights went on and guns fired star shells to show the planes the way home. It was a daring decision on Mitscher's part, since the lights made the Task Force a sitting duck for enemy submarine or air attack. But Mitscher would not abandon his flyers, and Burke approved of the decision.

Later, Burke would write that the TF 58 flyers "did their job unusually well that day because they had faith in their leader and confidence in the ability and desire of the force which was left behind to rescue them."

Recovery of the aviators permitted Ozawa to get away, however, and Spruance called off the chase. Mitscher and Burke were bitterly disappointed that they had missed this chance to sink the Japanese carrier force, and the fact that they had decimated some four hundred enemy aviators was little consolation to them. As far as they were concerned, they might have won the most decisive naval engagement of the war, had Spruance let them sail west on the night of June 18. On the other hand, both Admiral King and Admiral Nimitz believed that Spruance had made the correct decision in ordering Mitscher to stick close to Saipan to support the beachhead.

The debate can continue; but the Marianas Turkey Shoot was over on June 21, 1944. Burke was to spend much time in later years, speculating on the forces which drive a commander, under stress of combat, to make this decision or that one. Occasionally, when he could find a yeoman on the bridge, he dictated the reasons for his own combat decisions, revealing a tendency toward introspection which could come to the fore even during the strain of battle. Eventually Burke decided that it is a brave man—or an incautious one—who criticizes another man for the action which he took in battle, unless the action was an error caused by "an obvious lack of character."

In the weeks that followed, Burke began to know and respect many of his fellow officers on the Admiral's staff. At the same time, the other officers were getting to know Burke. In many ways, it was a remarkably gifted flag staff, with a full complement of rugged individualists. Mitscher had never been one to attract "yes" men. He liked men with nerve, who were quick-witted, the kind of men who made top-notch fighter pilots.

When Burke boarded the *Lexington* in March, the operations officer was a typical Mitscher selection, a black-haired, daring aviator named William J. "Gus" Widhelm. Gus was an inveterate gambler with as much style as a professional card player on a 19th-Century Mississippi river boat. Burke found Widhelm "full of bubbles," and he observed with interest that the brash flyer slept "boots and saddles," or fully dressed, at all times.

Later, Widhelm was replaced as operations officer by Commander J. H.

Flatley, a short, dark, intense Irishman who worked hand-in-glove with Burke in developing battle plans. A former fighter squadron commander, Flatley was inclined to be apprehensive and to take things hard. Born a Roman Catholic, he had lost his faith, then been re-converted. Despite his own ups and downs in matters of faith, however, Burke noted that he was impatient with those who disagreed with him.

There was Lieutenant Commander F. A. Dingfelder, who was, in Burke's opinion, "one of the best communications officers in the business." Dark, slender Dingfelder was not a graduate of the Academy. He had enlisted in the Navy in World War I and had applied for the Academy, but a CPO had sat on his papers until Dingfelder was over the age limit for entry. Dingfelder took it in his stride, and Burke respected him for it.

In June 1944, the Admiral's staff got a new Administrative Officer in the person of Captain W. A. "Gus" Read, son of a wealthy New York investment banker. Read had been a flyer in World War I and he was now USNR. One of Captain Read's duties was to present decorations for heroism on the spot, if he and the Admiral decided that a man was deserving of a medal. Previously, it had taken months for requests for citations to be approved, since the forms had to wend their weary way through dusty offices in Washington, D.C. All too frequently, the recipient of the decoration had been killed by the time the award was approved. On other occasions, the act of heroism for which the decoration had been intended had been superseded by a still more heroic action. It made far more sense, in Burke's opinion, for the Admiral's staff to judge whether or not a man deserved a decoration, and to present that decoration while the event was still fresh in the minds of all.

Gus Read managed to be a fashion plate, even in combat, and he always handled himself as if he were about to step into a corporation board meeting. Burke told a friend that "Read never looks as though he slept in his clothes, even when he has."

Commander North, the gunnery officer who didn't know that Burke was getting the deepfreeze from "Pete" Mitscher, was well liked by most of the officers. Courteous, with a good sense of humor, North had a long, expressive face, a tough beard, and a kind word to say for practically everybody except the Japs. For his part, North was struck by Burke's qualities as a naval officer and leader. He considered the Chief of Staff "a dynamo of energy, drive, and perfection," and he observed that, despite the intense pressure to which the staff was continuously subjected, the job was being done—and done well. Commander North also marked Burke's "personal interest" in various aspects of running the gigantic armada of which he was a part, and he tried to apply a number of Burke's leadership concepts to his own "gunnery business." (The Chief of Staff once wrote that "men are inspired by the personal interest and consideration of their commander more than by any other factor and, once they have become inspired, they will follow a leader into the most difficult situations . . .") Burke himself was the "quintessence" of personal interest, North felt, and his presence was greatly enhancing the effectiveness of Task Force 58.

Another of North's favorites was a frequent visitor to the *Lexington*, Captain Luis de Florez, one of the nation's outstanding inventors. Captain de Florez had made a fortune by developing a cracking process for oil, then had turned his talents to military invention. In 1944, de Florez was director of the Navy's Special Devices Division, and the year before he had won the Collier Trophy for inventing synthetic training devices for aviators and aerial gunners. Now and then, he flew out to the Task Force to check on the efficacy of his training inventions.

Lieutenant Pennoyer, the aide who had been so interested in Burke when the new Chief of Staff came aboard, was a pleasant and courteous red-head who seemed remarkably "polished" to a Colorado ranch boy like Arleigh Burke. For his part, Pennoyer finally decided that Burke was a "wonder" as a tactician. Many times, the young lieutenant watched in admiration as Burke hunched over the radar scope, TBS in hand, maneuvering, by seaman's eye, three or four carrier task groups simultaneously in position astern of replenishment groups.

The Admiral's navigator and assistant gunnery officer was Commander B. D. "Woody" Wood, Jr., who struck Burke as a shy man and a slightly apologetic one. But it may have been the force of Captain Burke's own personality that made Woody Wood appear to withdraw. For while Commander Wood thought Burke pleasant and affable enough as a rule, he also was struck by the man's tremendous physical and mental vitality and "the sharpness and quickness of his mind." Burke kept the entire staff on the alert to anticipate his questions, and he thought that each specialist should have the answers he required on tap at all times. If the answers weren't forthcoming in a hurry, Burke grew impatient—and he showed it.

The Chief of Staff also talked rapidly, and Wood observed that Burke's mind seemed to race far ahead of his words. Most members of the staff, in Wood's opinion, found it difficult, and sometimes impossible, to keep up with Burke's rapid-fire expression of thoughts and ideas.

There were many more on Mitscher's staff, 140 officers and enlisted men in all. They included Lieutenant Commander Johnny Myers, the aerial operation officer, a likeable, dapper, pilot with a smart moustache; Lieutenant Commander C. G. Steele, tall, good looking, a good writer and a hard worker; Lieutenant j.g. C. A. Sims, a Japanese-language expert, who once translated an order to attack the flagship one hour before the attack took place; Lieutenant H. S. L. Wiener, the son of scientist Norbert Wiener; and Lieutenant B. R. "Whizzer" White, a football star. There was the senior aerological officer, Lieutenant J. J. Vonk, who represented a vocation noted for its leisurely pace and notorious for hedging. Vonk's weather forecasts were precise and he never hedged, although he frequently disagreed with the other aerologists in the fleet. "Admiral," he would ask Mitscher, "are you going to believe those bastards or are you going to believe me?" More often than not, Mitscher would take Vonk's word.

Finally, there was Admiral Mitscher himself, a reticent commander, so soft-spoken that many pilots, temporarily deafened from engine noise and the clamor of battle, could not hear him during interrogations. Mitscher kept to himself, and he appeared sometimes to be nourished by his bitter, unyielding hatred of the Japanese people. He loathed the enemy as much as he loved his aviators, and this did not speak well for the enemy.

Pete Mitscher was a slight man, weighing only 135 pounds, and his three principal recreations were sitting on his special swivel chair, smoking, and, upon retiring, reading detective stories. A correspondent once wrote that the Admiral kept running out of "whodunit" fiction, and Mitscher was never short of crime stories after that. They were sent to him from all over the United States.

Aviators adored the Admiral, and his lighting up the carrier decks after the Battle of the Philippine Sea was only one of many reasons. Mitscher, they felt with some justification, was one of them. He rescued an amazingly high percentage of flyers downed in the water, and he was uncanny on occasion in predicting where their rafts might turn up. He fought the idea of night-fighter missions because he hated the thought of an aviator hitting the water in the dark. (It was Arleigh Burke, not Mitscher, who helped plan the first night-fighter mission, from the *Enterprise*.)

Mitscher's reactions were hard to predict. He could be unexpectedly gentle with aviators who had made bad mistakes; he also could be ruthless with those who failed his trust or who committed serious blunders. His initial distaste for Burke was unusual, however, for he generally was a just man, and his justice was tempered with mercy.

Task Force 58 and the Mitscher team continued to support the invasion of the Marianas throughout the rest of June and July. Saipan fell to the Marines on July 9, and the war cabinet of Premier Tojo in Japan fell soon after. The island of Tinian was the next objective, and it was conquered on July 31, one week after it was invaded. The conquest of Guam took longer, but it was returned to American hands on August 10. With seizure of the Marianas, the United States had bases from which the new long-range B-29's could strike Tokyo.

In August, Admiral Spruance and his teammates, Admiral Turner and General Smith, left the combat zone and Admiral Halsey was called up from the South Pacific. The principal naval force of the Central Pacific now was called the Third Fleet, with Halsey in command. Task Force 58 became Task Force 38, with Admiral Mitscher, by his own choice, still in command, and Arleigh Burke still Chief of Staff. The *Lexington,* under command of Captain Ernest Litch, remained their flagship. Burke welcomed the arrival of Halsey, whom he considered one of the great naval commanders.

With the change came new task group commanders to serve under Mitscher. There was Vice Admiral John S. McCain, with his "disreputable" green cap and wrinkled uniform, who was slated to relieve Mitscher until Mitscher declined to be relieved; Rear Admiral Ralph E. Davison, colorful, a good planner with seemingly inexhaustible energy; Rear Admiral Frederick C. Sherman, stubborn, precise, and meticulous, but a fighting commander, in Burke's opinion; and Rear Admiral Gerald F. Bogan, a short, pugnacious officer who hit the enemy hard and fast. These were the group commanders who soon would help lead Task Force 38 into the greatest sea battle in the history of the world.

Admiral Halsey, in his flagship *New Jersey,* joined Mitscher's Task Force and occasionally assumed tactical command. The first mission was to begin softening up the Philippines for the long-awaited invasion of those islands in the fall. On September 11, the Combined Chiefs of Staff, meeting in Quebec with President Roosevelt and Prime Minister Churchill, cancelled plans to invade Mindanao and ordered Admiral Nimitz and General MacArthur to join forces for an invasion of Leyte, farther north than Mindanao in the Philippines, on October 20, 1944. The Third Fleet was stripped to very little else but Task Force 38; other ships were transferred to the Southwest Pacific forces for the assault on Leyte. In mid-September, Task Force 38 supported landings on the islands of Morotai and Peleliu. Other troops invaded Angaur Island and Ulithi Atoll.

As summer ended, there were signs that Admiral Mitscher was beginning to mellow toward his Chief of Staff. One day a destroyer came alongside *Lexington,* and Mitscher, without cracking a smile, told his Marine orderly to "secure Captain Burke until that DD shoves off!" More civil words were passing between the two men now. Despite himself, the Admiral could not help but be impressed by Burke's ability, loyalty, and intelligence. In the middle of one major operational plan after another, Burke was proving that he could fight in the air as well as on the sea. He was open minded, pragmatic, forever questioning, forever receptive to new ideas and plans.

When he wasn't on guard, Burke still lost his temper, and he could turn the air blue with a seaman's invective like any veteran bosun's mate. He still could talk at length when he wasn't giving orders, but his orders were masterpieces of brevity. It was becoming part of his code to give as few as possible, since he had learned that once an officer gives an order on a particular subject, he must always give orders on that subject.

One day in the fall of 1944, Burke was riding a destroyer and was to transfer back to the flagship by high line. To Burke's annoyance, there was some delay in bringing the destroyer alongside the *Lexington* and she trailed in the carrier's wake for several minutes. Captain Fitch, the *Lexington's* skipper, promptly felt the sting of Burke's impatience, as he received the following visual from the destroyer: "MSG CAPTAIN. WHAT THE HELL. BURKE." The message got results in a hurry.

But all nerves were getting frayed. The difficult, exhausting, dangerous work of war and death continued for TF 38 without respite. The objective was to destroy enemy planes, and during the next sixty days, TF 38 was to shoot down twelve hundred enemy aircraft in devastating raids on the Philippines, Ryukyus, and Formosa. On the islands of Leyte, Cebu, and Negros, U.S. planes caught the enemy on the ground. On September 21, TF 38 plowed through tropical rainstorms to strike the eastern coast of Luzon. Two days later, Burke visited the *New Jersey* to talk about attacks on Okinawa, Formosa, and the home islands of Japan with Halsey's Chief of Staff, Admiral Carney. The plans they made began to be carried out in October, as Mitscher craftily followed a typhoon up to Okinawa and arrived off the shore of that island undetected. After a successful one-day strike, TF 38 planes struck airfields in Luzon on October 11 and arrived over Formosa at dawn on October 12 for a daring three-day raid. Halsey was looking for a fight, and Burke was with him heart and soul.

The first day of the Okinawa raid, TF 38 pilots destroyed many enemy installations and shot down more than two hundred fighter aircraft. On October 13, the enemy sent in torpedo bombers which managed to damage cruisers *Canberra* and *Houston* before the Americans shot them down in large numbers. With their usual weakness for boasting, the Japanese aviators reported that most of the Third Fleet was wiped out. The wily Halsey even heard a Radio Tokyo broadcast announcing his own death, and he tried to use this bit of intelligence to lure the enemy fleet from hiding. All his ruses failed, however, and the Imperial Japanese Navy continued to stick close to the home islands. But while the big game still eluded the Third Fleet, Burke noted that TF 38's carrier squadrons had shot down about 350 enemy aircraft in the five days between October 11 and 16. American losses numbered eighty-nine. After this four-to-one kill, the fleet proceeded to its position off Leyte to support the triumphant American return to the Philippines. Landed and protected by units of the Seventh Fleet, under Vice Admiral Thomas C. Kinkaid, who reported to MacArthur, more than sixty thousand assault troops and more than one hundred thousand tons of supplies were put ashore on Leyte by sunset on October 20, and a few troops had penetrated more than one mile inland. Halsey held his breath. Would this be the action that would bring the Imperial Navy out to fight?

It was—and Burke was to be in the thick of it.

CHAPTER 8

A Postgraduate Course in Suicides

It was partly the fault of the U.S. Navy that the Japanese had not come out to fight before. American submarines had been concentrating on sinking enemy tankers, and the Japanese fleet was badly restricted in its movements by lack of fuel oil.

When General MacArthur, supported by Admiral Kinkaid, struck Leyte in the Philippines, the Japanese fleet was split into three segments. A large force of battleships, cruisers, and destroyers was near Singapore, under command of Vice Admiral Takeo Kurita. Vice Admiral Kiyohide Shima was in command of a force of cruisers and destroyers in the Ryukyus. In Japan's Inland Sea were remnants of Vice Admiral Ozawa's once proud Mobile Fleet, the fleet with which he had planned to sink Mitscher's Task Force the preceding June. Ozawa was still suffering from a shortage of trained aviators.

Convinced that if Japan lost the Philippines, it lost all, Admiral Toyoda ordered all segments of the Imperial Navy into action. Both Kurita and Shima were to converge on the U.S. Seventh Fleet and stop men and supplies from reaching the beachhead of Leyte. Ozawa was to sortie with his carriers from the Inland Sea—pilots or no pilots—and draw Halsey's Third Fleet, including TF 38, far to the north. Only if this were done, Toyoda felt, could any hope be entertained of stopping MacArthur. In offering Ozawa as a decoy, Toyoda assumed that his Mobile Fleet would be destroyed. Japan was willing to pay that price to save the Philippines.

Of all the three segments of the fleet, Admiral Kurita's was by far the most formidable. It included five old battleships and two new ones, the two largest fighting ships in the world, *Yamato* and *Musashi*. In addition, there were eleven heavy cruisers, two light cruisers, and nineteen destroyers. They represented the most powerful striking force left in the Imperial Navy.

Admiral Toyoda's plan was for the main body of Kurita's ships, including the two superbattleships, to enter the Philippines from the west, cross the Sibuyan Sea, sail through San Bernardino Strait, north of Leyte, and to enter Leyte Gulf with this massive firepower on the morning of October 25. The Americans referred to Kurita's force as the Center Force.

Admiral Shima would join his force with a splinter of Kurita's and head for Surigao Strait, to strike at Leyte Gulf from the south as Kurita sailed in from the north. This was known to Americans as the Southern Force. Together, according to the plan, at any rate, Kurita and Shima would grip Kinkaid's Seventh Fleet in a pincers. Halsey would be far to the north, attracted by the decoy, unsuspectingly sinking the carriers of Admiral Ozawa's Northern Force. So reasoned the Japanese High Command.

What actually happened during the next few days should be as familiar to every American as the victory of Lord Nelson at Trafalgar is to an English patriot. On the morning of October 23, American submarines *Darter* and *Dace* spotted Kurita's massive Center Force. *Darter* promptly fired four torpedoes into Kurita's flagship, the heavy cruiser *Atago,* and watched the vessel sink in eighteen minutes. *Darter* then crippled a heavy cruiser so badly that she had to pull out of the attack and head for Borneo, with a couple of destroyers for company. Finally, *Dace* struck her blow. She put her torpedoes into another heavy cruiser, which exploded.

A shaken Kurita managed to escape to the superbattleship *Yamato* and he sailed on all day the twenty-third and all night. He must have sailed with foreboding, however, since he could be certain that the American submarines had notified Halsey of his arrival in Philippine waters. He also could be sure that Halsey and Mitscher would send out a welcoming committee.

Jubilant after the successful strikes on Luzon, Formosa, and Okinawa, the Third Fleet and its fighting core, TF 38, were taking a rest. Ships were refueling and rearming, one group at a time. Admiral McCain's group was moving toward Ulithi to refuel, when word came from *Darter* and *Dace* of Kurita's approach.

Pacing the bridge with excitement at the news, Halsey ordered the remaining three carrier groups of TF 38 to pull in closer to the Philippines, and Burke began to work out battle plans. Before 0630 on the morning of October 24, carrier scout planes were away and looking for Kurita and his associates. Aircraft from Davison's group soon discovered the van of the Southern Force, and the rear echelon of the force was spotted a short time later. But at 0810, a flyer from one of Admiral Bogan's carriers found the big one. He sighted Kurita's Center Force just as it entered the Sibuyan Sea. At last, this was the big game Halsey had been waiting for.

At 0827, Halsey bypassed Mitscher and gave the order to all task group commanders to concentrate their air armada on Kurita's Center Force.

McCain, still steaming toward Ulithi, was ordered to reverse course and to refuel at sea. On October 24, Halsey sent five air strikes against Kurita, who had practically no air cover at all, and by afternoon TF 38 planes had hit four enemy battleships and put a heavy cruiser out of action. On the final attack, nineteen torpedoes and seventeen bombs hit the superbattleship *Musashi,* which capsized, sinking with one thousand men. In the late afternoon, Kurita suddenly appeared to give up his attack. He reversed course and sailed back west.

But tragedy had struck TF 38 during the battle over Sibuyan Sea. One reason that Kurita had enjoyed no air cover was because the Japanese air command on Luzon had decided to attack the ships of TF 38, not its planes. The main attack was directed against Admiral Sherman's task group. Sherman scrambled his fighters and moved in under a rain squall, and, as during the Battle of the Philippine Sea the previous June, the American pilots proved far superior to the enemy aviators. Just when the battle appeared to be over, however, a lone enemy dive bomber came out of the clouds undetected and bombed the light carrier *Princeton.* It proved to be an unlucky hit, for several torpedoes loaded in Avengers exploded, causing tremendous damage. Burke was on the bridge of *Lexington* when the *Princeton* was hit. He immediately maneuvered the group to cover her. By afternoon, it appeared to all that *Princeton's* firefighters were getting the blaze under control, and cruiser *Birmingham* pulled alongside to aid in the firefighting and to make preparations to take *Princeton* in tow.

Suddenly, the nearly tamed fire reached torpedo storage, and a fearful explosion blasted away most of *Princeton's* stern and after flight deck. The *Birmingham,* alongside, with most of her crew on deck, took a deadly rain of steel and fire. In an instant, everyone still aboard the *Princeton* was either dead or wounded. Worse yet, more than two hundred on the deck of *Birmingham* were dead; more than four hundred were injured. The deck of *Birmingham* was a scene of bloody horror. Burke watched and thought that *Birmingham's* skipper, Captain Thomas B. Inglis, did a wonderful job of handling his ship after the disaster. Eventually, Admiral Mitscher sadly gave the order to torpedo *Princeton* and watched, as the first carrier he had lost since TF 58/38 was organized slipped under the sea.

The *Princeton-Birmingham* tragedy was being played out far from the scene of major action that October day. In the Sibuyan Sea, the planes of TF 38 continued to smash at Admiral Kurita as he regrouped his fleet and reversed course. From all reports, Halsey assumed that Kurita's ships no longer were in condition for a major fight and that the Japanese Center Force was retiring from the scene of battle for good. As all were to learn subsequently, this was not quite the case. Despite almost continuous attacks by some 250 carrier-based planes, Kurita's force still was extremely powerful. But the Japanese admiral had lost confidence in his antiaircraft gunners;

he had sent a message to Toyoda, reporting that he was "temporarily" reversing course until a lull came in the attacks by TF 38 planes.

The lull came shortly. In the late afternoon, soon after Kurita had altered his course, Mitscher's scout bombers finally located the Northern Force of Ozawa, 190 miles to the north, and Mitscher passed the information along to Halsey. That evening, the fighting commander of the Third Fleet made a major combat decision, one which was to prove as controversial as the decision of Spruance to restrain Task Force 58 at Saipan the previous June.

Halsey looked at all the pieces on the chessboard. He decided that Admiral Kinkaid could handle the relatively weak Southern Force as it sailed through Surigao Strait. His pilots had reported that the Center Force appeared to be on the run and that its guns and communications were seriously crippled. In the north was an unknown, a fresh enemy, the Mobile Fleet of Admiral Ozawa. That it had been sent as a decoy, Halsey did not suspect; that it had but a handful of trained aviators, Halsey had no way of knowing. He did see an opportunity to sink Japan's carrier fleet—all of it—and he seized that opportunity. He gave the order to all the ships of the Third Fleet—three carrier groups and a force of battleships and cruisers under Admiral Lee—to sail north. He decided to attack Ozawa with all the weapons at his command, rather than let Ozawa come to him and risk the possibility of shuttle bombing by Ozawa's planes using Philippine airfields.

Aboard the *Lexington,* Burke also had worked out a battle plan, but he was to learn the hard way that superiors do not always listen to a Task Force Chief of Staff. Burke had made his own estimate of the strength of Ozawa's Northern Force, and he felt that the carriers could handle the job with only two battleships. The rest could be left behind under Admiral Lee to guard San Bernardino Strait, in case Kurita changed course and came on through in the night. But when Burke offered his plan to Mitscher, the flying admiral shook him off. "Admiral Halsey is very busy and I am not going to bother him with your plan," Mitscher said. Burke's arguments failed to move him.

As Mitscher prepared to turn in on the night of October 24, Burke made one last try. He told his boss that they had better find out where Kurita's Center Force was, and Mitscher agreed. Shortly thereafter, Burke received a report from a plane from *Independence,* stating that Kurita was *not* sailing west, but was sailing toward San Bernardino Strait. The report was confirmed later, and Burke and Jimmy Flatley hastened to awaken Mitscher. "Does Admiral Halsey have that report?" asked the Admiral. Flatley said that he did. "If he wants my advice, he'll ask for it," Mitscher said finally, and he went back to sleep. He felt that Halsey had taken tactical command and that he had been left out of the picture. Burke was not convinced,

130

however, and he stayed awake all night, working on plans, ready to fill a command vacuum if one occurred.

During the night, Halsey formed Task Force 34, an impressive Battle Line, which included all six of the battleships attached to Third Fleet. TF 34 set out in front of the three carrier task groups. On October 25, at dawn, 180 planes took off from American carriers to find the Northern Force. They located Ozawa's ships at 0800 and moved in for the attack.

But far from Burke's ken, in the south, other momentous events were taking place on October 25. As Halsey had anticipated, the Seventh Fleet had proved ample to repulse the Japanese Southern Force as it attempted to slip through Surigao Strait during the night. It had been more than repulsed; the enemy van had been annihilated in what may have been the last great line battle at sea.

But the rest of the news wasn't so encouraging. As Burke had feared, Kurita's Center Force had indeed "pulled up its socks" and sailed through San Bernardino Strait during the night. Kurita still hoped to meet the ships of the Southern Force and disrupt the invasion of Leyte. And Kurita's fleet still was Japan's most dangerous weapon afloat. The enemy admiral had correctly surmised that the disappearance of TF 38 planes during the previous afternoon meant that Halsey had finally discovered the decoy fleet of Admiral Ozawa and had sent units north to meet him. Kurita had no way of knowing, however, how many of his carriers Halsey had taken with him. He supposed that the Third Fleet had left a number of units behind to guard the approach to Leyte Gulf, and he was prepared for a major battle. Actually, the only thing in Kurita's way were three Seventh Fleet task units, comprised of little "jeep" or escort carriers, destroyers, and destroyer escorts. This was comparable to confronting a professional heavyweight contender with a Golden Gloves flyweight (novice class). For the eighteen-inch guns of the Japanese, the action that followed should have been a shooting gallery set-up—and a ghastly defeat for the American forces.

Japanese luck, however, had run out. Perhaps it would be more correct to say that Kurita was so demoralized by the smashing blows he had received from American submarines and TF 38's planes that he saw phantoms. Peering through the morning mist, he saw a destroyer screen of American vessels and he saw the decks of several baby flattops on the horizon, with aircraft taking off. After taking the previous day's pounding from TF 38 aircraft, it occurred to Kurita that these carriers in the mist must be part of Mitscher's dread Task Force, and he had learned that his own antiaircraft gunners appeared to suffer from myopia. It is understandable, therefore, that Kurita did not view the carriers on the horizon as the sitting ducks they really were. He believed that he faced a formidable foe.

The American escort carriers and destroyers knew very well what they were facing, from the moment that they received a terrified report from one of their search planes. They knew that Kurita's Center Force had come through the Strait after all, and that it was about to blow them out of the water with its big guns. Admiral Kinkaid sent a message to Halsey, far to the north, yelling for help. Burke's hair began to rise as he saw the message, and he told Mitscher that he believed the matter to be serious.

Had Kurita not been so alarmed and confused by what he thought he saw from the bridge of his flagship, the matter would have been very serious indeed. But Kurita gave poor commands; he failed to coordinate his ships and to order them into battle line. Meanwhile, a sudden rain squall gave cover to the group of American escort carriers, and American destroyers and destroyer escorts displayed reckless, almost suicidal, courage by dashing out to attack the monster ships of the Japanese fleet. In one run, they actually put a heavy cruiser out of action. Maneuvering to keep out of the way of the destroyers, Kurita's flagship *Yamato* managed to maneuver itself clear out of the battle picture, so that the fleet commander no longer could make any decisions from personal observation of the combat. The Japanese fleet took a heavy toll of U.S. destroyers and escorts, but our valiant ships took the brunt of the attack and saved the day. For suddenly, when the end seemed near for the escort carriers of the Seventh Fleet, Kurita's powerful fleet turned tail and sailed away over the horizon. The Americans simply couldn't believe their eyes.

Why Kurita turned away remained a mystery until after World War II, when it was learned that another phantom had engaged him. Manila had informed him that a major carrier force lay off Samar, and Kurita presumed that the force represented the main strength of Task Force 38. Kurita set out to find that force. He did not find it, of course, because it wasn't there. It was another ghost, one of many that conspired to haunt and frustrate the Japanese on October 25, 1944. By evening on that day, Kurita gave up looking and retired from the field of battle, sailing back through San Bernardino Strait. Eventually, planes of two TF 38 groups did catch up with the Center Force and drubbed it some more, but Kurita eventually escaped with four battleships, three cruisers, and seven destroyers.

Meanwhile, Burke was with TF 38 in the north, off Cape Engano, finally putting his own battle plans into operation. Starting with the first launch on the morning of October 25, Hellcats from Mitscher's carriers polished off enemy planes while bombers and torpedo planes sank a destroyer and a light carrier. Another cruiser was dead in the water, and still another was hit so hard that she slowed to ten knots.

Admiral Halsey, tasting blood at last, was moving in for the kill when messages to come to the rescue of the Seventh Fleet began to come in thick and fast. With great reluctance, Halsey turned his back on his opportunity to sink every ship in Ozawa's fleet and headed south with his battleships and one carrier group. McCain was ordered to knock off refueling and to hurry to the rescue as well. Mitscher and Burke stayed off Cape Engano to destroy what they could of the remainder of Ozawa's Mobile Force. At noon, they began a new round of air strikes, and by the end of the day, TF 38 planes had damaged one carrier severely, had sunk another light carrier, and had put a heavy carrier under the sea. Surface vessels sank a crippled light carrier and a destroyer, and a damaged cruiser was sunk by an American submarine as she attempted to slip away from the battle. Mitscher, Burke, and company then headed south.

Unfortunately, there was one more round in the Battle for Leyte Gulf, for the Japanese, at the recommendation of Vice Admiral Takijiro Ohnishi, commander of naval air forces in the Philippines, had selected this day to inaugurate a new kind of tactic against American ships. Faced with the prospect of fighting the veterans of TF 38 with poorly trained and inexperienced pilots, the enemy admiral had established a new Kamikaze Special Attack Corps. The name Kamikaze, which means Divine Wind, was taken from the typhoons which scattered Kublai Khan's invasion fleets in the thirteenth Century, but to Americans the word would always mean "suicide." The non-commissioned flyers who volunteered for Kamikaze service agreed to crash dive their planes, each armed with a 550-pound bomb, into the decks of American vessels. In effect, their planes became guided missiles with human guidance systems.

On October 25, pilots of the Special Attack Corps located escort carrier units of the Seventh Fleet and began to hurl themselves to certain death. By evening, one escort carrier—the *St. Lo*—had been sunk, and six escort carriers had been damaged. Arleigh Burke, still in the north mopping up on Ozawa's fleet, did not witness the Kamikaze attacks that day, but he was going to come to know the meaning of the Divine Wind all-too-well during the next eight months. The Japanese were to experience no difficulty in finding plenty of volunteers for suicide missions.

By the end of October 26, the Battle for Leyte Gulf was officially over. In terms both of distance covered and the number of ships involved, it had been the greatest sea battle in the history of the world. Despite missed opportunities and a few regrets, the battle also represented the most overwhelming Navy victory in our country's history. The Japanese were finished as a sea power in World War II after Leyte Gulf. They had only enough left for one last suicidal sortie, and that was many months away.

Burke, as one of the planners of this massive naval engagement, was both a participant and a privileged observer. As usual, part of his mind was committed to the battle; another part, a cool and analytical part, set itself off from the battle and appraised it. Burke could learn from his experiences; he could weigh them and profit from them, although he was not always aware of the importance of this process at the time. And, during

Leyte Gulf, he learned, among other things, something more about the art of combat command. Despite the calculated risks involved in the decisions made during Leyte Gulf, he still believed strongly in audacity—the kind of audacity which Halsey represented. "The paralysis of fear and uncertainty," he wrote, leads to indecision and poorly conceived plans.

But he also observed that "responsibility for parts of a plan must be set forth clearly so that all are aware of their individual responsibilities . . . there must be no doubt in anybody's mind as to who is responsible for what part of an operation."

After the battle, Mitscher called Burke to his cabin and said that he wanted his Chief of Staff to be promoted to Rear Admiral. Burke argued against the idea, convinced that a premature promotion might injure his career permanently. He was just forty-three. At last, a compromise was reached. Burke agreed to accept a wartime promotion to the temporary rank of Commodore (equivalent to Brigadier General in the Army). In a few days, Mitscher turned the Task Force over to Admiral McCain and Burke, now a flag officer, returned to Pearl Harbor with his boss for conferences and a much-needed rest.

From Pearl, Burke and the Admiral flew to San Diego, where they were to meet Mrs. Mitscher and travel together to Washington. As they waited for her plane to arrive, Mitscher told Burke that he would not be going to the capital just yet.

"I'm going to go fishing," confided the Admiral. He gave Burke a sealed envelope which contained directions on how to reach Mitscher in case of emergency.

"Don't open it unless you have to," insisted Mitscher. "Then you can tell Secretary Forrestal truthfully that you don't know where I am."

After Mrs. Mitscher arrived, the Admiral asked Burke if there was anything special he'd like to have aboard his plane to Washington.

Burke didn't hesitate. "I'd like some tomatoes and fresh milk and ice cream and a pretty girl to serve them," he replied.

The Admiral laughed and turned away, and Burke boarded his flight to Washington and went to sleep. After a couple of hours, he felt somebody shaking his arm. Opening his eyes, he stared into the beautiful eyes of one of the most lovely Waves he had ever seen.

"I've brought your tomatoes and milk, sir," she smiled. After months of combat, the States looked too good to be true.

Upon arriving in Washington, Commodore Burke reported to stiff, rough Admiral King and discussed the operations of Task Force 58/38 with the testy CNO. After several minutes of talking, Admiral King suddenly broke out the operation order for TF 38. Unlike most op-orders, which were thick, voluminous documents, this was a thin one, reflecting a new style developed by Burke. A commander could tear off a single page of

Burke's streamlined op-order and have a week's operating schedule. Burke explained that the system gave task group commanders a lot of leeway, but the ex-destroyer sailor happened to believe in giving leeway, if he had faith in his men.

But all that failed to interest Admiral King. It was another feature of the op-order which held his attention. Burke had a habit of spicing up the covers of his orders with cartoons. Occasionally, they were political or military cartoons; sometimes, they were simply decorative. The cover of the particular op-order which Admiral King clutched in his hand was of the decorative variety, and female decoration at that. The Admiral pointed at the girls with ill-concealed fury.

"Did you write this op-order?" King asked.

"Admiral Mitscher signed that op-order," hedged Burke.

"I said did you write this op-order?" repeated King.

"You are holding Admiral Mitscher's op-order," Burke replied.

"Damn it," barked King. "I asked you if *you* wrote it."

"Yes, sir," Burke admitted.

"Well, just look at this thing," King shouted. "It's terrible. It lacks dignity. Look at those girls' pictures. Don't you know we are fighting a war?"

"Yes, sir," replied Commodore Burke, stiffening his back. "We are fighting a war." The CNO continued to dress down Burke for some five minutes until he had to pause to catch his breath.

Burke moved in for the attack. "Do you remember Admiral Turner's op-order in the amphibious forces?" he asked innocently.

"No," said King.

Burke asked if the Admiral would mind sending for it. It was brought in, a fat, thick document.

"Admiral, you haven't read this op-order, have you?" queried Burke.

King admitted that he hadn't.

"But you have read ours," Burke bored in.

"Yes, damn it," barked King.

"That's the reason for the pretty girls on the cover," said Burke, concealing his triumph. "All of our op-orders are read. Nobody reads Admiral Turner's."

King stared at Commodore Burke for several minutes before he could speak, while Burke waited for the CNO's reaction.

"Okay," said King finally. "Let it go, let it go." Burke felt the same sudden relief as he did when *Lexington* repulsed an enemy attack. He left, met Bobbie at last, and began a month's leave. Burke had earned the rest.

He was awarded a Gold Star in lieu of the Second Legion of Merit for his conduct as Chief of Staff during the preceding eight months. His citation read in part: "An inspiring and courageous leader, discharging his many and complex responsibilities with distinction, Commodore Burke skillfully planned and executed a long series of successful offensive operations in support of the reduction of the outer perimeter of Japanese defenses in New Guinea, the Carolines, the Marianas, Balmahera, and the Philippine Islands. Largely as a result of Commodore Burke's superb professional skill, tireless energy, and coolness of decision throughout these operations and during repeated air attacks carried out in strength against heavily fortified strongholds in enemy-controlled waters, the Pacific Fleet has been brought within range of the Japanese Empire itself to continue our relentless drive against the enemy."

Early in December, Burke parted from Bobbie once again to return to combat. In San Francisco, he met Mitscher and Jimmy Flatley, and they took him up to Mom Chung's place. Mom was a Chinese physician who had started adopting aviators with Chennault's Flying Tigers and had been at it ever since. Submariners followed aviators in her affections, and she tried to have something left over for surface sailors, too. Every Sunday night, she held a cocktail hour and dinner for "her boys."

As drinks were served, Mom Chung extolled the virtues of several recently returned submarine officers who were present and held a ceremony to make Admiral Mitscher one of her "beloved bastards." Jimmy Flatley had been so honored on an earlier visit. As Burke settled back into a corner, one of Mom's visitors spotted him and began to tell her about 31-Knot Burke's adventures as a destroyer squadron commander in the Solomons. Mom Chung was impressed, and she then and there dubbed the surface sailor a "Kiwi, number 246," which she defined for all those assembled as "exceptionally good bastard material, but one who does not fly." After dinner, Mom took Burke into her trophy room full of enemy souvenirs and presented him with a leather memo pad engraved with the following: "Commodore A. A. Burke. My beloved son, Kiwi 246." Burke was pleased, but he was also embarrassed by all the attention and felt that he was riding on Mitscher's shoulders.

On December 15, after he and Flatley had arrived in Pearl Harbor, Burke received a Christmas present from Mom. Like all her "sons" across the ocean, he received a good bottle of whisky, a silver ring, and a Christmas card with a plane at the top, a submarine at the bottom, and a picture of Christ in between, with the message: "May the Lord watch between thee and me while we are absent, one from the other." Inside the card was a flattering picture of his benefactress, with the following additional message: "May God always ride with you as co-pilot. May you always have blue skies, fair weather, smooth sailing, and happy landings. Wherever you are, my prayers for your safety and my love wing their way to you. Devotedly, Mom Chung."

There was still more. On the back of the card were the qualifications for becoming one of her "fair-haired bastards." They called for "a good guy, who can fly, who's not afraid to die; a courageous man who is loyal, tolerant; a square man who contributes to the progress and glory of aviation, who makes the world a better place because he lives."

Those were sentimental times, but they were also times of valor. Mom Chung was not only a physician, Burke discovered; she was an excellent psychologist.

After returning to Hawaii, Burke, Flatley, Gus Read, Dingfelder, Bob North, and others on the staff immediately were plunged into their most involved operational planning assignment to date. These were the plans for striking the Japanese mainland, and the staff took only one break—to welcome 1945. Soon after New Year's Day, Admiral Mitscher arrived, and a weary Burke and staff presented him with a superb set of plans. The Carrier Task Force was ready to go back to work.

But there were delays, as there always are in war. For Burke, ever restless and impatient, the waiting was always the hardest. His letters to Bobbie revealed his growing irritation.

"I went home after curfew," he wrote her on January 9 from Pearl Harbor, "and discovered that, as a commodore, I'm old enough to be out at night . . . Aside from that and being able to find my hat in a crowd, I have found no advantages to being a commodore."

Like so many other men in war who must face periods of inactivity, Burke turned his energy inward and gave himself a good working over. He worried about gaining weight. He worried about boring people with talk, and he observed in a letter home that "when I eat too much I talk too much." He lost a friend—a surface sailor—by praising aviators too much at dinner. And he decided that he was "too old, too stiff" to become an aviator himself. On January 13, after turning the plans over to Mitscher, Burke wrote Bobbie: "I find I'm bitter against most everything now . . . I am working on the edge of the big league, as it is usually referred to, and know I don't belong and never will."

But a day later, his irritation had increased to include not only himself, but those around him as well.

"We have so many socially inclined boys on the staff . . ." he told Bobbie in another long letter. "As a matter of fact, our staff is about one-fourth workers, one-fourth social, one-fourth experts, and one-fourth observers. I have never had so many drones in my hair before. I don't like it, since I'm not always available to explain things to people who have nothing to do but sight-see."

In a few more days, however, he developed some insight into the cause of his melancholy. "There isn't much to do out here now," he wrote, "but there will be soon."

In a letter on January 20, 1945, he wrote wistfully: "It will also be

137

good to be doing something besides pushing papers around. What I really mean, I guess, is that I'm no social staff officer. I can't play bridge, or golf, or horseshoes, or anything. I'll be glad to go to work, since I feel I've deteriorated quite a bit in the last few months—both physically and mentally. Maybe I can feel useful again by and by."

Orders finally came. Halsey's Task Force 38 was retired to paper, and Mitscher again took over Task Force 58, serving once more under Admiral Spruance, who was in command of the Fifth Fleet. The Task Force was assembled at Ulithi, where officers and men got some additional rest before striking the Japanese home islands.

From his Ulithi anchorage, Burke wrote Bobbie: "We are back home again, not in the same ship, but at sea. We have been here several days, days of long hard work and days in which I don't seem to do too well— nor do I know exactly why—except I'm a little slow in getting started. High-pressure work usually takes a little building up and we started off in high gear with no idling period . . ."

But as the waiting continued at Ulithi during the first part of February, Burke once again found time heavy on his hands. His boredom communicated itself to Mitscher.

"I told the Admiral today I wasn't so much interested in how far I went in the Navy, as when I could retire on $300 a month," wrote the future Chief of Naval Operations to his wife on February 1. "I don't think the Admiral understood it—or believed I meant it—but I do. Sometime I'd like not to have any schedules to meet on any work that had to be done . . . and very little responsibility."

By February 9, his restlessness had increased to the point that he had the chaplain send him two back issues of *Collier's* magazine and a copy of *Forever Amber*. The following day, Burke set sail from Ulithi at last, now aboard a new flagship, *Bunker Hill*. The first mission was a thrilling one: to strike Tokyo with carrier-based aircraft in the first such attack since the Doolittle raid. The purpose of the mission was to distract the Japanese from another event which would take place simultaneously; the invasion of Iwo Jima.

With typical daring, Mitscher took his Task Force to a point only sixty miles off the shore of Honshu before he launched his planes on February 16. But weather proved an even more treacherous enemy than the Japanese, and Burke's plans for a major and telling strike went awry. Despite storms, however, TF 58 planes managed to destroy forty or fifty enemy planes, and they put a few furrows in Japanese airfields. In addition, the raids distracted the enemy for a short time from the bombardment of Iwo Jima, which also began on February 16. After the strike on Honshu, Task Force 58 turned and raced to Iwo to help.

The forces attacking Iwo Jima needed all the help they could get. Victory was going to be costly on this small island, and as late as March 25, the Marines would still be killing Japanese. For a few days after the landing, TF 58 carrier planes gave the Marines valuable support.

"The Marines are doing their usual fine job—as are the flyers," Burke wrote Bobbie, without identifying the engagement in which he was involved. "The planned dope is going all right, and except for a few minor but spectacular busts, I'm doing fair. (*Author's note: Evidently a reference to the miscarriage of the Tokyo raids.*) Truth to say, I'm not a good staff officer, nor, I feel frequently, a particularly good naval officer. I'll certainly be glad when this war is over and maybe I can command a station ship someplace until it comes time to retire—and even before then I'm going to take things very easily."

On February 21, Burke finally saw the Japanese suicide squadrons in action, when the heavy carrier *Saratoga*, attached to the Amphibious Support Force for night operations, was hit by three Kamikaze bombers. *Saratoga* was one of five ships hit that night; the smaller escort carrier *Bismarck Sea* was sunk. Commodore Burke set his jaw. Now it was his turn to see one of his more audacious plans put into action.

After supporting the invasion of Iwo for four days, Task Force 58 returned to a position off Honshu to participate with two hundred land-based B-29 bombers in a massive raid on Tokyo and surrounding airfields. While the new long-range bombers dropped incendiaries and burned out two square miles of the Japanese capital, Mitscher's planes knocked down 150 enemy planes. The raid was a smashing success, and Burke's morale soared.

"The plans went much better than we thought they would," he admitted in a letter home after this raid. "I hope that it will continue to be so— but there is a lot to do yet. Perhaps in another six months the Japs will commence to get a taste of what war is really like, and a year from *there,* perhaps they will have had enough."

Following the Tokyo raid, TF 58 returned to Ulithi, its Pacific anchorage, to prepare for the next major invasion. The next target was Okinawa, by far the largest island yet to be invaded in the push across the central Pacific. Everyone knew that Okinawa would not fall in a matter of days, and everyone knew that the suicide pilots would be waiting for the American ships when the invasion began.

Preparations for Okinawa occupied TF 58 for a couple of weeks, and Burke once again had time to compose long letters home. Once, he attempted to explain to his wife exactly what it was that a Chief of Staff did for a carrier task force.

"Much of the fighting leaves me as an onlooker," he penned, in his boyish hand. "Usually by the time a fight starts, my work is done. Most of my headaches come weeks ahead.

"When the fight actually starts, there isn't much I can do about it—

or anybody else over here . . . Usually in one fight I'm working hard to win the next one, which sometimes isn't over ten minutes away. That's where the wear and tear on husbands come in—the decisions to dispose for the next battle at the expense of the present one."

A couple of days later—shortly before the Task Force was to sail, Burke was invited to a beer bust. He accepted joyously, for it was like a homecoming game and a family reunion, all rolled into one.

"At last the destroyer sailors took pity on me and asked me to a party," he wrote Bobbie. "It was good to be among friends again. It was good to sit on a smoky, dirty island and throw beer bottles about and not have anybody try to wear me down. Mostly it's good to be among people whose language I understand and who are not always panning somebody."

Burke still would have traded his Commodore's hat for a destroyer command once more.

On March 18 and 19, Task Force 58 helped open the Okinawa campaign with massive raids against airfields on Kyushu in the Japanese home islands and against what was left of the Imperial Navy in the Inland Sea. The enemy fought back desperately, bombing carriers *Enterprise, Yorktown, Wasp,* and *Franklin.* The latter was seriously hurt; it was a miracle that she remained afloat. The Japanese also shot down 116 American planes.

"Things are going fairly well, although due to many things not exactly according to plan," Burke told Bobbie. "The Japs have and are taking quite a beating . . . but even bad beatings cost . . . I'm still very sleepy. I still feel as if I'm working in a strange league without friends, and also feel that I'm not doing too well at it."

On March 23, TF 58 began its pre-assault strikes on Okinawa. D-Day was set for April 1, and the day before, a suicide bomber dove into the *Indianapolis,* flagship of Admiral Spruance, and Spruance had to find other quarters. By April 5, enemy bombers and suicide planes had damaged thirty-nine vessels, including an escort carrier, and the following day, a giant force of 355 suicide-bent pilots took off from Kyushu to hit TF 58. Despite valiant efforts of American flyers and gunners, the few planes that got through sank a destroyer transport, an LST, two loaded ammunition ships, and damaged twenty-two other vessels.

But the Imperial Navy was strangely quiet during these furious air battles. Burke had not forgotten that Kurita had sailed away from the Battle for Leyte Gulf in the largest battleship in the world, *Yamato. Yamato* was still afloat and still a menace to the U.S. Navy.

In a prophetic letter to Bobbie dated March 31, 1945, Commodore Burke speculated on the plans of the enemy fleet. "The Japs are fighting hard," he wrote. "They are bewildered and desperate, but they still fight. Perhaps this action will bring out their Navy in their last banzai charge.

We have been wondering what they will do. Their minds work so curiously that it is very hard to predict future movements, and, as a consequence, our own counter movements. So far we have won in the preliminary moves in this massive game of chess . . . I hope I can pump up enough energy to think of some good attack procedures."

The enemy, indeed, was nearly ready for that "last banzai charge." On April 6, just one week after Burke wrote his speculative letter home, the monster *Yamato* (she displaced seventy thousand tons) sortied from the Inland Sea, accompanied by the light cruiser *Yahagi* and eight destroyers. The men aboard *Yamato* had been told that they were on their way to fight the decisive battle of the Pacific War. Most had not been told that *Yamato* carried only enough fuel oil for a one-way trip to Okinawa, and that it was the intention of the fleet commander to fire upon the invasion beaches until the planes of Task Force 58 destroyed his ships. But while he distracted Mitscher, he believed that the suicide planes might have a chance to frustrate the Navy support forces. *Yamato* was taking a desperate, suicidal course, and as the great ship prepared to sail, and the navigator raised his sake cup in the traditional toast, the cup slipped from his nervous fingers and shattered on the deck. All hands interpreted this as an evil omen; as perhaps it was.

For on the first afternoon out, on April 6, the passage of *Yamato* was duly noted by two American submarines. The subs flashed a warning and Admiral Spruance alerted a battleship force to attack *Yamato* on April 7. But TF 58 did not intend to wait. After receiving the submarine's report, Burke worked all night with his charts and calipers to determine where *Yamato* might be by daylight. Then, he hastily drew up a battle plan and at dawn Mitscher sent off his search planes to find the Japanese fleet.

A British observer aboard *Bunker Hill* didn't understand. He wondered how Burke could be quite so sure of *Yamato's* location.

"We are launching against the spot where we would be if we were *Yamato*," Burke told him airily. Sure enough, TF 58 planes relocated the enemy force at 0800, and it was kept under constant surveillance from then on. At 1000, Mitscher launched his air group; nearly four hundred planes were launched in all.

Shortly after noon, when the silver-gray, "unsinkable," *Yamato* was halfway to Okinawa, the carrier planes appeared, circling in a clockwise direction, to put Burke's battle plan into operation. *Yamato* and companions opened fire and began to maneuver. The planes swept down on the super-battleship.

In the first aerial attack, a torpedo hit *Yamato* forward in the port side; two bombs hit aft. The great ship stayed afloat, without even a list. In the second attack, there were more bomb hits and *Yamato* took three torpedo hits on the port side. Torpedo planes also machine-gunned the bridge. The attacks appeared to have no effect. In the third wave, torpedo planes made five more direct hits, and, for the first time, the mighty *Yamato* began to list slightly. To restore balance, the Japanese commander ordered sea water pumped into the starboard engine and boiler rooms, drowning his crew in those spaces in violent churn of cold sea water and steam and boiling water from burst boilers.

Still another attack came from the sky. *Yamato* suffered more torpedo hits and more than ten bombs burst on her decks. All communications were knocked out; there was no radio. *Yahagi*, the lone cruiser in the force, was sunk and several destroyers were hit.

A fifth wave of carrier planes concentrated on *Yamato's* rudder. After that, *Yamato's* crew lost track of the hits. The world's largest fighting ship listed 35 degrees to port, and the electric power failed. Still more hits on the port side, and *Yamato* finally capsized. As the bilge keel rolled skyward, a group of survivors gave three cheers for His Imperial Majesty. A misty rain began to fall as the battleship sank. As the carrier planes left the scene of destruction, *Yamato, Yahagi,* and four destroyers were under the sea, and a fifth destroyer was on fire and dead in the water.

Commenting on this terrible day in a note to Bobbie, Burke wrote briefly: "Another battle down . . . This was a most remarkable one, for they came out to die—and die they did—without being able to inflict enough damage for the effort, let alone for the loss of their ships. The plans worked once again . . ."

But while the last remnants of the Imperial Navy had vanished, the suicide planes continued to come in seemingly inexhaustible supply. The terrible raid of April 6 and 7 was to prove to be the first of ten massive strikes which would take place during the next few months. The suicide raids would take the lives of 1,465 Japanese aviators and as many planes, but the Japanese would manage to sink twenty-six ships and damage 164. More than 3,500 Navy men would lose their lives as a result of the kamikaze attacks at Okinawa.

Burke's letters home during April 1945 reflected the strain of battle. "This has been a fantastic war, but we are whittling the Japs down, and though we don't expect to see them crack, it is possible. Very shortly they should be impotent at sea and in the air . . ."

"Would you like a battle report? It would start: the battle continues, forever and ever it seems. Suicides, torpedo planes, dive bombers, fighters, but they are losing a terrific percentage of the planes put against us, and if it continues, they will eventually use up all their planes and pilots . . ."

"The same old pace is being set. It's monotonous now—and it seems perfectly natural that people should always get up at 0330 and be called twenty times during the night."

"The war goes on and on, some battles nearly every day. Some are pretty heartbreaking in spite of us winning them all. Battles cost . . ."

It was on an April evening that Burke was listening on the circuits and heard "one of those freak communications things." It was a destroyer at one of the picket stations off Okinawa, and she was under attack.

What Burke heard, with a suffocating sensation of mingled horror and pride, was the destroyer's combat information officer reporting on damage to his ship. The officer, an ensign, stated that the bridge was demolished, the captain was killed, the executive officer was killed, the engineering officer was killed. The number one gun was blown out; the ship was listing badly. So far as he could determine, he was the only officer who remained alive on the ship, and he had taken command.

Clammy with sweat, Burke listened to the matter-of-fact recitation, as the officer reported all his casualties and added that he had two guns left in operating condition. He could still make about five knots, still make steerage way, he said.

Then he completed his battle report with words that would remain in Burke's memory for years to come, words that would keep trying to tell him something about the meaning of the U.S. Navy.

"I am an Ensign," said the voice. "I have only been on this ship for a little while. I have been in the Navy for only a little while. I will fight this ship to the best of my ability and forgive me for the mistakes I am about to make."

Then, as Burke listened transfixed, the destroyer was sunk. Burke never learned the man's identity, but he could never forget him.

There were few light moments during that exhausting spring off Okinawa, and the few that there were had macabre overtones. One day, as the *Bunker Hill* was under attack by suicide planes, Burke felt a slight chill and sent the steward for his "jacket." The nervous steward hurried back in a few minutes, in full view of both officers and men, carrying a rubber life jacket for Commodore Burke. Burke looked at the frozen faces of the men staring at him, then leaned back and laughed. The faces relaxed into smiles. The *Bunker Hill* was not hit—not that day.

She *was* hit on May 11. Two kamikazes blasted into the flagship, only moments apart; the second of the suicide planes flamed into the ship's island, close to where Mitscher stood. Burke got everyone out of Flag Plot and helped Dingfelder get his radiomen out of a smoke-filled compartment. Thirteen of the flag staff were dead, including three officers and ten enlisted men.

The flag staff transferred to a new flagship, *Enterprise,* but on May 14 she was hit with a tremendous explosion by a suicide plane. For the second time in three days, Burke transferred to a new flagship, *Randolph.* On May 19, he hinted to Bobbie that something had happened but said that "it is a little early to tell you about it, except that we are now graduates of the complete course in suicides, including the postgraduate course."

On May 20, the news was out in the States, and Burke wrote a more complete letter home:

"We were in *Bunker Hill* when she was hit. A good many of our staff were killed, including Charlie Steele, and many others were wounded, and some suffered from shock. Frank (or no, that was the next time) . . . We were hit by two planes . . . The fires were pretty bad, smoke was bad, and many people suffocated. The ship was saved by some courageous fire fighting. I was proud of our flag division. They did well and helped more than could be imagined . . . There were some fine stories of bravery came out of that burning, exploding mess with gasoline fires all over the decks . . . and tremendous explosions caused by our own bombs and ammunition exploding . . . The story of young Anderson—who is now taking Charlie's place as he (Andy) fought fires in the hangar deck and gradually, by pure guts and will power, brought them under control—of (Lieutenant B. R.) White and (Lieutenant E. C.) Cheston who also fought fires and brought out suffocated men. Of Frank Dingfelder, who went down after his radiomen and brought them out—and nearly didn't get out himself. There are many such stories. These men are wonderful."

"We finally transferred to *Enterprise*, Bud Hall's ship . . . stayed there two days, and one bright morning off Japan we were attacked by many Jap planes. One got through and hit *Enterprise*. The same story again, only because we didn't have so many men, we didn't lose so many. Also, it wasn't quite so bad. Frank was wounded, but not seriously. We—he and I—were standing on the lookout platform when it came in. Of course, we hit the deck, and I think the piece of metal that hit Frank was one that passed over me. We had more wounded and quite a few more shock— and then we transferred again to another flagship and are now in *Randolph*. These bastards take a lot of killing."

As usual, Burke was too modest to describe his own activities aboard *Bunker Hill* and *Enterprise* when they were hit. The citation accompanying Burke's Silver Star Medal tells that part of the story:

"For distinguishing himself conspicuously by gallantry and intrepidity in action with the enemy while serving as Chief of Staff of Commander First Carrier Task Force, Pacific on 11 May 1945. When the flagship on which he was embarked was hit by two enemy suicide dive bombers, he proceeded to a compartment in which personnel were trapped by fires and heavy smoke, and with complete disregard for his own safety, succeeded in evacuating all hands. He then arranged for transfer of the staff to another flagship and on 14 May, when this ship in turn was hit by a suicide plane, he set an inspiring example of coolness and courage, and again arranged for the expeditious transfer of the staff to a new flagship. In spite

144

of all difficulties, he maintained tactical control of the Task Force . . ."

Commodore Burke also received a Commendation Ribbon for his work on May 11 in saving the lives of his fellow officers. "His conduct," that citation reads, "was at all times in keeping with the highest traditions of the United States Naval Service."

But all men—even 31-Knot Burke—reach a limit to their stamina and endurance. After boarding *Randolph,* Burke wrote Bobbie: "If I can only get enough sleep I can keep going, and that's about all anybody can do. I'm tired, more tired than fearful, for fear is quickly over . . . I am convinced that any possibility of leave is only a dream." But on May 27, Admiral Halsey again took over the main force of the Pacific Fleet from Admiral Spruance, and Mitscher and his staff were told they could head for home. By May 29, the *Randolph* was sailing for Guam, with Burke, Flatley, Read, North, Dingfelder, and the rest of those who had lived through the battle off Okinawa. *Randolph* left the fleet, Burke wrote: "Tomorrow morning I sleep in after 0330. Do you know what it feels like to be able to sleep? I don't . . ."

From Guam, Burke flew to Pearl Harbor in Halsey's private plane. After thirty-one months of service in combat zones, Commodore Arleigh Burke was out of the shooting war, for the struggle with Japan was drawing toward its explosive climax. Burke would not again be concerned with war in the Pacific until the action in Korea.

CHAPTER 9

A Mind of His Own

Men reach the limit of their ability to grow at different ages. One man hits his stride at twenty-three; another does not reach possession of his full powers until thirty-six; still another man's destiny does not take shape until he passes forty. At the end of World War II, despite a chestful of medals and one of the most dazzling combat records in the U.S. Navy, Burke was in some ways still maturing, still was ripening, still was developing into the leader to come.

Like many complex men who must create their own view of the world, Burke needed time to think as well as to act. The battle of the Pacific had been his supreme test as an officer, but experience had piled on experience so quickly, as the events of the war unfolded, that Burke had enjoyed no time to reflect and to apply what he had learned. Burke was a man of action, but he was part intellectual, too. His adventures in the Pacific would not be completely meaningful for him until he had spent some time considering them.

When he got time, Burke, now a Captain again with the wartime rank of Commodore abolished, prepared a series of "after battle" reports, which he passed around inside Navy circles. In each report, he analyzed an engagement, much as a bridge champion reviews the playing of a tricky hand, and suggested ways in which the tactics might have been improved. After the war, some of the top Navy brass read these reports and lifted their eyebrows. Burke was showing them that he could do more than lead men and win battles; he could think and he could write as well. He began to be a marked man.

In an organization like the Navy, there are practically no skyrocket ascents to public notice and acclaim. The Navy takes its time in training a man, examining him, testing him, and allowing him to test himself. The Navy gives a leader enough room to master himself, and after the war Burke still was seeking the resolution of a number of internal clashes. The struggle of the man of action versus the intellectual was only one. There were a number of contradictions. Burke could be demanding and impatient; but he also was self-critical to the extreme, as a number of his letters have indicated. He insisted that those around him measure up to their own capabilities; he did not like to see a man sell himself short. At the same time, however, he drove himself more sternly than he ever drove a subordinate; his personal drive for improvement frequently left him temporarily exhausted. The former Colorado ranch boy set high standards for himself.

Burke was filled with restless energy; he was supremely devoted to the Navy and to his country. He also could know the taste of discouragement and ponder the benefits of retirement. Burke needed to be of use to the Navy; it was essential for him to put his gifts to work, because work was the only reality he recognized. It is possible that the battles which were waged inside Captain Burke are those which are waged frequently inside emerging leaders in the United States of America. In America, there is no aristocracy to give a young man the assurance that he is a natural-born leader. Achievement means everything in the United States, and, as a result, rising young men must test themselves continuously. They question their right to command others, as no Old World aristocrat would think of doing. They criticize themselves more harshly than any of their superiors would dare to do.

Following the war, as Burke's war record and written reports marked him for important missions, the Armed Forces unification battle began to take shape. President Truman and General Marshall favored merging the Army and Navy, but the admirals feared that the identity and effectiveness of the Navy would vanish under such a scheme. Among other things, they believed that the Army Air Force would control and neglect Navy Air. In the fighting against absolute merger which followed, the Department of Defense was created, along with the partial "unification" of today, which permits each service to maintain its own identity.

Burke, who was serving a brief stint in late 1945 as head of the Bureau of Ordnance's Research and Development Division, was hand-picked for an important role in drafting Navy plans for the pending unification battle, but Admiral Mitscher suddenly intervened. The former Task Force commander, who had so resented Burke's arrival on his ship less than two years before, now refused to consider anybody else but Burke for the post of Chief of Staff of the Eighth Fleet, Mitscher's new command. Shortly, Mitscher would be given command of the Atlantic Fleet, and Burke would stay with him to the end.

It may have proved fortunate that Burke did not become involved in the unification squabble in 1947. Serving with Mitscher once more, under peacetime conditions, gave him the time to reflect that he needed so desperately. The job also helped his self-respect, for Burke never considered himself much of a dry-land sailor. He couldn't help thinking that a Navy man belonged on a ship at sea.

In February 1947, Admiral Mitscher died, and Burke was called back to Washington. On his way back home, however, he became a peacetime casualty. In Trinidad, where he left the flagship *Pocono,* he squired around the wife of the Governor, a young woman who suffered terribly from arthritis. She accepted her infirmity with courage, however, and with Burke's assistance toured the battleship *Missouri* with the best of them. After a dinner party aboard the battleship, Burke saw her to the dock, an operation which required helping the young woman up a ladder. Burke bent down from the dock to help her, and felt something give way in his back. He saw the Governor's wife to her waiting car, then turned and passed out cold on the dock. His trouble was diagnosed as a slipped disc.

Burke flew back to Washington from Trinidad in excruciating pain, recalling that he had a speaking engagement to make in two days before a banquet of the Society of Naval Engineers. A youthful physician in the Sick Bay told Burke to forget about making his speech, but Burke insisted that he *had* to fulfill the engagement.

"All right," said the doctor. "I'll put a local anesthetic into your back. Then I'll get a room at the hotel and meet you there before the banquet with some pills to deaden the pain some more."

Burke wanted to know if the pills wouldn't make him too dopey to speak.

"Probably," admitted the doctor. "So about fifteen minutes before you start to speak, I'll give you a shot of stimulant. That will wake you up enough to say what you have to say. But you are going to be just like Cinderella. You are going to have to leave the ball on time. The minute you begin to feel a twinge of pain, get out of that banquet room, because your back will be worse than ever when all this stuff wears off."

That night, Burke took his shot of anesthetic and hobbled to the Statler in Washington. There, the doctor loaded him with sedatives, and advised the Captain to avoid alcohol, conversation, and food. Burke nodded sleepily through dinner, then trotted out for the shot to wake him up. The medical mumbo-jumbo worked. Burke was stimulated in the nick of time and rose to make an excellent speech. Amid applause, he sat down again, waiting for everything in his back to pull loose.

He waited for five minutes. Nothing happened. Ten minutes. Still nothing. His physician, like Cinderella's coachman, waited anxiously in the wings. Burke wiggled his back tentatively. Still nothing. He smiled and decided to try a highball. It was good. He turned to his host and said that he had reconsidered and would like to have some food after all. He demolished a hearty meal and tried wiggling his back again. Still no pain.

His back never bothered him again.

Burke's new assignment in Washington was on the Navy's General Board. By tradition a drowsy kind of club, the Board's function was to advise the Navy on its plans for the future. In practice, the Board accomplished little, but Burke managed to pump some new life into the organization. One reporter said that Burke "zipped into the General Board like a bee buzzing through a pasture of grazing cattle." He put the Board to work on a ten-year projection of the Navy and its relation to world affairs and military power.

Captain Burke had that assignment for fifteen months. In the latter part of 1948, he commanded the U.S.S. *Huntington* and participated in a goodwill cruise. It was Captain Burke's practice, a fellow officer aboard *Huntington* recalls, to call the crew aft at certain intervals and explain the ship's mission to them. The skipper invited and answered questions, and some of the sessions were spirited ones. Burke was putting to practice his growing belief in the value of communication between officers and men.

In December, 1948, Burke suddenly was appointed as an assistant chief of naval operations and returned to Washington. Waiting for him was a job which plunged him up to the ears in a bitter inter-service feud and nearly cost him his career in the Navy.

The Navy was far from happy with unification. A new Secretary of Defense, Louis Johnson, had replaced a pro-Navy man, James Forrestal. Secretary Johnson definitely was not pro-Navy. He favored strategic air power, and he promptly cancelled construction of the supercarrier *United States*. Secretary of the Navy John Sullivan resigned in protest and Francis Matthews, a man felt by Navy aviators to be unsympathetic to their side, was appointed to fill Sullivan's job.

The Admirals, particularly those who were former aviators, decided that it was up to them to save the Navy from extinction. A special information unit was created to develop policies, information, and defensive plays to support the Navy's position—a position that played up the role of carrier-based aircraft and played down the role of long-range strategic bombers, like the Air Force B-36. The unit was dubbed Operation-23, and it was to head Op-23 that Burke was recalled from the cruiser *Huntington*.

It wasn't long before the admirals were making speeches all over the country, describing the Navy aviator's position clearly and forcefully. The press was full of Navy stories. Navy Secretary Matthews was angry, and he was even angrier when he learned about the existence of Op-23. Late one afternoon, as Burke and his staff were preparing to leave for the day, Navy inspectors "raided" the offices of Op-23. Incredible though it seems, the inspectors actually refused to permit Captain Burke and those under him to go home. All were held incommunicado the entire night while inspectors frantically searched the files. The raiders, however, found nothing that they did not already know.

149

It appeared to Burke, who was being forcibly detained, that he was under arrest, but inspectors were careful *not* to ask him to turn over his sword. He kept his sword, and the Navy has not officially termed the "battle of Op-23" an arrest.

Captain Burke couldn't have been more furious if he had been arrested. The following morning, when the inspectors departed, he stormed into the offices of Secretary Matthews and demanded the right to see his boss. When Matthews eventually admitted him, Burke wanted to know why the Secretary had taken such an insulting and outrageous course of action. "If you wanted to know what I had in my files, I would gladly have told you," Burke said. He admitted that he supplied material for admirals' speeches, but he insisted that he supplied material for all kinds of speeches. "We are all on the same team here," he told Matthews.

The battle between the Navy and the Air Force over the future of carrier aviation finally exploded into national headlines. A civilian naval aide to the Secretary of the Navy wrote a memorandum hinting that the B-36 bomber was a weapon of dubious value and that politicians had foisted it on the American taxpayer. The aide was suspended, and later took back what he had written.

Then a Marine Captain risked his career by charging publicly that the offensive power of the Navy was being ruined. In early October, 1949, the captain handed the press confidential copies of three highly charged letters to Secretary Matthews. Authors of the letters were Admiral Louis Denfeld, Chief of Naval Operations; Admiral Arthur Radford, Commander in Chief of the Pacific Fleet; and Vice Admiral Gerald Bogan, formerly of Task Force 38 and now Commander of the First Task Fleet, Pacific. While their statements differed in particulars, the general view was that the Marine Captain was right, that the Navy was being stripped of its power, and that the Air Force was selling the country a false bill of goods. The sensational disclosure of these letters led to the Marine's suspension and a major investigation of the Navy-Air Force controversy by the House Armed Services Committee. As head of Op-23, it was Burke's job to brief the Navy witnesses.

The Navy's position in late 1949 was that carrier planes could carry atomic bombs to the enemy quite as effectively as long-range bombers, and that the mobility of carriers could prevent the enemy from finding the source of attack. The Navy also insisted that carriers were a powerful weapon against the chief weapon of the Soviet Navy, the submarine, as well as against surface craft. In addition, the admirals had reason to believe that the Army wanted to absorb the Marine Corps, and the Navy did not see why the high-morale Marines should disappear. In retrospect, the Navy arguments appear to be sound, and the bitterness of the interservice battle seems fantastic today.

150

Presenting the Navy's case before the Armed Service Committee was a dazzling array of witnesses, including Admirals Halsey and Spruance. Burke himself testified on the new carriers. Secretary Matthews waited patiently while the pro-aviation witnesses talked. He heard Admiral Radford call the B-36 "a bad gamble with national security." When the witnesses were through, however, Matthews expected Chief of Naval Operations Denfeld to take his seat as a witness and refute all the Radfords, Halseys, and Burkes in the U.S. Navy. But Denfeld upheld the flying admirals, and Matthews angrily fired CNO Denfeld and replaced him with Admiral Forrest Sherman. Then he set out to get even with Arleigh Burke and any other men who had opposed him on the issues confronting the Navy.

In the heat that followed, calming words came from General Dwight D. Eisenhower, who said that he would be no party to either side in the "unification" conflict, but who wisely reminded all concerned that "we are dealing here with distinguished Americans, men who have the country at heart, and we should not be too ready to call names on either side." But Secretary Matthews appeared to forget that 31-Knot Burke was a distinguished American and a war hero. He could only think of his role in Op-23 and the Navy-Air Force fight, and when a Navy selection board placed Burke on the list for promotion to Rear Admiral, Matthews had Burke's name stricken. But Admiral Sherman, the CNO, interceded with President Truman, and in February, 1950, Burke finally became a permanent flag officer.

The experiences of the preceding three years had taught him a great deal about the dangers that come from being able to think and write well. CNO Sherman found Burke a spot on the Research and Development Board where he wouldn't attract so much attention.

The job wasn't to last for long. In June 1950, the North Koreans invaded the Republic of Korea in the south, and the United States once again mobilized for war. Prior to the risky Inchon landing in Korea, CNO Sherman pulled Arleigh Burke out of mothballs and asked him how soon he could leave for the war zone.

"In two hours, if I can call my wife," replied Burke.

Admiral Sherman gave him until the next day.

At his own request, Admiral Burke took with him to Korea three young Navy officers—a crack jet pilot, a top gunnery man with amphibious training, and a first-class administrator. With his young assistants, Burke, acting as Sherman's personal representative in Korea, checked out every detail of the planned Inchon invasion and reassured Sherman that everything should proceed without difficulty. Then Burke and his small staff handled planning assignments connected with the Wonsan invasion and, later, with the evacuation of military and civilian personnel from Hungnam.

After completing these jobs, Burke took command of Cruiser Division

Five in the Far East. His flag flew on the cruiser *Los Angeles,* whose skipper was Captain Robert MacFarlane, and, as usual, Burke was delighted to be back at sea. One day, as they cruised off the coast of North Korea, MacFarlane spotted an enemy railroad bridge and prepared to fire on it with eight-inch guns.

Burke made an exception to his own rule of never interfering with the skipper of a ship and began to kibitz.

"You'll be wasting your bullets, Bob," he told MacFarlane. "You can't hit a bridge with eight-inch guns. The thing to do is to knock out the abutments on each side."

MacFarlane disagreed. "I can hit it," he replied stubbornly.

Admiral Burke thought for a moment.

"I'll make you a bet," he proposed. "I'll bet you can't hit that bridge with your first ten shots. If you hit the bridge with your first shot, I'll buy you nine cases of Scotch. If you hit it with your second, you win eight cases of Scotch . . . and so on to ten shots. But for every shot over ten that it takes you to hit it, you have to buy me a bottle of Scotch."

MacFarlane couldn't wait to shake on it. Then Burke sat back and watched while the captain fired thirty shots at the Korean bridge, without scoring a single hit.

"It's hard to hit a bridge," commented Burke mildly, as he collected his twenty bottles of whisky.

The primary mission of Burke's Cruiser Division Five during the spring of 1951 was to blockade the east coast and to support friendly forces on the land with incessant bombardment. Vice Admiral Lee Song Ho, later chief of naval operations of the Republic of Korea, recalled that Burke's "gunfire support was so deliberate and effective that friendly forces could easily resist enemy attacks along the coastline." The Admiral remembered that the survival of the First Republic of Korea Corps in the east, under command of General Paik Sun Yup, seemed "miraculous" as it faced the so-called "sea of human mass" of the Chinese Reds. That survival, he said, depended largely on the naval gunfire support of the United Nations Forces.

Burke frequently flew to the front by helicopter and surveyed any areas which he deemed strategically important. He had a working arrangement with General Paik. Several of Burke's officers worked ashore with the ROK Army, acting as a fire-control party. Burke's cruisers were the ROK artillery.

On one occasion, Lieutenant General James Van Fleet, commanding the Eighth Army, came over to inspect General Paik's First Corps, and Paik asked Burke to fly over for the inspection. After the Koreans had briefed Van Fleet on various phases of their operation, General Paik announced a briefing by his "artillery commander." Burke realized that Paik must be

152

talking about him, since the Koreans had no artillery except the U.S. Navy. With a straight face, Burke arose and briefed General Van Fleet on his artillery operations. The Koreans were delighted.

After the inspection, Van Fleet took Burke aside. "I understand," he said, "that you have a lot of ice cream aboard the *Los Angeles*."

"We do," answered Burke. "Since we have to fly up the line anyway, why not come out to the ship for ice cream before we leave."

Van Fleet quickly agreed, and Burke suggested that they use his Navy helicopter rather than Van Fleet's, since "Navy personnel know more about landing aboard ships at sea."

As a rule, that was true. On this particular day, however, the youthful aviation pilot handling Burke's helicopter knew a lot about flying—but very little about landing on ships. Also, Burke noted that the number of stars on General Van Fleet's shoulders appeared to rattle the young man.

Whatever the reason, the pilot brought the helicopter over the moving *Los Angeles* at too low an altitude to make a satisfactory landing. As the helicopter's wash came over the deck, it lifted the aircraft, tipping it over on its side. General Van Fleet and Admiral Burke saw that they were precariously balanced at the edge of the ship, half over the water, twenty feet below. Gasoline began to spill and run over everything, and several crewmen grabbed at the helicopter and just managed to pull it aboard to safety. By this time, the aircraft was half on its back, with General Van Fleet on top of the struggling bodies inside.

"What do we do now?" the general asked.

"What we do is kick out the side of this damn thing and get out," replied Burke, in muffled tones. The husky Van Fleet followed the suggestion and used Burke as a rug when he stepped down to safety. Then Burke crawled out, followed by the pilot, who was ready to hand in his wings.

Burke was so embarrassed that he didn't know what to say to the general. Both officers watched while the crew of the *Los Angeles* continued to grapple with the aircraft, which was about to go over the port side once again. Van Fleet stared at the operation in stony silence, while Burke gloomily considered how he almost had managed to kill the commander of the Eighth Army.

Finally, Burke could keep silent no longer. "What would you like on your ice cream, General?" he queried.

Van Fleet thought a moment. "Do you have pineapple?" he asked.

Burke said, "Let's go get it," but Van Fleet held him back.

"Maybe we'd better take the pilot along," he suggested. "He looks kind of down in the mouth." The three of them polished off two pineapple sundaes apiece.

When it came time for Van Fleet to go ashore, Burke decided not to attempt a return trip via helicopter. He told the crew to call away the landing boat. Since the beach was a tricky one, Burke accompanied Van Fleet ashore.

On the way in, the admiral casually asked the coxswain whether he had landed through a surf before. "No, sir," the man replied.

"Haven't you ever had any training?" Burke asked in annoyance.

"Sir," said the man in a frightened voice, "I have just been coxswain of this boat for two weeks."

Burke turned to the boat officer.

"What do you know about taking a boat through the surf?" asked the admiral.

The officer swallowed hard. "Nothing, sir," he answered shakily. "I am just the Junior Officer of the Deck and I don't know anything at all about boats."

"Does anyone aboard know anything about landing through surf?" shouted Burke. Nobody moved.

"Well," said the admiral, turning to General Van Fleet, "you are going to witness something that very few people have ever seen. You are going to see an admiral bring in a landing boat."

"Do you know how?" asked Van Fleet, with evident concern.

"I'm a sailor, dammit," declared Burke. "I'll take this boat in all right." And he landed through the surf into a small inlet.

Van Fleet looked properly impressed as he bade Burke farewell, but a few minutes later Burke had reason to be thankful that Van Fleet was no longer aboard. He discovered that it was going to be far more difficult to get the boat back out through the surf than it had been getting it in. The engineman was as inexperienced as the rest, and Burke had to shout orders to him on engine speed while handling the rudder himself. When he finally got the boat out again, the admiral promptly instituted coxswain drill and boat drill. He promised himself that he would never again let a coxswain take a boat that didn't know how to handle a boat. And he kept that promise!

After his experiences as a Korean artillery commander, a soda fountain operator, and an admiral-in-charge-of-a-landing-boat, Burke next tried his hand at running a heliport.

He called in a member of his cruiser division staff, Lieutenant William Jeffers, a former aviator, and told him to keep an ear glued to the helicopter circuit.

"One of these days," said Burke, recalling Mitscher's concern over pilots in the drink, "you are going to overhear a helicopter pilot in trouble. Those boys are flying a long way from our bases now, and our cruisers are a lot closer than their airfields. When you hear a pilot say he can't make it home, you direct him to come in here."

Bill Jeffers said he would do just that, and a few days later, while riding the helicopter circuits, he heard a pilot in distress. Jeffers guided him in, and in a few minutes an Air Force helicopter dropped in on the deck of the *Los Angeles*. The pilot was most grateful; he had run low on fuel and he would have gone down, without the offer of hospitality from the Navy. In fact, after a good meal and a decent bunk, he actually became enthusiastic about life aboard a cruiser.

"I think I ought to operate from here," the pilot told Admiral Burke the next morning.

"Sounds like a good idea," the Admiral told him.

"Yes," said the pilot, "I can do as much work from here as I did from the airfield. You're on the same circuits we're on—in fact, your communications are a lot better than ours."

Burke smiled at the Navy's newest convert and reported the aviator in. The following day, another Air Force helicopter arrived, and two Marine helicopters landed before the week was out.

Early in 1951, Burke was invited to visit the Naval Academy of the Republic of Korea. While touring the struggling new school, he discovered that the Academy had no library and that the midshipmen sorely needed textbooks and reference books. Burke promptly wrote an appeal entitled, "Books for Korea," which appeared in the June 1951 issue of *U.S. Naval Institute Proceedings*. As a result of this one article, more than twenty thousand books were presented to the Academy by individuals, naval organizations, American colleges, universities, and libraries. These donations became the cornerstone of a new Academy library.

On June 24, 1951, an event took place which would take Burke from the sea again and plunge him into one of the most responsible, exasperating, and fascinating assignments of his career. That day, almost one year from the start of the Korean War, Jacob Malik, Soviet delegate to the United Nations, broadcast what was interpreted as an armistice proposal. Malik said: "The peoples of the Soviet Union believe it is possible to defend the cause of peace. The Soviet peoples further believe that the most acute problem of the present day—the problem of the conflict in Korea—could also be settled. This would require the readiness of both parties to enter on a path of peaceful settlement of the Korean question. The Soviet peoples believe that, as the first step, discussions should be started between the belligerents for a cease-fire and armistice providing for mutual withdrawal of forces from the 38th Parallel. Can such a step be taken? I think it can, provided there is a sincere desire to put an end to the bloody fighting in Korea."

Following this broadcast, General Matthew Ridgway, Commander-in-Chief of the United Nations Forces in Korea, was directed to propose a military armistice conference. He did so, suggesting as the site for the conference the Danish hospital ship *Jutlandia*. Replying, the North Koreans and

Chinese Communists suggested that the town of Kaesong on the 38th Parallel be the site of the cease-fire meeting. As an indication of the good faith of the United Nations Command, General Ridgway accepted Kaesong as the meeting place.

As senior delegate to the conference, Ridgway selected Vice Admiral C. Turner Joy. The other UN delegates were Burke; Major General L. C. Craigie, Deputy Commander of the Far East Air Forces; Major General H. I. Hodes, Deputy Chief of Staff, Eighth Army; and Major General Paik, Commander of the First ROK Corps and Burke's good friend. The first meeting was to begin at 1000 hours on July 10, 1951.

The day broke damp and cloudy. General Ridgway and others in the UN Command delegation drove to the helicopter landing area to wish the negotiators "Godspeed." After posing for hundreds of photographs and after dodging scores of unanswerable questions from reporters, Burke's helicopter took off, skimming over white-clad Koreans planting rice in their paddies. The farmers looked up and waved, and looking down upon these people, Burke realized that he was heading for the most important conference of his life. Like others in the delegation during that flight, he prayed that the enemy would meet the UN half-way.

In a short time, the helicopters landed on a field near the Kaesong Methodist Missionary Compound, and the delegates were met by a North Korean liaison officer. Communist photographers and newsreel cameramen were everywhere. Burke and his companions hopped into U.S. Army jeeps, and noticed that the Communists also were driving several jeeps with U.S. Army markings. One bore the letters "Wilma" across the hood, and there were two bullet holes through the windshield on the driver's side. Gloomily, Burke realized that the Communists had purposely driven these vehicles to the scene to show their contempt for the UN negotiators.

The party was led down a road lined with armed guards to an old house, later dubbed United Nations House. Like the road, the dwelling was surrounded with guards armed with machine guns, and, as Burke went up the front steps, a burp gun in the hands of a young North Korean lad was pushed into his face. Burke calmly pushed the muzzle of the gun to one side and entered the house. It soon was discovered that the UN team had come early; the Communists were running on a different time and would not arrive for one hour.

At 1050 (ROK time) the party was escorted to the conference site, a once splendid mansion several hundred yards away. Here, too, the house was surrounded by officious North Korean guards, all armed. Burke, the other negotiators, and the staff were ushered into the conference room, where they noticed that the Communists had provided beer, candy, and cigarettes as refreshments. There was a moment of extreme tension as the two enemies faced one another across the room. Burke thought they all

156

looked like circus animals set free in an arena. Then one of the Reds spoke.

"I am Nam Il," he said.

"I am Admiral Joy," the UN senior delegate nodded.

Three North Koreans and two Chinese confronted the four Americans and one ROK officer. Burke observed that the North Koreans were in Soviet-type uniforms, with smart gray blouses with red piping and big blue trousers. The Chinese officers wore woolen khakis devoid of all insignia.

The American Admiral could not help noting that uniforms of the enemy were of two grades—very poor and resplendent. The delegates and a few staff officers wore fine uniforms; the others wore inferior stuff. On the other hand, the United Nations delegation—officers and enlisted men alike—wore khaki. It occurred to the admiral that the "classless" society of the Communists was practicing class distinction to a far greater extent than the "capitalist" countries.

The delegates exchanged credentials. The enemy's senior delegate was General Nam Il, Chief of Staff of the North Korean Army. He had taught school in the Soviet Union and was an ardent, Soviet-trained Red tactician. The other two North Koreans were Major General Lee San Jo, who had become a Communist in 1940, and Major General Chang Pyong San, who had once served, it was rumored, as an enlisted man in the Soviet Army. Evidently he had been added hastily to the delegation, and he contributed little to the proceedings.

The senior Chinese delegate was Lieutenant General Tung Hua, deputy commander of the Chinese Communist Forces in Korea. An old-line Red, he had been political officer of the First Army in 1930. The other Chinese delegate was Major General Hsieh Fang, a sharp-witted man of forty-seven, who reportedly had held positions in the Northeast Military District of Manchuria and in the Chinese Communist Ministry of Information and the Political Bureau. He was rumored to have attended a university in the Soviet Union.

The enemy faced the UN across a table covered with green felt, and interpreters sat behind their respective delegations. Admiral Joy placed a small UN flag in front of him on the table. (That afternoon, General Nam had a North Korean flag fluttering from a slightly higher standard.)

Admiral Joy made an opening statement, which was translated into both Korean and Chinese, in which he said that hostilities would continue until agreement on the terms of an armistice could be reached. He assured the enemy that the UN Command was prepared to do its part in trying to work out an agreement for the cessation of hostilities in Korea under conditions which would make certain that the conflict would not resume.

Nam Il and General Tung replied. They presented three proposals at the outset. First, that both sides issue orders simultaneously to cease all

157

hostilities; Second, that the 38th Parallel be established military demarcation line and that both sides withdraw their troops ten kilometers from the Parallel; and, third, that the armed forces of all foreign countries be withdrawn from Korea as soon as possible.

This so-called "agenda" of the Communists actually consisted of conclusions, not topics, and it was unacceptable to the United Nations negotiators. But Admiral Joy said he would study the Red proposals. In the meantime, he said, he wished to call the attention of the enemy to restrictions which the Communists were imposing on the movements of the UN staff. Guards were keeping UN delegates from moving freely between United Nations House and the conference site. Joy also said that the UN wished to include twenty newsmen as an integral part of its delegation, since Communists continued to pop in and out of the room, taking both still pictures and moving pictures. The enemy replied that these things were "minor matters" and that they would consider them.

The UN's own proposal for an agenda was a true agenda, as Westerners understand that term. It consisted of topics to be negotiated, not conclusions. For example, where the Reds had included insistence on the 38th Parallel as a demilitarized zone as a part of its agenda, the comparable United Nations agenda item said simply: "agreement on a demilitarized zone across Korea." The UN had no intention of agreeing to the 38th Parallel as the line of armistice.

Burke himself felt strongly that a military armistice must spring from military realities and be based on those realities, not on politics. A cease fire is nothing more or less than a suspension of hostilities between belligerents for a period of time and under conditions agreed upon. An armistice conference is not a peace conference; an armistice is a military problem requiring a military solution. And the 38th Parallel was not a line which had much to do with the current military situation. It was a political line.

But the Reds appeared to be just as determined to include the 38th Parallel demarcation line as a condition of the agenda. It was apparent to all that agreement even on the question of agenda topics would prove tedious and difficult.

But before even the agenda negotiations could proceed, there was the matter of the UN newsmen to resolve. On the morning of July 12, twenty reporters and photographers joined the convoy of UN delegation jeeps, but they were halted by the Reds at Panmunjom. The newsmen were not admitted to the Kaesong area. That was the straw that broke the camel's back. General Ridgway promptly sent an open letter to the Communist commanders, calling a recess until the question of admittance of the newsmen could be resolved to his satisfaction. Ridgway also proposed that both the Reds and the UN agree on a neutral zone at the center of Kaesong, from which all armed personnel would be barred.

Many of the reporters were astonished and regretful at being the cause of breaking off cease-fire negotiations, and they treated the matter gravely. But Burke wholeheartedly approved of Ridgway's decision to call a recess over the question of admitting the press. The time to insist on equal treatment for the UN delegation, he felt, was at the start of the conference —not later.

On June 15, the Reds agreed to the Ridgway proposal, and that afternoon American newsmen were roaming the conference site, picking up bits of information and taking photos of a Miss Paik (no relation to the South Korean general), who was one of the most ardent of the Communists in the area. After further negotiations, the liaison officers for both sides arranged a neutral zone in Kaesong, and the armed guards vanished. The long, tough struggle for adoption of an agenda then began in earnest. It was not adopted until July 26, 1951—eleven days later—and it read:

1. Adoption of agenda.

2. Fixing of military demarcation line between both sides so as to establish a demilitarized zone as a basic condition for the cessation of hostilities in Korea.

3. Concrete arrangements for the realization of cease fire and armistice in Korea, including the composition, authority, and functions of a supervisory organ for carrying out the terms of cease fire and armistice.

4. Arrangements relating to prisoners of war.

5. Recommendations to governments of countries concerned on both sides.

It had taken nine days for the two negotiating teams to agree that they would even attempt to reach a meeting of minds on these five points.

As the negotiations proceeded that summer, Burke and the others began to realize that they were facing an extremely clever and determined enemy team. While General Nam's arguments were based on dubious Communist premises, they flowed logically from those premises and they exploited every weakness they could find in the UN position. In time, the UN delegates compiled a list of expressions to avoid and they learned to use short, uncomplicated sentences in explaining their position.

Burke discovered that there is no singular or plural in Korean, and that the interpreter was having difficulty in translating exact meanings. Occasionally, Burke or one of the others would rephrase a statement in the interest of greater clarity, only to find later that the interpreter had translated the phrase approximately as it had been stated in the first place. Delegates began to understand the expression: "It all sounds the same in Korean."

The Communists, who could be clear when they wished, also were masters at changing the subject and at making long, political speeches to stall for time. Despite the serious nature of the conference, delegates couldn't help a faint smile when General Nam would say such things as: "I'd like to hear your opinion of my opinion of your opinion of yesterday."

But it was not language difficulties which were the real cause of disagreement between the Reds and the UN. The difficulty was over item two in the agenda, the establishment of a demilitarized zone. In agreeing to remove their demand for a zone along the 38th Parallel from the agenda, the Communists had not altered their view that the 38th Parallel was the only possible demarcation line. They insisted that their view "must be accepted."

Again and again the UN negotiators insisted that an armistice must be based on military realities. One reality was that the present battle line was not coincident with the 38th Parallel. Except in the most western sections, the lines were well north of the 38th Parallel. Another reality was that the 38th Parallel was not a defensible position. At many points, it could be overrun easily. Still another reality was that the Parallel followed no easily discernible features of terrain, such as rivers, roads, ridges or towns. An imaginary, geographical line, it had no meaning on the ground as a line of military demarcation.

Burke and others insisted that a demilitarized zone should possess the following features: (1) It should be located geographically in relation to the existing overall military situation; (2) It should be outlined by easily recognized terrain features; and (3) It should include suitable defensive positions on both sides close to the zone.

By mid-August, the sessions were deadlocked. The Reds would make no proposal other than the 38th Parallel and they refused to discuss any adjustment. The UN team was unwilling to accept the 38th Parallel as a basis for the demilitarized zone. Finally, the UN negotiators suggested the creation of a subcommittee charged with finding a way to break the deadlock. The Communists quickly agreed, and appointed General Lee, of the North Korean Army, and General Hsieh, of the Chinese Communist Forces, as their two subcommittee members. Admiral Joy selected General Hodes and Burke, although Craigie was to alternate with Burke now and then.

Burke went to the first subcommittee meeting on August 17, full of high hopes and vigor. Prior to the meeting, someone had referred to the subcommittee meetings as "informal, round-table discussions," and the Reds had taken the UN at its word. In the corner of the conference room, surrounded by several tired-looking easy chairs, was a small round table —about the size of a nightclub cocktail table. The Reds had decided that if the UN wanted a round table, it would get a round table. They couldn't understand why Burke and Hodes laughed when they saw it.

During the next few days, the American admiral and general got plenty of time to study the two men who faced them across the two-foot round table. General Lee was thin, very dark, and he wore an air of perpetual dissipation. Now and then he looked as though he were nursing a mam-

160

moth hangover, but it didn't matter a great deal to the progress of the negotiations. Lee Sang Jo let the Chinese delegate carry the ball. Lee either read what his staff officer had written for him to say or agreed with Hsieh Fang.

Hsieh was a small, neat, and quick Chinese. He knew Chinese history and he knew Communist history. In time, Burke learned that the man also knew American history. He was widely read and he had been trained in the art of Red negotiation. Now and then he resorted to temper tantrums, although he did not pound his shoe on the table. Once, when Hsieh lost his temper, Burke stated firmly that he had always been brought up to believe that the Chinese people were courteous, friendly, and logical. In past dealings with the Chinese, he said, he had found that his upbringing on this point had been correct. But Hsieh, he pointed out, was not acting in a Chinese manner. His negotiating technique was neither courteous, friendly, nor logical.

"I had heard that the Chinese Communists had thrown away respect for their ancestors and had turned their back on close family ties," said Burke, "but I did not realize, until these negotiations began, that they also had thrown away their logic and common sense."

Hsieh responded furiously by calling Burke a "turtle egg," a name which carries vile connotations in Chinese. Burke replied that the name meant nothing to him. Through the interpreter, Hsieh pointed out that the name was very much worse than any name which Burke could imagine. Burke replied that he was unmoved. (On an earlier occasion, one of the enemy had referred to ROK General Paik as "a dog in the house of the dead," and the good general had not taken the insult as calmly as Burke took "turtle egg." "It is hard to maintain Oriental calm in the face of such provocation," he scribbled on a note to the admiral.)

But all was not vituperation. The Reds gave up the use of temper as a technique when they discovered that the UN team could not be shaken by such adolescent attacks. And Burke frequently had the feeling that Hsieh might be a civilized person behind his Red façade. Now and then, he revealed a sense of humor and a delight in the use of words which failed to correspond with the harsh face he generally turned toward Burke and Hodes.

Once, when Hsieh pressed Burke hard to agree to some vague point, Burke told the Chinese delegate that he had not explained it thoroughly enough.

"You are asking me to bet on a horse that I haven't even seen," said Burke. "You want me to bet on the horse just because of your description of the horse."

Hsieh seemed amused by the metaphor. He replied that Burke should go ahead and place the bet. It was a wonderful horse, he said. It was a fast

161

horse. It was a jumping horse, and it was a beautiful horse. The Chinese said that he thought Burke should bet on his horse even if he hadn't seen it.

Each morning as Burke entered the conference room he greeted Hsieh civilly with "Neebahow," the Chinese equivalent of good morning. And each morning, the Chinese delegate stared back without replying. Burke had greeted him for nearly two months when suddenly Hsieh replied, "Neebahow," and smiled. This brief thaw was the closest that the Chinese delegate ever got to being friendly. He was a Communist to the core, and he could never afford to drop his guard.

In four days of negotiating, Burke and Hodes failed to make any headway with the Reds on the subcommittee and they decided that the enemy delegation had no authority to consider any alternative to the 38th Parallel. The Reds refused to budge off that line. On the night of August 22, 1951, the Communists staged a fake bombing incident in the Kaesong conference area, and used this as a pretext to break off negotiations. Although there had been previous incidents, this time it appeared that the Reds were in no hurry to resume the armistice conference.

Months later, Burke referred to notes he had made during the conference and wrote down a number of observations on how Communists operate, negotiate, and obfuscate. Taken together, his comments would fill a book, but a few of the most interesting follow:

"The Communists have a habit of burying the most important part of their statement in the middle of long propaganda creations . . . When dealing with Communists, it is essential to remain firm. Statements should be truthful and logical and have other important qualities, but they must, above all else, be firm . . . Once vacillation or compromise starts, the Communists come to the conclusion that there is positive evidence of weakness and become more and more demanding."

"In common with all Americans, our delegates became impatient periodically . . . The heritage of our people is to want results, effective and rapid results, without beating around the bush. Maybe if the Communists stood fast on their demands, the press and people at home would become restive and eventually insist on an armistice under any terms. The Communist propaganda machine was geared to create such a frame of mind . . ."

"It was felt rather strongly that the United Nations Command should not be duped by the Communists into concessions without comparable concessions from them. Like blackmail or appeasement, once started, it would be most difficult to make the Communists realize when we had come to our final position and would give no further . . ."

At the request of General Ridgway, Burke took charge of the UN armistice camp each time that the Communists broke off talks. He and the men slept in tents in an apple orchard, since nobody, with the exception of General Hodes and Burke himself, anticipated that the conference would last for long. Most believed that an armistice agreement would be signed within a month.

As the year wore on and winter came, Burke had wooden floors installed in the tents, and oil stoves were added for warmth. Unfortunately, the stoves were so risky (there was danger of carbon monoxide, as well as explosion) that they couldn't be left on at night. Burke tried putting another tent over the top of his first tent to keep the wind out and he staked down his tent heavily and threw dirt over it to keep air from entering at the bottom. He put six blankets under him and six over him. He also slept in long Army underwear, with a pair of long woolen socks. Mixing his uniform, he pulled a Navy watch cap over his head when he retired.

The sailor was learning something about life in the Infantry as he tried life in a tent, and it wasn't long before he found a way, Navy fashion, to improve on Army life. It occurred to him that the lights went out in the camp as soon as the movies ended. Power came from a diesel generator. Burke had a brainstorm. The next time that a yeoman went to Tokyo, he had him pick up an electric blanket. After taps each night, the land-locked admiral plugged in his electric blanket and slept more comfortably than he had in weeks.

Burke had used his new blanket only a few days when General Hodes caught him plugging it in.

"A soldier would never stoop to the things that a sailor does when he comes ashore," said the general bitterly. "I refuse to have one of those blankets." It wasn't long, however, before he tried to borrow Burke's.

During the periods when there were no negotiations, Burke had to find work for the men who made up the armistice team's support unit. It was a motley collection of servicemen. There were Army clerks, cooks, and signalmen. There were similar specialists from the Air Force and Navy, as well as a few yeomen, storekeepers, and radiomen. Burke got everybody a weapon, and then he proceeded to organize the whole camp like a ship. He even had a general alarm ship's bell installed.

Most of the time that he ran his dry-land vessel, Burke wore an Army uniform, and as many of the troops addressed him as "general" as called him "admiral." It was the closest that Burke ever got to "unification." Before long, he was marching his Air Force, Army, and Navy units out to the rifle range for target practice, and eventually the mess sergeant came to him and said: "General, it's sure good to get back into the old Army again. We haven't done things this way for twenty years."

"General" Burke looked at him closely and decided that the cook was both sincere and complimentary. His sincerity was proved that evening when Burke's plate was laden with a brace of pheasant. From that day on, the admiral ate as well as he could in a first-rate hotel.

The cease-fire conference, which had been broken off in August at the instigation of the Communists, did not resume for two months. During this period, the Reds continued their usual pattern of twisting, accusing, dictating, and distorting in order to make it appear to the world that the United Nations Command had broken off the talks. Throughout this period, General Ridgway remained calm and purposeful, always ready to explore any honorable approach which might lead to resumption of talks.

Late in September, General Omar Bradley, chairman of the Joint Chiefs of Staff, accompanied by Charles Bohlen, State Department expert on the Soviet Union, visited the Far Eastern Theater and held long discussions with Ridgway and the negotiators on the armistice problem. One major point of disagreement emerged between Burke (and Hodes) and the Joint Chiefs. General Bradley felt that the UN Command should draw its final proposal for the location of a demilitarized zone on a map and present it to the Communists as a final proposal and a firm position.

Burke and Hodes felt just as strongly that the United Nations could negotiate an armistice only in terms of the battle line where the troops would be when the negotiations ended. If the UN handed the Communists a firm proposal now, and the UN troops won battles between the fall of 1951 and the date the armistice was eventually signed, it would mean that UN soldiers would be surrendering terrain which they had spilled blood to gain. In addition, Burke and Hodes knew that they would be giving up a good deal of leverage as negotiators if they agreed with the Reds on a demarcation line before there was agreement on other agenda items. They wanted the Reds to know that they would lose more territory the longer they stalled on the cease-fire. They wanted the ever-changing battle line to put pressure on the Reds to force them to negotiate. As far as Burke and Hodes were concerned, Washington was making it impossible for them to bargain effectively with the enemy.

Looking back on the affair, General Hodes recalled: "Why anyone thinks you can negotiate with Communists is something way over my head . . . The only way to get anything is to talk to them from a position of strength and adhere to the bitter end to your proposal. We (the sub-delegation) had the rug pulled out from under us by Washington so many times, that we outlived our usefulness, and Burke and I got relieved from the talking job. I took an Infantry Division and found shooting much more satisfactory than talking."

When the conference resumed, late in October, at the new site of Panmunjom, Burke and Hodes were not among the negotiators. Both had asked General Ridgway to be relieved of their duties because they felt that they had been discredited. Both had told the enemy that they would not settle on the present battle line—and now they were being forced by Washington to do so. "We estimated," said Burke later, "that if we ever

164

took the pressure off, the thing would drag out and out." And that, as the world knows today, is exactly what did happen.

In General Hodes' view, "Burke contributed as much as anyone on the team. He was always strong and he understood Communist ways of attacking any subject. There are not many people in the United States or in the world who understand Communist tactics. If I ever had to head up another delegation or sub-delegation, you may be sure that I would want Burke first."

Somebody else wanted Burke, too. Admiral Sherman, the CNO, had died in July 1951, but before he had gone, he had made arrangements for Burke to receive one of the top posts in the U.S. Navy; indeed a post which some believe is second only to CNO in importance. He was named Director of Strategic Plans. It was a job that would put him through a mental and physical wringer.

CHAPTER 10

Chief of Naval Operations

The Burkes had bought a pleasant house on Hawthorne Street in northwest Washington, and the new Director of Strategic Plans found that he now worked there almost as many hours as he spent in the Pentagon. Eight hours a day, six days a week, wasn't nearly enough time to swim through the waves of work which deluged the Admiral's desk. He worked so much at home that he grew weary of the sight of his upstairs study, and he set up a second workroom in the basement, complete with globe and world maps, so that he could refresh himself during long homework sessions by moving to a new locale.

Burke's new job was to prepare the Navy's official position on every conceivable subject affecting the Nation's present and future security. The reports went to the Secretary of Defense, to the Joint Chiefs, to the State Department, the National Security Council, and the President. In effect, Burke was recommending the moves on the Nation's naval chessboard, and the pressure exerted by the Soviet Union in 1952 and 1953 meant that the Admiral had to solve a "chess" problem at the rate of one per hour during the day, or forty-eight strategic problems per week. It was a job which involved crushing responsibility.

For once, Burke had found a task which demanded of him all that he could give. His global sea experience, his combat experience, his frustrating experience in attempting to negotiate with the Communists—and his slow, steady experience in learning to master himself—began to bear fruit. The fighting Admiral began to hit his full stride.

Once, in a magazine article published in the old *Collier's,* Burke wrote: "Boredom comes from lack of work. Outline for yourself work to do each day. Make sure that you achieve something in your career each day." Burke certainly did not suffer from boredom in Strategic Plans, and neither did his associates. Like his former colleagues in Task Force 58/38, they soon came to respect his boundless energy and enthusiasm, and his stubborn insistence that men take time to think and to do the "very best" job of which they are capable.

During his first months in the planning slot, he was nagged increasingly by the realization that the world situation gave him and his men very little time to think about anything but putting out brush fires around the globe. Eventually, he set up a new branch on strategic studies and withdrew several of his best thinkers from the "front line" of decision-making, sticking them in a back room, so to speak, with orders to think about the future of the Navy—five years ahead, ten years ahead. Picked to head the branch was George Miller, a young man that Burke had discovered while serving in the Far East and who had won the Admiral's respect.

"Think. Just think. And don't stop thinking," Admiral Burke told Miller and his staff. Many more were to hear this advice during the next decade.

By early 1954, the overtime thinking of Burke's strategic plans set-up had helped streamline many Navy concepts, and America's sea service was moving rapidly to adjust to the realities of the atomic—and hydrogen —age. But Burke, who never spared himself when he felt he could be of value, was temporarily worn out. He himself did not realize the full extent of his exhaustion, but like many men who rarely take vacations (he had not taken leave for years), he would have to be out of the job before he realized that he was tired. His associates and superiors, however, knew that he needed a rest, and they were concerned about his health. The new Chief of Naval Operations, Admiral Robert B. Carney, an old friend from the days when Carney was Halsey's chief of staff and Burke was Mitscher's, found him a job that would not overtax him for a few months. With some relief, Burke went back to sea in early 1954, in command of Cruiser Division Six, in the Atlantic. Incidentally, the new job, which was to last nine months, finally gave Arleigh and Bobbie a chance to tour Europe.

While CNO Carney did not discuss the matter with Burke, he felt that his friend definitely was slated for eventual promotion to vice admiral. However, the Navy traditionally is in no hurry to push young men ahead too fast. Burke was only fifty-three years old when he left for Europe; that is not very old, as the Navy figures a man's age. Admiral Carney was going to do all he could to see that Burke kept moving along to jobs of increasing responsibility, including command of a fleet, if possible. Meanwhile, Rear Admiral Burke had time to catch his breath, a military luxury which is not so common, in today's uneasy peace, as many laymen might think.

Burke met Bobbie, who had preceded him, in Spain, in Cadiz, and she helped him to break down the typical Spanish reserve at a reception the first evening that they were there. After several chill minutes in the receiving line, Burke noticed that crowds of Spanish ladies were gathering around his wife, and he broke away to see whether she was telling fortunes or regaling them with dialect stories. He discovered that Bobbie was attempting to speak Spanish, an endeavor which enlists Spanish sympathy, appreciation, and cooperation wherever the tongue is spoken. The women were helping her, and soon they brought their husbands into the group to assist them. From that evening on, the Burkes found the Spanish most hospitable.

In January 1955, a fully rested and well traveled Burke got a job that he had been wanting for many years. He reported as commander, Destroyer Force, Atlantic. This was a big job for a two-star admiral, and one that reunited Burke with his favorite ships. At last, he was "king of the tin cans." To say that the admiral was delighted would be an understatement. He understood destroyers; he understood the talk of destroyer sailors. Admiral Burke was home again.

It gets to be axiomatic, in any of the military services, that when a man gets a berth he enjoys, watch out! But Burke, rested and refreshed after his two years as the Navy's director of strategic plans, saw no reason why he would not complete a full stint aboard his favorite ships. The first warning, however, came after only a few months. One spring day in 1955, while his flagship was in port, Burke received a call from Admiral Radford, Chairman of the Joint Chiefs of Staff, who suggested that Burke fly up from Florida to Washington and call on him. Burke protested, but came anyway.

When he called on Radford, the vice admiral took him along to confer with Secretary of the Navy Charles S. Thomas. Thomas led the parade along to see Secretary of Defense Charles E. Wilson. By the time the delegation arrived in Wilson's office, Burke was completely mystified. He was even more confused when he was asked to explain his idea about keeping aircraft carriers in the Mediterranean to protect supply ships to Greece, Turkey, and Italy. He could have covered this in a written report. Burke began to talk, but after a few moments he observed that Secretary Wilson didn't seem too interested. After ten minutes, all excused themselves from the presence of the former General Motors head and padded back to Secretary Thomas' office. If Burke expected all to be revealed to him, he was disappointed. Thomas talked about destroyers for an hour, then bade Burke farewell. The admiral tried pumping Radford for an explanation, but he failed to extract any information. Then he dropped by to see the CNO, his old friend Mick Carney. Carney was as mystified as Burke. Shrugging, Burke returned to Florida to resume what he once termed "the most interesting job in the Navy."

A few weeks later, on May 9, 1955, Burke was attending a dinner at Newport, Rhode Island, when he was called from the table to receive a telephone call from the Secretary of the Navy.

"Where are you?" asked Secretary Thomas.

"Newport," Burke replied.

"Can you come to my office before 1000?" Thomas asked. "I've got to be on the Hill in the morning."

Burke replied that transportation might be difficult and asked if noon would be all right. Thomas snapped an okay and hung up.

The following morning Burke landed in Washington, where an aide drove him to the Pentagon. Upon arriving at Secretary Thomas' office, an aide, Captain Jackson, asked the rear admiral to remain in the Secretary's office until Thomas returned from testifying before a Congressional Committee.

"The Secretary has asked that you not see anybody in the Navy or on the Secretary staff until after you have talked with him," Jackson insisted mysteriously. Burke cooled his heels in the Secretary's big office. At lunch, he had a sandwich with Jackson, who said he didn't know why Burke had been summoned.

At 1330, Thomas returned and led Burke through an inner passageway from his own office to that of Undersecretary of the Navy Thomas Gates. The men got right down to business.

There had been differences of opinion, they said, between Admiral Carney and the Secretaries of Navy and Defense. They felt they could no longer work together as an efficient team, they explained, and Admiral Carney would not be reappointed CNO at the end of his two-year term that summer. Anyway, they said, they felt that CNO should rotate every two years.

Burke drew a deep breath and listened while Secretary Thomas explained the "difference of opinion" he had had with Admiral Carney.

Burke sat very still and kept his mouth shut tight.

Thomas talked on. He said that he thought the Navy needed younger officers in key spots, and he wanted a hand in picking the flag officers for major commands. "There are many things going on that I do not know about and for which I feel responsible," he complained.

Suddenly the Navy Secretary paused and stared directly at Burke. "Do you know of any reason why you should not be CNO?" he asked suddenly.

Burke was startled. It took him a minute to collect his thoughts. Then he said, yes, he knew of several reasons why he should not be selected as Chief of Naval Operations.

First, he explained, he was a friend and admirer of Admiral Carney.

Furthermore, Burke continued, he did not feel that he could accept the job if Carney were to leave under a cloud. Carney's departure, he insisted, would have to be accompanied "by full honors and the respect due him."

The Secretary of the Navy agreed. Now Burke brought up more objections.

He had been active, he reminded Thomas, in the notorious B-36 investigation. He had been head of Operation 23, and, "as a result, gained

169

much notoriety." What's more, he declared, he still felt that he had done the right thing in heading Op-23.

Burke then insisted: "I am not an easy man to deal with. I agree that younger officers should be assigned billets where they can be trained for more responsible Navy jobs. I agree that there should be greater emphasis upon new developments in the Navy. I am not averse to reorganization if it will improve the combat effectiveness of the Navy as a whole."

"But I am not tactful. I have a habit of saying my piece on a problem and laying my views on the table. I am sure that if I became CNO, you and I would have differences of opinion, and I will state my opinions freely and sometimes loudly."

Thomas said he had no objection to that either. He said that he *wanted* frank opinions.

Finally, Burke asked permission to see Admiral Carney and to tell him the whole story. Thomas agreed.

Burke "felt like hell" when he called on Mick Carney. He promptly told his old friend that he was being considered for CNO. Carney listened quietly, then surprised Burke by telling him the reasons that Thomas wanted him out.

Admiral Carney also claimed that Secretary Thomas did not understand the selection system with regard to officers of flag rank. He felt strongly that the Secretary of the Navy should have no influence over the selection of officers for high command (witness the fight over Burke's own promotion between Admiral Sherman and Secretary Matthews). Promotions, insisted Carney, were a military, not a civilian, matter. The military, he felt knew the worth of officers from years of association, including association under combat conditions; the civilian secretaries knew the worth of most officers only through occasional contacts, such as a cocktail party, or through hearsay.

Many commentators on the Pentagon scene have attempted to give personal overtones to the running controversies between the civilians in the military establishment and the professional military men. As a rule, such an interpretation is in error. It would be more accurate to say that the civilian-military controversy is inherent to the situation. A professional Navy man, who has given his life to the service from Annapolis on, and whose best friends are other professional Navy men, naturally resents advice and interference from civilian newcomers. But this Nation places *policy* control in military matters in civil hands. At best, it is frequently difficult to tell where *policy* leaves off and where purely military decisions begin.

Secretary Thomas had nothing but respect for Admiral Carney as a man; Carney likewise had a high opinion of Charlie Thomas personally, for he knew that Thomas could make double or triple his Secretary's salary in private industry. Their clash was an official one, and it is the kind of clash which can be minimized only through the oil of diplomacy and politics.

After talking with Carney, Burke had one more session with Thomas and Under Secretary Gates on that memorable May tenth. Burke recommended four other men for the CNO job and Thomas told him four reasons why the men were not acceptable either to him, to Secretary Wilson, or to President Eisenhower.

"Well," said Thomas finally. "Stick around Washington for a few days and we'll talk about this some more. Carney is going to be relieved in any case."

It was early evening when Thomas and Burke finally parted, but Burke caught Carney before he could leave the Pentagon. Carney wanted Burke to drive home with him.

As they headed into traffic, the events of the day began to crowd in on Burke and he admitted to Carney that he was apprehensive.

"Secretary Thomas seemed to agree with everything I said," he said, "but I'm not sure he hoisted aboard the real import. After all, I don't know Mr. Thomas or Mr. Gates or Mr. Wilson or Mr. Anderson (Under Secretary of Defense Robert Anderson) or the President. I don't know any of the hierarchy who have picked me out of the list.

"I'm afraid they are selecting me," he added, "because they think I'm a pushover."

He said he feared that he probably wouldn't last two years and that he didn't think he was prepared to deal with matters of high policy.

Carney listened carefully and gave Burke a much needed drink when they reached the CNO's official residence in Washington, the Admiral's House. Then Carney spoke candidly. He told Burke that he had expected him to be picked as CNO someday—perhaps in two years. "By that time, you would have been prepared," he explained in a kindly manner. Carney added that he thought it was "regrettable" that Burke was getting the Navy's highest post "prematurely." Nevertheless, he advised Burke in the strongest possible terms to accept the post, and he offered to do all he could to help. He predicted that, after the initial shock, the Navy would "rally round." (There were ninety-two officers on the list ahead of Burke, including the vice admirals.)

Then Carney told Burke something more about Secretary Thomas. "He is the best informed Secretary of the Navy we ever had," the CNO insisted. "He has more statistics on the Navy at his fingertips than any other Secretary in the DOD ever had. What bothers him is that he doesn't know those things that it takes a lifetime in the Navy to learn. He wants to be the whole show, and that is beyond the capacity of any individual."

On May 11, Burke was in Thomas' office before 0900, ready to talk some more. Even before he arrived, however, he had seen Carney again, who had insisted that he impress on the Navy Secretary that "the fleet has a high opinion of what I have been trying to do." Burke began to feel the oppressive weight of high-level politics and infighting. He repeated Carney's latest message to Thomas, and both men went up one level in the hierarchy to call on Secretary of Defense Wilson. When Wilson let them in (after fifteen minutes), Thomas asked Burke to tell the former car maker what the Navy wanted him to do as CNO,

Burke spoke briefly and outlined four main tasks—

1. Reorganize the high command so that younger flag officers could be trained for positions of responsibility, insure that all billets were held by capable people, and keep a flow of good prospects available at all times.

2. Make sure that everybody in the Navy "gets the word."

3. Put greater emphasis on the speedy development and installation of new weapons.

4. Increase the spirit, vitality, and combat effectiveness of the Navy.

These are the things he understood Wilson and Thomas wanted him to do, Burke said.

Wilson admitted that Burke had the general idea, but added that he had "oversimplified."

He told the rear admiral that at General Motors, he and Alfred P. Sloan could put any man they wished into any position, but that they knew that the man would be effective only if he could get the cooperation of his associates and the loyalty of his subordinates.

The Navy career man, the hero of the Solomons and Task Force 58/38, listened quietly to the homey sermon from General Motors.

"That's the problem in the Navy," summed up Charlie Wilson. He said there had to be better cooperation between the military and the civilians, and he called for a "rapid evolution rather than a revolution."

Burke continued to keep his mouth shut tightly, mainly because he had no idea what to say. Many men before and after Burke have learned that this frequently is the best course to follow when having a "discussion" with a prospective employer.

Many people, said Wilson, had said that Burke was the best qualified officer for CNO because he could accomplish things, gain alert service, and retain the loyalty and support of the rest of the Navy.

Burke thought nervously that these were the specifications for a "puppet," and he stated cautiously that he appreciated Mr. Wilson's remarks but that he had a "bad quality of having strong opinions at times and of being willing to fight for those opinions while laying them on the table."

Secretary Wilson looked down at his papers and said that was okay.

Next Burke met Under Secretary of Defense Anderson, who congratulated 31-Knot Burke on his appointment, but Thomas hastily warned that "there are a lot of formalities to go through yet." He told Burke to keep himself available because the President would want to see him.

But even then, Burke could not elude his new companions. Under Secretary of Navy Gates wanted to talk about what was needed in the Navy. Burke explained to Gates his own idea of leadership:

"It results from the cumulative effects of thousands of small actions and ideas," he pointed out, "each of which is significant in itself, and all of which generate an alive, vigorous outfit. This takes time to develop."

Again, before Burke could get out of the building, he had further talks with Carney and a long discussion with the Vice Chief of Naval Operations, Vice Admiral Donald B. Duncan. Politics—even Navy politics— is mostly talk, it seemed.

Back in Newport on May 16, Burke heard from Washington again. This time, President Eisenhower wanted to see him. It would be Burke's first meeting with the President.

On May 17, 1955, Burke, Wilson, and Thomas were driven from the Pentagon to the West Entrance of the White House and were ushered into the President's visiting room. After but one minute, Mr. Eisenhower entered and Thomas introduced Burke as the man they were considering for CNO. He told Mr. Eisenhower that Burke was young enough, popular in the service, a good leader with good judgment, and would do the most for the Navy. He added that Burke was *reliable*.

The President was affable. He said that it was a good thing to go down and select somebody young now and then, just as a matter of routine. He added that the practice broke up the idea that automatic selection as CNO came at a certain age.

Selection by seniority is good up to a certain stage, but beyond that, one had to be careful, the President pointed out. But he added that the ninety-two people passed over must be spared all possible distress and made to realize that what was happening was for the good of the organization. The concern pleased Burke. They were the honest sentiments of a fellow military man, the admiral thought.

Finally, the President offered Burke his two rules for behavior in top administration jobs. Many Eisenhower appointees heard similar words. First, the Government is a *team,* and while the President expected Burke to fight hard for his ideas and the Navy, he also expected Burke to support a decision, once it had been taken "in the family." Mr. Eisenhower recalled the unification battle after the war, and said that it brought out the worst in military people when they took their cases to the public via the press.

The President also said that the chief responsibility of a service chief, in his opinion, was to shape military policy on the Joint Chiefs of Staff.

173

Try to delegate your service responsibilities to the Vice Chief, Mr. Eisenhower told Burke, so you can be free to handle JCS responsibilities.

Finally, the President said that the appointment suited him. Burke was on the "team."

Burke shook hands and said that he understood.

The President prepared to send Burke's name to the Senate, and as Burke returned to Newport to arrange to move to Washington, he noticed something strange. While all his meetings had been held in secret, he noticed that he got a plane with unusual promptness. When the plane blew a cylinder and had to return to Washington, another plane was provided promptly for the rear admiral. People were deferential, ultra-courteous.

"The skids were greased," Burke wrote a friend. "Those people *knew* —but how the hell it happened I don't know."

Many others wondered "how the hell it happened" when word got out officially. In the words of one vice admiral (who had been passed over with the rest of the three-star admirals), the whole Navy was "stunned." In the words of one reporter on the Washington scene, "the Navy rolled as though it were caught in a thundering typhoon." All the things that Burke had said about himself—"a premature appointment" and "not enough top-policy experience"—were said about him by others now. But Burke was too busy being briefed to pay any attention.

For the press, it was a big story. Most of the "secret reasons" which Thomas had for not reappointing Carney now appeared in news stories. Columnist Doris Fleeson noted that "weeks ago, Secretary Thomas confided to friends that his CNO was running the Navy to suit himself . . . The Secretary indicated that his peeve extended to other senior admirals. He said he was looking among the younger officers for Admiral Carney's successor . . ."

Miss Fleeson had reliable information, though she, in common with other members of the press, shared the early delusion that Arleigh Burke was Irish. He was not only Irish in the news stories, but he had "a friendly Irish grin" and possessed "a puckish Irish humor." One reporter called him "a wild Irishman." All these Emerald Isle attributes disappeared in a hurry when his Scandinavian ancestry became known to the press, and reporters were equally quick to note that he had "a Swede's grin" and that he looked like "his Viking ancestors." Such is the price of fame.

One newsman discovered that Burke was the author of a service pamphlet entitled, "Discipline in the United States Navy," and he predicted that the book would become a best-seller among officers and enlisted men alike. Burke had written in the booklet:

"Officers must have confidence in the promotion system, or discipline will be jeopardized. Unless the best officers are promoted, faith of other

174

officers and enlisted men in the integrity of the system will be shaken . . . The rest of the Navy must have absolute confidence in those selected."

During June and July, Burke was thoroughly briefed on his duties as CNO, and he made a whirlwind tour of Southeast Asia and Formosa, where he conferred with Chiang Kai-shek.

At Burke's request, his swearing-in ceremony was to take place at Norfolk, Virginia, aboard the aircraft carrier *Ticonderoga* to dramatize to the American public the fact that not all sailors sit behind desks. It was to be the first time that the Chief of Naval Operations ever had taken the oath of office aboard a ship. Unfortunately, Hurricane Diane frustrated this historic ceremony, and sent the *Ticonderoga* scurrying to sea the day before. The swearing-in was hastily transferred to the Naval Academy, another first, where full honors were accorded to Admiral Carney, to Admiral Burke, and to Secretary Thomas. Burke described the outgoing Carney as "one of the most able naval officers in the history of the world."

The oath of office was administered in the Academy's Dahlgren Hall, where Burke had been commissioned as an ensign thirty-two years earlier. Now he was a four-star admiral.

Addressing the top Navy brass, including many of those he had passed over in receiving his promotion, Burke pledged "to push with all my energies those policies which Admiral Carney has initiated to contribute further to the combat readiness and fighting trim of the U.S. Navy."

Those were not mere words on Burke's part. He inherited a great deal from Admiral Carney's two-year tenure as CNO. Carney had been influential in getting more funds from Congress for the Navy's woefully lagging shipbuilding program. The budget for this program was virtually doubled during Carney's tenure. He had pushed for practical application of new technology in the fields of nuclear power, missile development, and antisubmarine warfare (ASW). He had improved the Navy's personnel program and its public relations activities. He had intensified efforts in the direction of better fleet maintenance.

All this was part of Burke's inheritance from a man he respected and admired. But Burke was his own man; he was different in outlook and drive and temperament from Admiral Carney, and, with his usual zest, he plunged headlong into a dizzy round of activities which might have felled a lesser man. The new Navy was just beginning to emerge as Burke took office, and he saw that there was plenty to be done.

It was a Navy that bore little resemblance to the service which Midshipman Burke had studied at the Academy in the early 1920's. It had, in fact, changed considerably since he had sailed with Pete Mitscher to the shores of Japan. The *Nautilus,* the world's first nuclear-powered vessel had been launched and had completed its maiden voyage successfully. New supersonic Navy planes were on the drawing boards or in production, and weird new missiles—Terrier, Sidewinder, Talos, Petrel—were being fired at the Navy's Missile Test Center in the California desert. Atomic Energy Commission scientists had boiled down the size of a nuclear warhead small enough to be fired from a cruiser's guns or to be carried by a fighter plane or bomber. New carriers were on the way, and in the planning stage were nuclear-powered ships, designed to plow through the water at thirty knots. And there were new, top-secret developments in ASW—antisubmarine warfare—an activity that was receiving top priority from Navy research teams and strategists.

It was this emerging Navy, a revolutionary new Navy, which Burke inherited and which he would guide to near-completion during the next six years. He would also order work begun on the most revolutionary Navy weapon of all.

Arleigh Burke took on the job of CNO with his eyes open. Burke has said that he didn't even want the job. His critics have laughed long and loud at this, claiming that the admiral may have appeared modest on the outside, but that he actually was praying for a crack at the post. The truth is probably somewhere in between. Burke was delighted with his job as Commander, Destroyer Fleet, Atlantic. Certainly he would have liked to be CNO—someday. Nevertheless, he was wary of receiving the job while he was so young, and he was suspicious of the conditions under which it was offered to him. Most importantly, he was cognizant of the awful responsibility which such a job entails in the nuclear age.

At the same time, it is far from unpleasant for a man to hear that he has been chosen over ninety-two other admirals for the top spot in the service to which he has devoted his life. Burke was a competent worker, and he *knew* that he was a competent worker. As a man now fully mature and confident, he felt strongly that many of his own ideas were as good or better than the notions of his associates, and he naturally felt heartened by the prospect of being able to put his ideas into practice.

At the outset, Burke's view of his relationship with the civilian Secretaries differed sharply from the view of Admiral Carney. First, Burke stepped back a little and shed his traditional military prejudices. He took a good look at the kind of men who accepted civilian positions. He decided that they are exceptional men, as a rule, who are motivated by good impulses. Sometimes they take Federal jobs for prestige, but, more often, they accept appointment because they want to be of service, because they want to do something for their country. Frequently, they already have enjoyed a degree of success in private endeavor; they are ambitious; they have drive. Many have money; they could retire, but they choose to work.

But Burke also saw that the civilians have their faults. For one thing, he noticed that they tend to assume that a military establishment is like a civilian company—only with uniforms. They tend to discount the intense loyalties and devotion to tradition generated in a military service. There are no class rings in General Motors or Proctor and Gamble. And it is not considered line-of-duty for a paint sprayer or a soap chemist to give his life for his employer.

Like Carney before him, Burke also feared that the Secretaries try to learn too much in too short a time. But unlike Carney, this fact didn't dismay him. To CNO Burke, all his conclusions about the civilians jelled into one politic rule: Keep the Secretaries thoroughly briefed; keep them "cut in" on what is happening; help them to understand the importance of what they are doing and the long-term importance of their decisions.

Burke also faced the truth he himself was not in charge of running the U.S. Navy. He could name scores of people who were running the Navy: the Congress; the Secretary of Defense; the Under Secretary of Defense; the Assistant Secretaries of Defense; the Secretary of the Navy and his assistants; the Joint Chiefs of Staff; the Bureau of the Budget, and, of course, the Commander-in-Chief himself, the President of the United States.

"The thing isn't even run by a committee," Burke thought. "It is run by a group of independent committees. It may be that the only thing I can do is to try and keep the whole business moving in the right direction. Perhaps I should just give the flywheel a pat every now and then."

But, while the admiral's observations on his role in peacetime undoubtedly were true, he also knew full well that in time of war, the full burden would lie on his shoulders. The professionals in the Navy would turn to him; the Chief of Naval Operations would bear the brunt of the outcome of battle. With his typical sense of realism, Burke did not decry this situation as unfair. He simply faced it and set about doing what he could to live with it and to bend it to the purposes of the Navy.

Besides getting along with the civilians, Burke knew that he also would have to learn to work with the other service heads, the other members of the Joint Chiefs of Staff—at least enough of them to be on the winning side now and then. Number one topic of conversation in the summer of 1955, as Burke took over the CNO slot, was the construction and use of ballistic missiles. Everybody talked about them in the Pentagon; everybody was an authority; everybody had a different notion how a good missile should be built. Most people foresaw tremendous missiles, of great complexity, moving about from one place to another on equally tremendous roving launchers.

The Killian Committee took a long look at ballistic missiles and their use aboard ships. Some in the Navy predicted that something on the order of Vanguard could be fired from a surface ship. (Few people considered firing missiles from submarines, since liquid propellants and liquid oxygen, which were essential to firing a rocket in 1955, were dangerous to handle in the confined spaces of a ship, and out of the question in a sub. Also, the missiles were too large to fit inside any undersea craft.) While the Vanguard-type missile proponents were in the minority, they made plenty of noise. There also was a large body of Navy opinion which insisted that the service should stay clear of ballistic missiles. Missiles, in the words of Arleigh Burke, are "expensive beasts," and the Navy had other needed items on which it could spend its money.

But Burke himself was pro-missile. About a month after he took office, in September 1955, he attended a meeting of the Armed Forces Policy Council at which everybody's favorite subject was discussed. Major topic was the intercontinental ballistic missile (ICBM). The Air Force, which already had authority to build both an ICBM and an intermediate-range ballistic missile (IRBM), believed with all its airborne heart that the ICBM was the important thing. A long-range missile could reach out and strike enemy cities in a hurry if the United States ever were attacked. But Burke had a few reservations about that. He thought that a shorter-range missile could be developed much more quickly than the ICBM, and that the experience gained on the IRBM project would help scientists in developing an effective long-range missile later. At the time, however, the Navy, working hard on Project Vanguard, had neither an ICBM or an IRBM on the drawing boards.

The Air Force was in the pilot's seat. With carte blanche to build both an ICBM and an IRBM, the flying generals were in no mood to bargain with anybody, least of all the Navy. But Burke decided that he would have a look at the IRBM question anyway. He directed the head of the Navy's missile section to prepare plans for a 1500-mile IRBM. While the Navy had no money for such a project, Burke felt that first things should come first.

During the month, the service chiefs had more talks. The Air Force continued to insist that, since missiles were airborne, the Air Force deserved the primary role. Burke insisted that the Navy had a legitimate interest in developing a seagoing intermediate range ballistic missile to strike at enemy installations from the sea. While the Air Force conceded that Burke might have a very small point, it insisted that the Navy couldn't possibly have an intermediate-range missile ready before the Air Force completed its own ICBM, since the Navy was a traditionally slow inventor. As Burke was to observe several years later, "This turned out to be not quite correct."

But the fighting Admiral had to concede that the Air Force had scored a point. The Navy *had* been a slow developer of new hardware, mostly because it proved its components step by step. It also set conservative deadlines for itself. Both the Terrier and Talos missiles were good, but they had been slow aborning. Burke realized that, if the Navy ever got a chance to try for a big ballistic missile, he would really have to push construction. The Navy would have to make some drastic changes in its research and development techniques. (Later, for example, Burke was to give the order to build a Polaris-carrying submarine before Polaris was perfected.)

With the Air Force unwilling to talk about development of a seagoing missile, Burke turned to the Army. He suggested courteously that the Army and Navy work together on an IRBM. While the Army had no particular interest in helping the Navy build its missile, it did have an interest in getting a good IRBM program. And the Army felt that the Air Force was crowding it a bit. As a result, in late September, the Army agreed to a joint endeavor with the Navy in developing an IRBM suitable either for land-based or sea-based operations. In October, the two services obtained approval for the project from the Secretary of Defense. Burke had put the Navy into the IRBM business!

In mid-November, the Secretary of Defense decided that the Army's Redstone Arsenal was to be the development agency for the Fleet Ballistic Missile, as Burke's baby was now called. Meanwhile, all manner of conflicting reports and suggestions were funneling into the CNO's office. Some said that the liquid-propellant missiles would be practically impossible to launch from ships. Solid-fuel propellants were the thing, said a few. Burke decided that scientists should proceed to develop a solid fuel with all possible haste. Then he set about establishing a special organization to develop the missile.

Both the Bureau of Ordnance and the Bureau of Aeronautics wanted to make the missile, and, after red-hot discussions, CNO Burke finally gave the job to BuOrd, with orders to use all available talent from BuAer. To head the new organization, and to pour some oil on the troubled waters, Burke recommended the selection of dynamic, personable Rear Admiral William F. "Red" Raborn, a naval aviator and former deputy director of guided missiles. Late in 1955, Raborn came to Washington to take over the new Special Projects Office (which was to develop the Fleet Ballistic Missile) and Burke gave his missile man an extraordinary memorandum which became known as "Red Raborn's Hunting License." Signed by Arleigh Burke, the memo permitted Raborn to "kidnap" any personnel he wished from other Navy jobs and to put them to work on his missile. It also stated that if Raborn "runs into any difficulty with which I can help, I will want to know about it at once, along with his recommended course of action . . . If there is anything that slows this project up beyond the capacity of the Navy and the department, we will immediately take it to the highest level . . ."

But Admiral Burke warned Raborn that he was not giving him overriding authority. Indeed, he explained that such a thing was not his to bestow. The only way that Raborn could get the job done, said Burke, was to obtain the cooperation of all the people who were going to work under him.

"You cannot order people to think," Burke insisted. "You cannot order people to cooperate. People have to want to do these things."

As far as the "hunting license" was concerned, Burke told Raborn that he could use it to get any *forty-five* officers he wanted in the Navy—but no more, and Raborn would be completely responsible for management of the project. There wouldn't be any place to pass the buck.

"If the project is a success," said the CNO, "it will be to your credit and the credit of your organization. On the other hand, if you fail . . ." He paused and puffed on his stubby pipe a moment . . . "it will be your neck."

Burke prepared to bow out of the operation and leave it to Raborn. Before he did, however, he participated in the decision to proceed with a solid-propellant missile. He also asked that certain cut-off points be established—points at which research problems either had to be overcome or the project would be killed. There was a cut-off point on fuel. There was a cut-off point on the ability to control the missile in flight. There was a cut-off point for the guidance system and one for the navigational system. Still another killing-point was established for the fire-control system.

Then Burke left it to Raborn. Today the world knows that Raborn succeeded. The Fleet Ballistic Missile which Raborn and his Special Projects Office developed was *Polaris,* and the first submarine to carry this deadly weapon was the *George Washington.*

So many people claim the distinction of having thought of building a Polaris missile, that a Navy wag printed a little wallet-sized card which reads as follows: "I was the first man who thought of the Polaris. I am responsible for the idea. I want credit for my idea. I also want credit for thinking of the death ray, if anyone can make that work, too." There is a line for anybody's signature and a picture of a daffy bird crying, 'Mine, all mine.' "

But if the ancestry of Polaris remains in doubt, there is no doubt whatever in Burke's mind about the men responsible for its development. After the missile was fired successfully, and after the whole project was completed years ahead of deadline, Admiral Burke wrote: "The confidence which we had placed in Admiral Raborn and his group was very well placed indeed. The success of this missile was not due solely to this group, of course. It is due also to the enthusiastic support of a great many contractors and a great many laboratories, both Naval and commercial. But it could not have been done without the expert guidance of Admiral Raborn and his magnificent group."

Burke's major job, as he saw it later, was to keep giving Raborn new and impossible deadlines and to do his best to keep other people off Raborn's back.

Getting the Navy started on its first intermediate-range ballistic missile was only one of many formidable tasks which Burke shouldered during his first few months as Chief of Naval Operations. One Navy officer said that Burke reminded him of the famous *New Yorker* cartoon showing Mayor LaGuardia entering City Hall and the Hall blowing its top until "the Little Flower" left again.

"That's exactly how it was when Admiral Burke came to work," the officer said. "You could hear the sighs of relief all over the Pentagon when he finally went home for the day."

Like Mayor LaGuardia, Burke made good copy. Human dynamos usually do. His salty comments made him a favorite of reporters and their editors.

"The only man who ever had his work done by Friday was Robinson Crusoe," complained Burke, stuffing his briefcase for home.

To a reporter, he explained: "You don't solve international problems; you just act on them."

He pointed out to a fellow officer: "When you're trying to get something done, don't worry about stepping on someone's toes. Nobody gets his toes stepped on unless he is standing still or sitting down on the job."

As ever, Burke worried over communications, and he wondered if it wouldn't be harder than ever for him to find out what was going on in the lower echelons of the Navy. After all, he decided, nobody tells the CNO anything. Burke decided to open up a few personal news channels.

As he had done on his trouble-shooting mission for Admiral Sherman at the outbreak of the Korean War, Burke selected several hand-picked "bright young men" to be his eyes, ears, and sometimes, his voice. These special emissaries traveled about the Navy, finding out for Burke how senior officers felt about things and telling the officers in turn how Burke felt about the Navy. What did Burke want done, anyway? The answer was simple. He still wanted people to "think, just think, and keep on thinking."

On several occasions, Admiral Burke invited an assortment of young and old Navy officers to join him on a flying trip. The officers always accepted eagerly. They hopped aboard the plane, expecting to read, gossip, or play cards all the way to their destination. After all, wasn't this the traditional freedom from care enjoyed by every traveler? Not on a trip with Burke, it wasn't! No sooner was the plane airborne than Burke came charging down the aisle, handing out essay assignments like a cheerful, conscientious schoolmaster. Weaponry, personnel problems, international relations, discipline—these were just a few of the subjects assigned to the brass hats.

181

"Write down everything you know," Burke would say. "Take your time. Take three hours." And *some* of the officers would begin to organize their thoughts for the first time since they left the Academy.

Burke didn't assign these essays as discipline. As CNO, he wanted to know what the men thought about the various subjects he handed out. He was picking their brains; he needed the information to make his own decisions. At the same time, he wanted to stimulate the officers; he wanted all of them to start thinking again. Occasionally, he discovered that he was too late. An officer had forgotten how to write his thoughts down on paper. That, too, was useful information for the CNO.

Burke developed a habit of asking surprising questions of his fellow officers. "What are you proudest of on your ship?" he would query innocently. Skippers would tell him. Now and then, he would pop out of his office in the Pentagon and snag an unwary Navy officer for a "chat," or a third-degree. He picked up sailors who were hitch-hiking, actually managed to put them at their ease, and asked them what they thought of the Navy, of their food, their weapons, their life aboard ship in general. Before long, the Navy "got the word," as Secretary Wilson and Secretary Thomas had desired. The tempo of Navy life was being increased; there was a new boogie beat. But there was no massive organizational "shake-up," as so many of the three-star admirals had feared when the relatively youthful Burke took over. Many younger men eventually did get key positions, but the spots were filled as the older admirals retired. Nobody was pushed around; there was no elaborate new command chart, full of new boxes and lines. As a matter of fact, when it came to organizational changes, Burke definitely was a conservative.

He wrote a friend: "Every time anything goes wrong in the U.S. Government, somebody thinks the organization ought to be changed. Actually, when things go wrong, it is usually because somebody in the organization does not do his job properly."

Every now and then, Burke noticed, a new Government organization is set up to look after another organization that has failed to do its job properly. "All this does is to establish a second outfit to help the first one *not* do its job," the CNO commented. "Organizations are run by people, and not by charts. *People* are what make things tick, not chains of command."

Admiral Burke began to see organization as a necessary evil. He admitted that it is necessary to divide the work load and that it sometimes is necessary to control the work of other people. "But that is about all an organization does," thought Burke.

"There has been more damage performed in the name of changing organizations than most people realize," he wrote. "Government is over-organized now, and it could do with less organization and more personal interest in work."

For his part, Burke found the Navy "a very loose organization," and he decided this was a virtue, not a fault. "It always has been loose," he told his friend, "and that is true of all navies. It is because we depend so much on individuals."

Because Burke believed both in communication and in the importance of the individual, he decided to revive those "fantail talks" he had enjoyed with the crew as skipper of the U.S.S. *Huntington.* He even went a step farther, and began to explain the reasons for his orders in a series of bulletins, so that the men "would know, not only what they were doing, but why." He cut a long-playing record on the growing importance of the Navy, and had copies sent to all ships and shore installations. Never before had enlisted men in any service been brought face to face with the rationale behind command decisions. From all reports, they were fascinated by the experience. More importantly, they developed a better understanding of the meaning of their jobs.

He also set about helping the flag officers, the admirals themselves, develop a better understanding of *their* jobs. In a hard-hitting pep talk which the admirals present will never forget as long as they live, CNO Burke told a group of flag officer selectees:

"You were selected because you have the stamina, the guts, the enthusiasm, the drive, the intelligence, the judgment, the health . . . the Navy expects to get a hell of a lot of work out of you—and I'm sure it will . . . There is another thing which you may not realize yet. It will come as a shock to you. You are old men. You are near the ends of your careers. There isn't much time left . . . You can't afford to waste any of that time. The Navy wants to get every drop of energy and enthusiasm and drive that you have to give . . . There is just no such thing as a mediocre flag officer. You are either good or you aren't. And if you aren't good for any reason, you do a lot of harm . . . Many of you will be looking for guidance. You aren't going to get much; there just isn't much guidance available . . . We have to do our own thinking; we have to make our own decisions . . . So, when you *do* ask for guidance, submit *your* recommendations at the same time.

"Usually it takes 20 per cent more work to get 1 per cent more result. If your principles are good, and if you have a good idea, and *don't act on it,* no one else is going to either, and chances are the thing won't get done . . . You must *act.* Make sure you're right; then get the Navy behind you. Sell your idea.

"You don't solve budget problems. Even after you spend the money, you are not through with them. You still have to explain *how* the money was spent and *why.* This is good. It keeps us on our toes and others on their toes, too . . . Many of the problems you'll meet are not completely soluble. All you can do is work *toward* solutions; live with your problems

183

successfully; stay on top of them, and make solid progress toward a better Navy . . .

"It's not enough only to know your job—and to have the right ideas. You must communicate those ideas to other people and convince them that you are right . . . The Navy's big weakness has been this inability to get our ideas across to other people. We must believe in the Navy and make certain that other people do too, and *know why they do."*

The admirals "got the word." There were no ivory towers left in the U.S. Navy.

Early in 1956, Burke began work on what he considered one of his primary missions as Chief of Naval Operations; he tried to convince the Congress that the United States needed a new kind of Navy, and that they needed it in a hurry. He testified before a Congressional subcommittee that the Soviet Union had grown into the major naval rival of the United States. Russia's drive to become a sea power, he insisted, was "the most significant development in Soviet grand strategy since World War II."

As 1956 began, Burke told the lawmakers, the Soviets already had four hundred submarines and were commissioning new ones at the rate of seventy-five a year. They were building more destroyers and cruisers than the rest of the world combined. Burke asked for a stepped-up U.S. ship construction program, including another supercarrier and a nuclear power cruiser. The Navy is full of independent thinkers, but just about everybody in the service was agreed in 1956 that our shipbuilding program was too small and too slow for the Navy ever to have modern ships.

Burke was so anxious to increase the rate of shipbuilding, that he was willing to cut the size of the operating Fleet to get more money for new construction. Like everything else in the country, the cost of maintaining ships had risen—and so had the cost of personnel. On Burke's orders, Navy budget reviewers brought tremendous pressure to bear on officers and men to cut costs, to scrimp. As a rule, budget pressure is unpopular, but this time the Navy was cooperative. All hands knew that scrimping was necessary to get more ships.

To reduce costs further, Burke put the last of our battleships out of commission. Like many other Navy planners, he considered them excellent training ships, but they took a lot of men to run them—and a lot of dollars, too—and it seemed obvious to all but a few diehards that the battleship would not be of much use at the outbreak of any future war. The battle wagons went into mothballs.

But if battleships were not going to be the answer, what kind of ships were? For one thing, Burke was convinced that aircraft carriers still had a major role to play. He pointed out that "massive destruction capability will not prevent creeping aggression—the type the Communists have used in the past and will probably try again in the future."

184

While Secretary of State John Foster Dulles was talking of "massive retaliation," Admiral Burke was worrying about the "little war," the brush war, like Korea. He was coming around to the notion that "the punishment must fit the crime." He didn't suppose that we would bomb the U.S.S.R. in a limited war.

"In limited war especially," the admiral insisted, "carriers, with their effective aircraft, provide a capability which cannot be provided by any other force. It must be borne in mind that, although a limited war will not necessarily be fought with the Russians, it will be fought against Russian-produced weapons, particularly modern high-performance aircraft."

He defended the carrier against all critics (there were many) and, through the press, he carried the battle to the public. He insisted that the hydrogen bomb had not made the carrier obsolete, any more than it has made a city or a land-based military installation obsolete. He pointed out that a modern carrier task force, dispersed over a large area of the ocean, could survive a nuclear attack far better than a city, which cannot disperse its factories and inhabitants. And a carrier can carry planes and missiles close to any enemy's shores, he insisted, and strike more quickly and with more accuracy than any other kind of weapon.

In 1957, Burke told the American people that the Navy definitely was not obsolete, and he reminded the public that it was the Navy who had landed the Marines at Inchon; it was the Navy who had blocked the Chinese Red's invasion of Formosa; it was the Navy who had removed 300,000 refugees from North Viet Nam; it was the Navy who had taken out three thousand American citizens from the Suez fighting zone. And Americans began to develop new respect for our seagoing service.

Admiral Burke wanted more carriers—and he wanted more aircraft and submarines. But he also wanted new kinds of ships to hunt enemy submarines and to guard the carriers. "We are going to have to design a completely new ship around the equipment that goes into the ship," he declared.

Burke and his associates took their time and speculated on the capabilities of this ship of the future.

Here are a few of the things they decided—

She would have to be able to shoot down a long-range enemy bomber. She would have to be able to shoot down any type of enemy aircraft at high altitudes and at high speeds—perhaps as high as Mach 2.

The ship would have to possess equipment to "see" an airplane or missile on the radar horizon three hundred miles away—or more. After "seeing" the attacker, she would need to employ a fast computer mechanism and an identification system to identify the airplane in a hurry and to shoot it down at long range.

She would have to be armed with an effective surface-to-air missile, like one of the Typhon variety, to intercept the attacker.

The speculations continued. Burke and company also knew that the ship of tomorrow also would have to protect itself from submarines—and the best submarine defense is an offense. The new ship would have to seek, find, and destroy an enemy submarine before the sub could find the ship.

This meant that the ship would have to have a long-range sonar and a variable-depth sonar to go through the thermal layer. More fast computing equipment would be needed to figure out what the submarine is doing, from the data acquired by the sonar.

After that, the ship would need a weapon capable of reaching out quickly to destroy the submarine—something like an airborne rocket or a homing torpedo with a nuclear warhead. Or perhaps a nuclear depth charge . . .

She also would have to fight enemy surface ships. Perhaps the antiaircraft missiles would be effective against other surface vessels . . . or perhaps a few guns might still be a good idea. Guns, after all, might be used to help support troops ashore.

Obviously, thought Burke, such a ship wouldn't be particularly useful in a general war, but it might be very useful in a limited engagement like another Korea. She would be a big ship—only slightly smaller than the World War II cruiser, but she wouldn't look like any warship ever built. She might look more like a merchant ship . . . only she would be stuffed with electronic gear instead of cargo.

But the ship of the future had to await improvements in the equipment that went into her. Burke told a friend that he'd dearly love to have a nuclear destroyer division, but that he'd a lot rather have a good sonar. He saw that it was essential to strike a balance between immediate combat readiness and future combat capability . . . He saw that he would have to spend every penny wisely . . . He saw that the decisions ahead would be life-and-death decisions.

The Navy, therefore, began to put more emphasis on designing new equipment. Big improvements came in sonar. New digital computers were perfected for rapid data transmission. New missiles replaced guns, and the Tartar missile proved small enough even to put aboard a destroyer. (The missiles were needed because the ships of the New Navy were going to have to operate independently and there would not be enough aircraft to cover all the ships. They had to have missiles to defend themselves against airplanes and subs and other missiles and anything else that the enemy might throw against them.)

The new equipment went into new kinds of ships, and Burke influenced the design of several of them through detailed memoranda to the other admirals. The first frigates were coming along when the new CNO came along, and he liked the look of them. Somewhat larger than destroyers,

186

frigates can operate in the heavy seas of the North Atlantic and they can operate alone. They were armed with Terrier missiles, a longer-range missile than the destroyer's Tartar, and they were equipped either to assist aircraft carriers or to operate independently.

In cooperation with the Marine Corps, Burke assisted in the development of new amphibious techniques and landing craft. In 1957, he had a series of talks with the new Secretary of Defense, Neil McElroy (whom he described in a letter to a fellow officer as "receptive, keen, hard-headed, pleasant, and quick to spot dust."), about overhauling ships. Burke explained to the new Secretary that by overhauling old destroyers, it might be possible to give them a few years longer life. Like everything else, of course, it would cost some money. McElroy was enthusiastic, took hold of the idea, and carried it one step farther. He recommended a complete modernization program for old destroyers—a program to extend the life of an old ship from five to eight years. The idea became the highly successful FRAM (Fleet Rehabilitation and Modernization Program). "I wish I'd thought of it," said Burke.

Under the CNO's leadership, the shipbuilding and conversion programs of the Navy began to increase. In fiscal year 1955, which ended shortly before Burke took over, the Navy spent $893 million for new and converted ships. In 1956, the programs hit $1.4 billion; in 1957, $1.8 billion; in 1958, $1.5 billion; in 1959, $1.8 billion.

Burke was making headway.

Before stepping down as CNO in 1961, Burke was to see a large share of this spending money hit the water in the form of new ships. In 1956 came the first guided-missile frigates; in 1957, the first surface ship with nuclear power, the cruiser *Long Beach,* and the first guided-missile destroyer; in 1958, the *Enterprise,* the first nuclear-propelled aircraft carrier, which Burke called "the largest ship of any kind ever built by any nation"; in 1959, the first nuclear-powered guided-missile frigate, *Bainbridge;* in 1960, Polaris was fired successfully from the submarine *George Washington.*

This procession of Navy "firsts" may give some indication of the revolution which was taking place during Burke's tenure. A whole new concept of seapower was emerging: new ships, new equipment, new strategy, new tactics. Like most executives faced with an endless chain of revolutionary problems, Burke repeatedly was forced to take arbitrary positions to separate the wheat from the chaff and to emphasize the directions he wanted the Navy to take. And as he looked at all the threats to the United States, he decided that the submarine threat should receive top priority.

"Our greatest technical problem now is antisubmarine warfare due to the tremendous submarine-building program of the Soviet Union," he wrote Admiral Nimitz in 1956. In another letter, he said, "We must detect, identify, and destroy a submarine at ten thousand yards with an integrated weapons system . . . and we must have such equipment quickly."

He was even more specific in a letter he penned in 1956 to Dr. E. A. Walker, chairman, Committee on Undersea Warfare, of the National Academy of Science. "We can defeat any enemy air attack that can be launched against our ships at sea," Burke wrote confidently. "We even can see some possibilities against a guided-missile attack . . . we have no fear of ballistic missiles . . . we can handle their surface attacks . . . even their high-speed motor torpedo boats . . . Our most difficult problem will be to defeat the enemy submarine threat."

Out of Burke's concern developed the Navy's modern antisubmarine warfare (ASW), a complex, highly coordinated combination of destroyers, aircraft, and other submarines (a sub is one of the best antisubmarine weapons) which can work together or separately to locate enemy subs and destroy them. Details are classified and ever-changing, but suffice it to say that Burke found he could sleep more soundly as he neared the end of his tenure as CNO.

The ASW experience taught him a thing or two about human nature, as well as about technics. When he went into office in 1955, the Navy was building a number of conventional submarines, which would operate as antisubmarine agents. Although the *Nautilus* had proved successful, the high initial cost of nuclear-powered submarines—as well as their higher maintenance cost—had led the Navy to plan on making very few subs of the atomic variety. But Burke soon learned that it was easier to get money to build a nuclear submarine than it was to get dough for a conventional model. The nuclear submarine had caught the public's fancy. Children played with plastic models of them in the bath tub. The nuclear sub appeared on a postage stamp. Burke directed that the Navy go all-out for nuclear submarines and convert as many of the previously programmed conventional subs to nuclear power as possible. The Navy did—and was successful.

In 1957, Burke was reappointed CNO, and this time the swearing-in took place "on-the-job" in the Pentagon. Despite his man-killing schedule, Burke managed to give visitors—and his fellow Joint Chiefs—the impression of an affable, sunny, informal sort of sailor, sucking calmly on one of a half dozen stubby pipes like a cheerful skipper of a Swedish fishing boat. As his visitor leaned back, and Burke chuckled, a Filipino mess boy served either coffee or tea from a silver service. The visitor watched his smiling host and wondered how a man could be so relaxed while running an organization like the U.S. Navy.

The answer was that Burke was not relaxed. His aides watched the scene through peepholes, ready to come in and receive Burke's notes on the interview as soon as the visitor left. The admiral's own little notebook recorded the visitor's arrival and departure and gave the event a number in his personal classification system. In all likelihood, a chain of memos followed the visit, and perhaps a dozen suggestions. Burke always milked every conversation for every scrap of information he could squeeze out of it, and he invariably put the information to work.

While he frequently spoke bluntly, he was careful never to write a letter—or to sign one which his aides had written—which contained a single harsh word. Letters, he had learned, could be dynamite; people were likelier to misunderstand the written word than they were the spoken word, since they couldn't see your expression or hear the tone of your voice.

As he began his second term as CNO, he wrote a colleague: "Particularly in this job, I can't get anything done by an order. I can only get things done by persuading a lot of people . . . You don't get anything done by putting things out and saying, 'This is the way it shall be,' because people just don't do it."

About the same time, he wrote his predecessor, Admiral Carney, saying, "This job really is more hectic now than it has ever been since I've been in it. I used to have to jump sideways; now I just quiver in place!"

In addition to all his other duties, Burke set about establishing friendly, working relations with the heads of other free-world navies. He made friends in Belgium, Norway, Denmark, the United Kingdom, Italy, West Germany, Japan, Korea, the Republic of China, Turkey, and Greece. He worked closely with Latin American naval forces. He tried to impress on the smaller allies of the United States the importance of the job which smaller navies can perform in a war—jobs like mine sweeping, without which we couldn't get the necessary supplies to Europe in an emergency.

He arranged for an exchange of midshipmen with several Latin American nations, and he told their naval chiefs that south-of-the-border navies, particularly if oriented toward antisubmarine warfare, could play a vital role in a limited war. Burke also saw to it that loans of ships to other countries included first-class ships, not cast-off scrap.

"A good ship in the hands of one of our allies is ready if war breaks out," Burke reminded critics of the foreign ship-loan program. "That same ship in mothballs in the United States couldn't be made ready for action for thirty to ninety days."

Most of Burke's major battles were fought behind closed doors during his years as CNO, but a few of the more important ones he decided to wage out in the open. One of the most important, as far as the future welfare of the United States is concerned, was his relentless fight against a national general staff, à la Germany and so many other nations. The Army, which is organized along general-staff lines, saw nothing wrong with such a plan. The Air Force, with a modified general staff of its own, also seemed willing to go along with the idea. But Burke and the Navy were vehemently opposed.

Basically, a general staff consists of four or more principal staff groups —personnel, intelligence, operations and training, logistics (and civil affairs, in our Army). Each staff group is headed by one officer who directs the work of his group and is the single point of contact between the chief of staff and the commander, on the one hand, and his staff group, on the other.

Burke had long felt that general staffs tend to suppress all points of view except the view of one man. They prevent consideration of alternatives by the commander, since the commander hears only one recommendation—that decided upon by the general staff. This could lead to poor decisions and possibly to fatal mistakes, in Burke's opinion.

The admiral also felt that general staffs tend to plan along rigid lines and that they traditionally attempt to expand their influence and control over a nation's foreign and economic policies. (Witness the general staff's activities in Hitler Germany.) He also noted that general staffs have a long record of losing wars, while our system has a record of winning. Finally, he was convinced that, under a general staff system, the Navy's point of view would be suppressed and that naval capabilities would be given inadequate consideration (as also happened in Germany).

These were Burke's views when a Rockefeller Fund report came out for handing more authority to the chairman of the Joint Chiefs of Staff, including control over new unified battle commands. The Administration reportedly favored the idea. An angry Burke sought a public forum.

Early in 1958, he got his forum at a luncheon of the National Press Club in Washington. There, after the traditional steak, browned potatoes, and apple pie had been consumed, the admiral warned that putting "one man, a military Solomon" in power would lay the foundation for national disaster.

Burke said that he liked the Joint Chiefs of Staff the way it was. "It is particularly responsive to the requirements of modern global war," he told more than two hundred reporters. "It is in harmony without form of government. The dual status of the JCS members, who are also the uniformed chiefs of their services, is the inherent virtue of the system."

The dual status of the chiefs, he insisted, does something that no supreme general staff ever accomplished—the combining of authority to plan with the responsibility to carry out those plans.

"It assures reality," the admiral pleaded. "It avoids the fatal ivory tower."

He summarized his position clearly and with force. "There are proposals," he declared, "all leading in one way or the other toward more and more concentration of power, more and more autocracy by military policy and military decision, more and more suppression of differences of judgment, and more and more of what is described as 'swift efficiency of decision' as a substitute for debate and discussion of the military aspects of national policy."

After his speech made headlines all over the country, Burke continued his fight against the single military chief and against the pyramid of military power.

"Bigness in itself doesn't cure anything," he wrote. "There are evils which come with just being too big. The head of such an organization would not know all the things he should know. It would likely be a yes-man organization. It would eliminate desirable competition. It might lead to a single strategy which the enemy would soon learn, and learn to counter."

And Burke wasn't through. In June 1958, he testified before the Senate Armed Services Committee that he couldn't support two out of three recommendations in the President's Pentagon reorganization bill. He opposed giving greater power to the Secretary of Defense and he opposed downgrading the status of the Secretaries of Navy, Air Force, and Army. (Through Secretary McElroy, President Eisenhower had sent word to all top officers that he wanted them to back his bill. As usual, Burke felt that loyalty to country preceded loyalty to one man.)

A few days later, a reporter needled McElroy into calling Burke's testimony "regrettable." The Defense Secretary called Burke "a fine officer," but he said that he was disappointed in him.

"Admiral Burke is a man; he has a right to make a decision," McElroy stated. "I wish he had supported the President's position, but nobody's going to tell Admiral Burke what to say if he doesn't believe it."

Early in 1959, it was announced that Burke was slated to receive an unprecedented third term as CNO. Burke himself didn't think much of the idea, but the word came that President Eisenhower himself had asked for the reappointment. The admiral told an interviewer later why he had hesitated: "I wasn't sure it would be a good thing for the Navy for one man to run the show, to have things done his way, for so long a period. And I am still not sure."

Late in 1959, he passed the record as CNO set by Admiral William Shepard Benson, who had served from May 11, 1915, to September 24, 1919, during World War I.

More and more, in 1959, he took the opportunity to express his personal views of how Communists operate. After his experience in Korea, after heading the Navy's office of strategic plans, and after nearly four years as CNO, he was getting to be something of an expert on Soviet military thinking. In one speech after another, he reiterated his view that the Communists are more likely to involve us in a limited war than in a general war, and that the weapons that can win a general war are not the same weapons which are useful in a limited war. He also insisted that general-war capabilities, including hydrogen warhead missiles, have not prevented Communists expansion in the past and will not prevent such expansion in the future.

He told the Chamber of Commerce of Charleston, South Carolina, in 1959, that: "It is not saber-rattling to say that the Soviets know that the United States has the ability, right now, in being, to destroy the Soviet Union. We can do it in several ways, and several times over, with our powerful Strategic Air Command of the United States Air Force, with carrier striking forces of the United States Navy, with tactical air, and with Intermediate-Range Ballistic Missiles, which are now being installed in certain European sites.

"Therefore, the probability of general nuclear war is remote, for it would be suicide for the U.S.S.R. . . . We know that Soviet expansionist policy is continuing. There have been local aggressions, local uprisings, local crises in the past, which could not be dealt with by the use of mass destruction capabilities . . . These will continue to face us in the future and we will be able to deal with them effectively only by measures which fit the local circumstances."

In Kansas City, he declared: "General war is most unlikely because the Soviets know we are capable of destroying them in such a war."

But he told a Naval War College audience that the Soviet nibbles around the periphery of the free world "are going to come faster and faster and faster."

Burke liked to quote a 1931 statement made by Dmitri Manuilsky, an old Soviet warhorse. "War to the hilt between communism and capitalism is inevitable," Manuilsky had stated. "Today, of course, we are not strong enough to attack. Our time will come in twenty or thirty years. The bourgeoisie will have to be put to sleep, so we will begin by launching the most spectacular peace movement on record. There will be electrifying overtones and unheard-of concessions. The capitalist countries, stupid and decadent, will rejoice to cooperate in their own destructions. They will leap at the chance to be friends. As soon as their guard is down, we shall smash them with our clenched fist."

In quoting this terrible threat, Burke pointed out his concern because Americans did not seem to realize that the Soviet aim is a ceaseless war of attrition and an avoidance of any dramatic military setback.

"One of the best ways to control limited aggression," he told a management group, "is to use mobile forces, forces that can be moved quickly to the scene, in the precise strength needed, to back up our many friends in all parts of the world. When the action is over, these forces pull out, and stand by to take on the next aggression, wherever trouble flares up."

In the summer of 1961, Burke's third term as CNO drew to a close, as did his naval career. There had been no general war, but there had

192

been Lebanon and Suez, Formosa and the off-shore islands, Viet Nam, Berlin, and Cuba. In every crisis, the Navy had moved quickly and effectively. Burke had presided over the emergence of a new Navy, and Navy men and women—as well as the American people—were prouder of their seagoing service than ever.

On the evening of July 26, 1961, the Commandant of the Marine Corps and Mrs. David M. Shoup gave a reception for Admiral and Mrs. Burke at the Commandant's House, and a moonlight parade of Marines ended with the Marine Band playing "Auld Lang Syne" and "Taps," in farewell to the CNO.

On July 27, Burke received another Distinguished Service Medal—this one from President John F. Kennedy, a reserve Navy officer himself. In presenting the medal, the President said that he knew of no American more devoted to his country and "who more appropriately typifies the best qualities in the American serviceman." He also presented Burke with a plaque made of wood and a spike from the *Constellation*. The plaque bore the following inscription signed by President Kennedy: "These relics from the first U.S. Navy ship, the frigate *Constellation,* presented to Admiral Arleigh A. Burke, U.S. Navy, on his retirement, with high esteem and deep admiration for his distinguished service."

That night, the former destroyer sailor attended a farewell dinner held for him in the Bethesda Naval Medical Center Officers Club, which also was attended by Vice President Lyndon B. Johnson. Highlight of the evening was the presentation to Burke, by Secretary of the Navy John B. Connally, of an oil painting of Destroyer Squadron 23 in action off Guadalcanal.

On August 1, 1961, Burke returned to the Naval Academy at Annapolis to turn over his command to Admiral George W. Anderson, the new Chief of Naval Operations. Secretary Connally told the retiring admiral that "you have the thanks of a grateful Nation and the enduring affection of sailormen everywhere, and from all of them I relay to you a sincere and heartfelt 'well done.' "

Burke's personal flag was struck, and it was presented to him. And with that simple act, a career that had begun when a Colorado youngster reported at Annapolis came to an end.

Following the change-in-command ceremony, a reporter asked the departing CNO what he considered the most important things he had done for the Navy. Was it serving an unprecedented three terms as CNO? Was it fighting to keep the Navy alive during the B-36 squabble? Was it the job as Director of Strategic Plans?

"None of those," replied Burke, drawing himself up. "It was the battles. It was the battles to which I contributed the most—those of Destroyer Squadron 23 and those of Task Force 58/38. That always is what counts to a military man—the battles he has fought . . . and won!"

Index

196

Lee, Vice Admiral Willis A., 112, 115, 117, 120, 130
Lee Sang Jo, Major General, 157, 160–161
Lee Song Ho, Vice Admiral, 152
Legion of Merit, 37, 135
Lexington, U.S.S., 109–110, 112–115, 118, 121, 123, 125–126, 129–130, 135
Leyte, 114, 117–118, 125–128, 131
Leyte Gulf, 128, 131, 133–134, 140
Lincoln, Abraham, 29
Litch, Captain Ernest, 125
Lodge, Henry Cabot, 18
London, 10, 12, 14–15
Long Beach, Calif., 68, 74
Long Beach, U.S.S., 187
Longfellow, "Jenks," 73–74
Longstreet, General James, 26
Los Angeles, Calif., 74
Los Angeles, U.S.S., 152–154
Luzon, 126, 128–129

MacArthur, General Douglas, 110, 114–117, 125–127
McCain, Vice Admiral John S., 125, 128–129, 133–134
McClintock, Ambassador Robert, 15, 20–21
McClory, Dr., 24–25, 42
McElroy, Neil, 187, 191
MacFarlane, Captain Robert, 152
Macomb Street, 10
Mahan, Admiral Alfred Thayer, 15
Major, Harlan, 80
Majuro, 116
Makanami, S.S., 102, 104–105, 107
Malik, Jacob, 155
Manchuria, 157
Manila, 132
Manuilsky, Dmitri, 192
Marianas Islands, 82, 114–115, 117, 120–121, 124
Marines, United States, 15, 17–21, 115, 117–118, 139, 150, 185, 187, 193
Marshall, General George C., 147
Marshall Islands, 115
Massachusetts Avenue, 2, 10
Matthews, Francis, 149–151, 170
Mediterranean Sea, 4, 12–13, 17

Melton, Melton, 83
Merchant Marine, American, 20
Mercury, U.S.S., 13
Merrill, Rear Admiral Aaron S. ("Tip"), 94–97, 100, 101
Merriwell, Frank, 42
Methodist Missionary Compound, 156
Michigan, U.S.S., 53–56
Michigan, University of, 78–79
Middle East, 2–3, 6–7, 9, 17
Midway Island, 110
Military Sea Transport Service, 13, 103
Miller, George, 167
Mindanao, 114, 125
Missouri, U.S.S., 148
Mitscher, Admiral Marc A. ("Pete"), 72, 109–139, 141, 147–148, 167, 175
Mitscher, Mrs. Marc A., 134
Mole de la Traverse, 14
Monterey, Calif., 67
Monterey, U.S.S., 112
Montpelier, U.S.S., 100
Moral Rearmament, 103
Morgan, Maude, 42
Morotai Island, 125
Mugsford, U.S.S., 82, 84–87
Musashi, 127, 129
Mussolini, Benito, 15
Myers, Lieutenant Commander John, 123
Myoko, S.S., 97–100

Naganami, S.S., 98
Nam Il, General, 157, 159–160
Naples, 12–13
Nasser, Gamal Abdel, 2, 6, 13, 17
National Academy of Science, 188
National Geographic Society, 79
National Press Club, 190
National Security Council (U.S.), 7, 9, 11, 14, 16, 166
Nautilus, U.S.S., 175, 188
Naval Academy, United States, 42–47, 49–50, 59, 78–79, 84, 122, 175, 193
Naval Engineers, Society of, 148
Naval Gun Factory, 87–88
Naval Intelligence, Bureau of, 90
Naval Observatory, 2

KEN JONES

author, lecturer and world traveler, went to sea at the age of eleven with his father, Captain Jack Jones. Since then his writing career has taken him to such strange places as the bottom of Pearl Harbor and Equatorial Africa, and earned him the title "Mr. Adventure." His personal adventure stories have appeared in *Life, Reader's Digest, Coronet,* and many others. Ken Jones served in the Navy during World War II and went to Korea as a War Correspondent, writing for major magazines. His other books include DESTROYER SQUADRON 23, a study of the combat exploits of Arleigh Burke's gallant force.

HUBERT KELLEY, JR.

after being graduated from the University of Kansas City (Missouri) in 1952, won the first annual J. C. Nichols Award in city planning and moved to Washington, D.C., where he has remained ever since. He has been assistant information director of a Federal agency, managing editor of a trade magazine, special writer for the National Inventor's Council, and chief of his own capital news bureau, covering Congress for business and technical magazines and newspapers. His articles and stories have appeared in *Harper's, The Sunday Star,* and many other publications. Kelley is a veteran of World War II and saw service in the Pacific. He is married, has one child, and lives in Bowie, Maryland.

CPSIA information can be obtained
at www.ICGtesting.com
Printed in the USA
LVOW03s1204260218
567888LV00001B/321/P